Publish and be damned
www.pabd.com

Slamthology

John Lister

Publish and be damned
www.pabd.com

First published in Great Britain 2005 by John Lister.
The moral right of John Lister to be identified as
the author of this work has been asserted.

Designed in London, Great Britain, by Adlibbed Limited.
Printed and bound in the UK or the US.

ISBN: 1-905290-10-1

To Norma

About this book

Two things have defined my professional and personal life: writing and wrestling. I couldn't even begin to guess how many hours I have spent writing about the industry. This collection is intended not only to entertain the reader, but to document the development of how 'hardcore' fans in Britain have thought, debated and written about professional wrestling in the last decade and a half.

The collection opens with a comparatively recent piece in which I took on the challenge of covering the entire history of American wrestling in exactly 1500 words. It is the piece I'm most proud of, simply because it required such brevity and clarity of writing, and gives what I consider a more accurately representative account than you will ever find in 'mainstream' journalism.

Following this, the first half of the book is taken up with the epic trilogy of special editions of my *Hulk Who?* fanzine, covering three trips to and around the United States. These remain the longest pieces I have ever produced, and they still bring back fond memories. They are also a sobering reminder of just how much the wrestling world has changed in less than eight years.

The rest of the book is taken up with a selection of articles and columns from throughout my writing 'career'. Bear in mind that they are in chronological order, so both my writing styles and understanding of the business go through several transformations over what amounts to half my lifetime.

My thanks go to my editors, my writing colleagues, and to everyone who has read my work over the years.

A 1500-word history of American pro wrestling (*Pro Wrestling Press*, January 2003)

The first wrestling matches before a paying audience were in the late 19th century with the 'Harry's Hill' bar in New York running regular Saturday shows from 1867 under 'collar and elbow' rules. This style (whose main star was William Muldoon) had dropped from fashion by 1893 when 'catch as catch can' (freestyle) champion Evan 'Strangler Lewis' beat Greco-Roman champion Ernest Roeber to become the first 'American mixed style' titleholder (what we now know as pro wrestling). In 1905, European champion George Hackenschmidt beat American mixed champion Tom Jenkins to become the first world heavyweight champion.

Around this time, the nature of the con in wrestling began to change. Previously, traveling wrestlers manipulated finishes with one another to make it appear challengers from the audience stood a chance, then destroyed the local in a legitimate contest while cleaning up on bets from spectators. By the time American champion Frank Gotch dropped his belt on a 'fluke' to Fred Beel, regaining it just 16 days later, the emphasis was on working finishes to draw large paid audiences. Gotch became the first true superstar of pro wrestling, defeating Hackenschmidt for the world title in 1908 and winning a rematch in 1911, both before huge Chicago crowds.

Following Gotch's retirement in 1916, business struggled until two promoters created pro wrestling as we know it. New York-based Jack Curley introduced concepts such as time limits and one fall matches while forming promotional cartels with former business rivals. And Toots Mondt, assisted by 'Gold Dust Trio' partners Ed 'Strangler' Lewis (the greatest legitimate grappler of his era) and Billy Sandow introduced the idea of a traveling roadshow of wrestlers visiting towns regularly and working finishes to build up future bouts.

Business boomed, but rival promoters soon became bitter at Mondt and company's domination. When the Gold Dust Trio put the world title on former football star Wayne Munn in 1925, Stanislaus Zbyszko was persuaded to go against a planned finish and steal the title from the unskilled Munn. The incident set off a decade of chaos as promoters formed and broke allegiances with one another and double-crosses led to the world title splintering into up to a dozen different branches. Amidst the chaos, charismatic (if unskilled) Jim Londos became the biggest star of the 1930s. He drew at least five crowds of more than 30,000, including a 1934 match with Lewis sold as 'the last great shooting match in history'; the 'smart fans' of the day wrongly assumed Lewis would never lay down for his opponent.

After the second world war, St Louis promoter Sam Muchnick persuaded his rivals to set up a national allegiance (or cartel to the cynical) under the National Wrestling Alliance banner. NWA promoters agreed to respect each other's territorial boundaries, recognise a single touring champion, and work together against local challenges from 'outlaw' independent promoters. After initial champ Orville Brown's career ended in a car crash, Muchnick buried the hatchet with St Louis rival Lou Thesz, who became the flagship champion for much of the following 20 years.

In the late 40s and early 50s, wrestling became one of the first success stories on television, with up to 10 hours of nationally televised action each week, creating such small screen superstars as Gorgeous George. The glut of television lead to a boom period, but inevitably ended in overexposure at the expense of live attendances; promoters soon switched to producing studio-based television shows designed specifically to promote arena events.

While the NWA dominated the American wrestling scene, there were two significant breakaway groups. Mid-west promoter Verne Gagne formed the AWA (complete with his own world title) in 1959, while Vince McMahon Sr (assisted by Mondt) used recently dethroned NWA champion Buddy Rogers (arguably the first heel to master explicitly working crowds) to give Bruno Sammartino the new WWWF version of the world title. NWA promoters appeared happy to tolerate McMahon's territory (which ran from Boston to Washington) and for part of the 1970s the WWWF was readmitted as an NWA member.

The 1970s saw success across the country, with Gagne and Nick Bockwinkel the main headliners in the AWA, Bruno Sammartino, Pedro Morales and Bob Backlund having lengthy reigns in New York and the Funk brothers, Jack Brisco and Harley Race travelling the NWA territories as world champion. The only serious challenge to the national cartel came from baseball big-shot Eddie Einhorn who attempted to go national with his IWA group, but proved to be a decade or so too early and soon folded.

The claim that wrestling was a struggling local business in 'smoke filled halls' when Vince McMahon Jr took control of the recently renamed WWF is far from true. 1983 was arguably the most successful year for business across the country. But it was clear cable television was going to change the industry: Ole Anderson, whose Georgia promotion was seen nationwide on TBS had already begun experimenting with shows outside of his territory on the back of TV exposure.

But McMahon was not taking the cautious approach. Instead he built on his national exposure on cable's USA Network and began paying heavily for local television across the country. His policy was simple: sign up a local territory's stars, swamp the area's airwaves with hours upon hours of television, and then invade the area with live shows based around local favourites and headed by star attractions Andre the Giant and WWF champion Hulk Hogan. Within a year he had bought out the Calgary and Toronto promotions as well as taking control of the Georgia group and its prestigious TBS Saturday night slot.

At first WWF shows were rejected by local fans in many markets (McMahon lost something close to $7 million in 1984), but after he persuaded the New York based media that wrestling was now the in thing, it became a self-fulfilling prophecy. While Jim Crockett's Mid-Atlantic group had tasted success on closed-circuit broadcasting with 1983's Starrcade, the WWF's WrestleMania in 1985 was the first such event to make big money nationally. McMahon followed up with a regular network slot on NBC and after two mildly successful pay-per-views, hit the financial jackpot with 1987's WrestleMania III, headlined by Hogan vs Andre.

Jim Crockett mounted the most serious challenge, pulling long-term NWA champion Ric Flair from other promoters and taking over the promotions in Florida, Georgia, and St Louis as well as Bill Watts' UWF group (bought for its substantial syndicated television network). But Crockett found himself second in a one-horse race, with the potential income from his first two pay-per-views wiped out by McMahon power-plays. Crockett spent himself into a corner by giving huge guaranteed contracts to keep stars such as Lex Luger and the Road Warriors from jumping to the WWF and, as television ratings (and advertising revenue) plummeted in 1988 after botched booking wasted a potential NWA-UWF feud, Crockett was forced to sell the company to TBS owner Ted Turner.

With two national groups left (the outdated AWA having faded away by 1991), the WWF boom of the 80s began slowly declining before a sex and drugs scandal saw an overnight collapse in April 1992. Hogan left the WWF in 1993 and signed for Turner a year later; his WCW reign had little immediate business business benefit outside of pay-per-view, but the move led to WCW chief Eric Bischoff securing a seemingly insane TV slot for new show *Nitro*, head to head with the WWF's flagship *Monday Night Raw* show.

Nitro shocked observers by holding its own in the TV ratings before the 1996 nWo angle (boosted by a roster of smaller, faster competitors, many of whom had been given their first exposure by flourishing Philadelphia indy group ECW) lead to two years where WCW became number one in all aspects of business. McMahon fought back with a deliberately controversial product, regaining the top slot after the celebrity rub from Mike Tyson helped Steve Austin become a mainstream superstar. The WWF followed up with the most profitable run the business has ever seen.

By the end of 1999, recycled angles and creative bankruptcy had seen WCW begin an inescapable slide, with even huge new star Goldberg losing his appeal thanks to backstage politics. ECW had a brief spell as only the third group to make regular pay-per-views a viable venture, but an unsuccessful move to national television on TNN ended any chances of financial stability and the group folded in early 2001. Within a few weeks, the sale of Ted Turner's empire saw new bosses from AOL/Time Warner cancel WCW programming. With the wrestling division now virtually worthless, the promotion that had made $60 million profit just three years earlier was snapped up for barely a couple of million dollars by Vince McMahon.

But while a week later McMahon promoted the most successful show of all time (WrestleMania X7), his reign as the sole national promoter of pro wrestling has seen the twin evils of ego and panic reflected in a continuing drop in business, with the long-term future of American wrestling as we know it far from certain.

Hulk Who? Goes Extreme (August 1996)

Tuesday 2 July

"But that was weeks before the ECW convention, wasn't it?" I hear you cry. Yes, dear reader, but before we hit Philadelphia, we had to make a quick visit to the Fairfield Halls in downtown Croydon for the monthly All Star show. With Sasuke and company back in Japan, one might wonder what we were doing there, and the 20 man battle royale main event certainly wasn't the attraction. For reasons that will become clear later on, we had gone to see Jason 'Dirt Bike Kid' Harrison against Ian 'Doc' Dean for the vacant European Junior-Heavyweight title.

The story began the night before as *Suckerpunch*'s Ross Hutchinson and his camcorder arrived at my deluxe hall of residence. A quick trip down the off licence and we started work on the captions for *Hulk Who? - The Video II*. Pretty soon the alcohol started to kick in, the collection of Boyzone posters left on the kitchen wall by my former flatmates was ritually sacrificed, and before I knew what was happening it was 2 am and Ross was broadcasting to the nation on *Talk Radio*. The rest of the night descended into a national debate on wrestling's merits, I gave Rey Mysterio Jr his first national exposure in Britain, Brian from Liverpool claimed he could do a shooting star press, and the last *HW?* promo was filmed at 6.30. At least we had one thing in common with ECW then.

Sleep was something of a non-factor, and come lunchtime we joined Kenny McBride and Rob Butcher on the old M6/M1 lark. Despite hitting London at rush hour peak with no idea of directions other than to turn off the M25 if we saw Croydon, we finally wound up in the hallowed arena. Jason showed up with the title belt, and very impressive it was too. Purchased at cost price through some guy named Sabu, it would retail at around £1,300. All professionalism aside, the camera came out and I was in the history books as the first person to hold the belt.

Undercard. Um. Er.

This is meant to be an ECW based journal, so I'll gloss over the actual in-ring activity. Suffice to say the highlight was our party joining a half dozen other travelling 'hardcores' in playing the role of honest marks by reacting with outrage to every dastardly heel move and managing to incite a near-riot. Oddly the security staff didn't appreciate this and kept stopping Kenny from 'trying' to storm the ring.

During the interval, Ross and I walked backstage (journalistic privileges at their finest) just in time to see promoter Brian Dixon explain to Jason that the hall management had become a bit suspicious when he walked in the artist's entrance carrying a table. This left him needing an alternative finish, and meant that Ross and I became a makeshift booking committee. Understanding the need to get Jason over in the hardcore style, we soon sounded like Konnan in Tijuana, and looking back I suppose I can understand the ring announcer's confusion as he walked past and saw Ross smashing a metal ashtray over his head.

Unfortunately none of our efforts were of much use as, contrary to the public view of wrestling being choreographed to the slightest detail, Jason had yet to meet Doc Dean... ever.

To cut a 30 minute story short, Doc was stiffer than a Von Erich and the plan for Jason to win the title went by the wayside. Instead the match went to a 1-1 draw after ten rounds and Dirt Bike was handed the title as 'a mark of respect'. That said, I had taken photos from ringside (Colin Bowman and company now have my full sympathy) and Ross had filmed the bout. Footage therefore existed of Jason wrestling a match and leaving as European Junior-Heavyweight champion, so part one of 'Plan DBK' was complete.

Before leaving we had to sit through a battle royale. Now, finding 20 British legends in 1996 is difficult at the best of times, but once you allow for the European tournaments and Billionaire Ted's mighty chequebook, things tend to get a bit desperate during the summer. I am not making this up: the competitors included a subscriber to my newsletter and one of Rob's tape trading customers. Remember this later on, say just after the words "The mystery partner was..."

Naturally the British wrestling experience concluded with a five hour drive home with us arriving hungry and tired in Preston at around 3.30am. Waking around 11 and thinking of repeating the process that night in, for example, Kings Lynn, I had a moment of sympathy for the likes of Ricco the Gladiator. Only a very brief one though...

<u>Tuesday 30th July</u>

Bischoff's law meant that five days after the Croydon trip I returned home to Stevenage (an hour from Croydon), but three weeks later I was back on the train to Preston for a Manchester flight via Rob's house. My plans to get a good night's sleep before the trip had fallen apart somewhat by my celebrating co-editor Matt Brannigan's 19th birthday on Monday evening; without going into grizzly detail, I didn't enjoy the train journey much.

The wrestling portion of the day came when Rob want out for the evening, leaving me with copies of the Great American Bash and Bash at the Beach. The former was something of a shocker to me, taking four times the usual half-hour to watch with a finger poised on the fast-forward button. An enjoyable Malenko-Mysterio affair, a hilarious Benoit-Sullivan brawl in the gents, a seemingly drunk Steve Regal having the time of his life against Sting, a shocking lack of humiliating job for the Horsemen against the footballers, and of course Uncle Eric being introduced to a table.

The most surprising entertainment came in the commentary of Heenan and Dusty Rhodes. Goldust's old man has apparently gone beyond the point of incoherency. Much like the infinite monkeys writing *Hamlet*, every so often Dusty accidentally makes an intelligent and insightful comment regarding the actual wrestling!

As for the second show, how could one not enjoy seeing Hulk Hogan receiving the chorus of boos he so clearly deserves?

A quick read through Rob's extensive *Observer* collection, a glance at his prized 1984 edition issue 3 of *Gong* (£1 from a Manchester market), and it was time to get to bed some time after midnight...

<u>Wednesday 31st July</u>

...which was a tad unfortunate as we had to be up by six the next morning. The usual airport business passed without anything remarkable to report and shortly after 10 am. we were taking off on a British Airways jumbo. First up on the excellent in-flight entertainment was a short music video of all things Americana. As well as the predictable

Statue of Liberty, Stars and Stripes and cheerleaders, the clips included a short stocky fellow walking around a ring and carrying an urn.

The weather on arrival was eerily reminiscent of Manchester, and queues at Immigration were stretching back an hour. The woman supervising explained that the weather had meant that only two officials had made it into work. This had a lot to do with the airport having been under four feet of water just an hour before we had arrived. Memories of the blizzard which wiped out a show at the February ECW convention came rushing back to Rob and, as you'll see in a moment, we were beginning to panic.

First up, though, was immigration itself. Believe me when I say this was the most frightening two minutes of my life. An Anglo-Italian pen-pusher sat there in the most intimidating fashion possible until even I began to suspect I might be an illegal immigrant.

The dodgy part really started here as, thanks to massive overbooking for some overblown Sports Day down in Atlanta, we hadn't been able to book a flight to Philadelphia. Instead we were now sitting in JFK airport, New York City, with no idea what to do next. (Apologies if this sounds like a typical student travel story.)

After the joys of a night stranded in Euston station back in February, we felt ready to find some brave and cunning solution to this situation. But Britain's transport problems aren't replicated across the Atlantic, and the wonders of capitalism meant we faced very little challenge after all. In fact we simply walked over to a help desk, asked how to get to Philadelphia, and five minutes lated we were booked on the next trip with Limelight Limousine.

Rather predictably this turned out to be a misnomer, as the vehicle in question was a minibus, carrying ourselves and two Philadelphia natives. The 100-mile trip turned out to be a bit longer than one might assume as it took us an hour to actually get out of JFK airport itself. Then came the real fun.

The usual route of driving down the Belt Parkway, the main route out of JFK, was out of the window as all of the underpasses around the airport were still flooded. Not to fear though; our driver had a cunning plan, which involved a lengthy detour around the seedier parts of Brooklyn.

Now this was an experience. The whole area closely resembled the site of the old Men on a Mission videos, and Steve Lombardi wouldn't have lasted ten minutes. It's one thing to chatter knowingly about America's ethnic divide, and another entirely to drive for over 30 minutes without seeing another white person.

After that eye-opener to American culture, we eventually made it across Staten Island and, after two hours, we were barely twenty miles from the airport. The interstate proved faster though and in no time we were speeding through a pothole-filled New Jersey and excitedly recognising hick towns where Dennis Coraluzzo had held independent shows.

Dropping the other two passengers off involved a guided tour of various parts of Philadelphia, and it all seemed quite respectable. Then we headed to our South Philadelphia hotel.

Imagine if you can a couple of very basic hotels surrounded on various sides by Spaghetti Junction, Heathrow Airport, an industrial estate the size of most British towns, and finally Sellafield's big brother. Now pump the temperature up to the high eighties and replaced the oxygen with sulphur dioxide. 'Philadelphia' itself was barely visible on the horizon. Lovely.

In the interests of balance, I should point out that the fare for the minibus (equivalent to arriving at Manchester Airport and getting a taxi to a hotel in Birmingham) was a ridiculous £20. Good work fella!

With the time difference it felt like midnight now, so after a visit to the hotel restaurant where I found myself charged about £6 for a dish known as the 'All American' (quarterpounder and fries, rather than any part of Ron Simmons' anatomy), and we met up with fellow Brit Mark Smith, we hit bed around 10.pm, which was about three in the morning in the ravaged system I call a bodyclock.

Thursday 1 August

The local TV channel bade us good morning with the news that a shop worker had been shot dead in a robbery. Fellow Brit conventioneer Antony Howells had a worse tale though: in Los Angeles the week before, he'd woken up to see a TV report on a shooting outside a local hotel that morning. Specifically, the hotel he was staying in... Meanwhile, the Philadelphia John Kettley said humidity was expected to hit 93%. Croydon this wasn't.

The highlight of breakfast was the waitress asking if we were paying in food coupons, assuming we were stranded holidaymakers (though admittedly our football shirts and cut-off shorts did stand out a little). After turning down the chance to complete the Doom connection with a dish called 'The Natural', we got talking to an Australian tourist who gave us an interesting insight into the sport from the point of an outsider.

"Do they still have wrestling in Britain then?" "I remember that Big Daddy fellow." "If you ask me, I think some of it might have been a put-on."

Ho hum. The 20 or so television channels didn't have much to offer beyond *Barney and Friends* and *Blinky Bill*, and all the hotel had to offer in the form of entertainment was the phone book. The sheer size of Philadelphia means the opportunities for lame prank calls are almost limitless. If you're ever in town, give Ron Garvin (233-0239), Michael Hayes (224-3451) and Vince McMahon (765-4384) a bell.

There was nothing left to do but take a train into the city centre and hit the shops. From a wrestling perspective, the video stores threw up a few laughs, including a WEWF tape titled *Off The Top Rope*. Nothing to do with Eddie Ellner, it featured "high-flying action including Adam Bomb vs Yokozuna and Lex Luger vs Tatanka". Skytwister presses aplenty no doubt.

The best offering, though, was *ICP Stranglemania*. This was apparently a collection of ECW and IWA matches with commentary by an L.A. rap group. It looked like Oliver Humperdink had been at work with the match listings, which included Cactus Sac vs Lama Namanemai in a Barbed Wire Bed Broken Glass Fat Boy Death Match!

A quick glance round the tourist sights proved disappointing, though it did bring back memories of a classic edition of *All American Wrestling* when 'Mean Gene' and 'the Brain' hit town. After a trip down the lively South Street, as recommended by the driver of the courtesy bus which took us to the airport to catch the train, we walked up 10th Street until we found the intersection with Sansom Street.

Yes, there it stood. Every wrestling fan's favourite jewellery store, Carver W Reed. Unfortunately we didn't hang around to see if J.T. was on duty, mainly because hanging around that particular establishment for too long could well have required a bullet-proof vest and an intimate knowledge of UFC techniques.

Back at the hotel we met up with convention organiser Tom Misnik (looking worryingly like Tom Anderson on *Beavis & Butthead* fame), who calmly mentioned that South Street was the home of one Scott Levy. He also told us that Tommy Dreamer had a mystery partner for the ECW Arena show and made what proved to be a correct guess at his identity.

Other conventioneers began a arriving , and our nationality instantly raised either of two questions from each American: "Are you those guys who got banned from writing about that H********k group?" or "Are you those guys who get New Japan on TV but with godawful commentary by Oliver Humperdink?" Yes to both, my transatlantic friends.

The evening's get-together meal was similar in value for money to a WWF house show, but did get us an invite to spend the evening in the hotel room of some guys from Florida. Accepting proved a wise decision as the half-dozen youths sharing a double room had invested their spending money down the liquor store and filled the bath with bottles and ice. As well as the usual T-shirt and change of pants, they'd somehow brought a video recorder and Super Nintendo. Abandoning our original plans to catch Deep South Wrestling on the telly, we caught the last three episodes of ECW TV (i.e. Heatwave 96). Four hours and 72 bottles later we were playing Super Mario at 1 am. with people we'd never met before, while one of them told a tragic tale of how he was $5,000 in debt, bankrupt, and rather than let the liquidators get it, had spend the last of his cash on going to the convention!

Friday 2 August

The convention proper began with a distinct absence of organisation. We spend the day watching fans gradually turn up in the hospitality suite (two bedrooms with an extra sofa), complain about the absence of the complimentary beers (no comment) and hang out watching tapes. For whatever reason, most of these ended up being bad weekly TV shows from the mid-eighties, including the legendary 20 minute Ron Garvin squash. You had to be there. The day's highlight was a 1986 edition of *Wrestling Challenge* where Randy Savage destroyed a hapless youngster by the name of Troy Martin!

The relaxation began to drag a bit in the afternoon as the rooms started to get overcrowded and we got fed up with people complaining that all they got on local TV was WWF and WCW television. There was some comedic relief in Mark Smith's reaction when the infamous Kathy arrived. For those who haven't had the pleasure, Kathy is certainly an acquired taste. "I've got a picture of Bruiser Brody..." Overbearing is not the word. Again, you have to experience this one for yourself.

Eventually it was time to head out to that monument to British pop music, the LuLu temple, in the otherwise unknown town of Plymouth Meeting. The hour's bus trip was highlighted by a great video compilation of ECW TV and previous conventions, ending in the uncut Beulah vs Francine catfight. Wahey!

The tedium of waiting for the doors to open was eased by the arrival of New Jack, who talked to the convention mob for 20 minutes or so. Despite the stories, he seemed a real friendly guy without a bad word to say about anyone. Except perhaps, Jim Cornette. Unfortunately, until Matt completes his legal training, we'd better not print the tale involving New Jack, Cornette, Cornette's girlfriend and a box of tissues.

Inside the building we were quite surprised at how, erm *nice* it seemed. Why they would want to allow ECW in their temple is quite a mystery. The Brits had taken over the front row (with Mark carefully sat next to his old pal Kathy) giving a great view of the main stage, where most of the workers and management appeared at some point to watch the matches, and all that was left before bell-time was the merchandise.

Apart from the obligatory 'programme' (a no-frills three-page affair), there was a surprisingly wide range of T-shirts. I walked away with two different Raven designs, a Brian F'n Pillman and a great Eliminators shirt. The only problem was that whomever designed the shirts had been a bit sloppy, asking us to *quote* rather than quoth the Raven, and referring to Sabu as *homo*cidal (*2005 note:* It appears the man responsible was none other than Taz. Given his professional rivalry with Sabu, things become clearer!)

Apparently the variety of shirts is because each wrestler is responsible for putting out their own merchandise and then takes the profits. Each sale was recorded and it was quite amusing to hear the merchandise crew keeping track of who was winning out of Missy, Beulah and Francine in the signed photo stakes.

Eight o'clock soon rolled around and, with the old TV music playing, it was time to get extreme.

1) European Junior-Heavyweight Title: Dirt Bike Kid vs Mikey Whipwreck

Yes, the belt won on the same bill that featured the Brixton Brawler was not to be defended on the undercard of an ECW show. Jason came out in a new set of biker threads, complete with Extreme logo. Mikey's entrance produced the first shock of the night, similar to than experienced at the first Michinoku tour back in February: he was just so small! Standing next to him, you realise how his gimmick works: you really do think you could take him in a fight!

The match was decent enough, competent rather than awesome. Dirt Bike provided the night's first highspot, a plancha that knocked the barrier, and ourselves, back several feet. Plenty of stiff-looking moves ended with Mikey landing a belly-to-back superplex to win the belt and become champion of our fine continent.

2) Bad Crew vs Bruise Brothers

Oh, Ron and Don Harris,
They grabbed those Bad Crew men,
They marched them off into a wall,
And they marched one back again.

The one left behind staggered up,
But the one that they slammed stayed down,
The referee made the count of three,

And Ron and Don left town.

3) Devon Storm vs Axl Rotten

First thing to mention is that Buh Buh's comment on Lady Alexander was certainly accurate. The young lass did look a bit chilly in that outfit. Not to complain though... Axl wasn't such a pleasant sight though, as the scars from the Bad Breed feud are still plain to see, a la Sabu. The match itself was nothing special, though interacting with Storm's manager Damien Kane was quite amusing. Axl got the pin with a front face slam.

4) Taz vs El Puerto Ricano

Bill Alfonso's gimmick seems to have run its course, as he came over as a comedy character, with everybody getting into his frantic whistleblowing. Taz didn't seem like the kind of fellow one would want to mess with.

Not really a match, this was more a suplex demonstration, concluding with a Tazmission.

5) Raven & Steve Richards vs Sandman & Scorpio

As is normally the case with ECW spot shows, we'd had to wait a while for a 'proper' match. We had to wait a few minutes longer, though, as the ring announcer introduces Richards and the Blue Meanie under the guises of Stevie Stanley and Meanie Gene Simmons. Yes, with the addition of Super Nova and Don E. Allen, Kiss were in the house!

While the fans fell about laughing, Raven came to the ring with Lori and Tyler Fullington. I'd been shocked seeing him on television, but nothing had prepared me for the sight of Tyler in the flesh. He acts exactly like Raven, but Raven as a tiny angelic child. You almost feel sickened at the morality of allowing a child so young to take part in this angle, but he portrays stone cold so well that Raven seems like the Meanie in comparison.

After Sandman had made his entrance with a very suspicious looking roll-up (which Scorpio also appeared to have had a puff on), Raven finally addressed the issue of the crutches he was walking with. Citing his foot injury (though serious pneumonia and dehydration the week before were also to blame), he explained that he was unable to compete. Cue Tod Gordon who announced that he would be let off tonight but risked forfeiting the belt at the Arena show if he didn't compete. Cue angle.

Stevie announced that he had a replacement partner, at which point the crowd all joined in an impromptu rendition of *Fly Me To The Moon* while J.T. Smith walked down the aisle, delighted to find Antony Howells waving a miniature Italian flag.

J.T. introduced Sal Bellomo and the opening bell rang. Sandman hit Bellomo with the cane, Scorpio landed a beautiful highspot, and Bellomo was pinned. J.T. explained that Bellomo wasn't actually the replacement and introduced Big Guido.

Sandman hit Guido with the cane, Scorpio landed a beautiful highspot, and Guido was pinned. J.T. explained that Guido wasn't actually the replacement and introduced himself.

Sandmen hit Smith with the cane, and I assume you're starting to get the picture. J.T. Allen, Nova and Meanie all met the same fate, and Stevie was looking to be up to his neck in it. What he really needed was a solid working wrestler with international experience who Scorpio and Sandman wouldn't be ready for.

And so it was quite fortunate that Britain's own All Japan grappler Johnny 'better than his cousin' Smith turned up. The course of the match was pretty basic. Sandman, in between attempts to remove something from his eye, would occasionally step in for a quick brawl with Richards, but most of it was decent grappling between Scorpio and Smith, while Richards played a wonderful heel routine on the apron. The personal highlights was a cane shot so hard that a piece of the stick broke off and landed at my feet. Cool souvenir! Scorpio got the pin with an incredibly graceful moonsault, and everyone disappeared to the loo for ten minutes.

6) Louie Spicolli vs Buh Buh Rey Dudley

Poor, poor Louie. Despite Sign Guy Dudley's Olympics gag. and Chubby Dudley sharing his crisps, it was pretty clear that the Dudley gimmick has passed its sell-by date. (*2005 note: Seriously, that was the perceived wisdom at the time.*) Buh Buh didn't actually perform anything that one might describe as a wrestling move, but Spicolli smashed him very hard with a chair, so the fans got what they wanted.

Louie got the pin after D Von ran in with a chair, and the obligatory post-match D Von-Big Dick angle was highlighted by Buh Buh completely missing a plancha and crashing to the floor.

7) Rob Van Dam vs Hack Myers

The crowd was starting to get a bit tired of squashes by this point, yet this proved a surprisingly enjoyable match. The pair managed to come up with a bout that put Van Dam across as a strong heel, but still provided ten minutes or so of excitement. Unfortunately the highlight took place out of our sight, but we could still tell what had happened from the crowd reaction. Mr Van Dam had apparently decided that the best place to perform an Asaisault was from the steps leading to the main stage.

While this was all going on, ring announcer Rocky Mustapha (excuse the spelling) came over for a quick chat and said Johnny Smith was really grateful for the pop we gave him and hadn't expected anyone to know who he was. Glad to be of service. Van Dam got the predictable pin with an Arabian facebuster before grabbing the mike for a quick promo for the Arena match against Sabu.

8) Elimination Match: Shane Douglas, Brian Lee & The Eliminators vs Tommy Dreamer, Pitbull 2 & The Gangstas

I'm not exactly the world's greatest Shane Douglas fan, but when comes down to the ring, he's in the greatest wrestling promotion in the wrestling world, he's got a beautiful woman with him, and Deep Purple's finest moment plays in the background. In other words, my entire desires in life. Bastard.

A quick look about shows two decaying tag belts, complete with

Gangsta-supplied Xs, a stunningly small Perry Saturn (5'9" tops, but still damn scary looking) and an ultra-hot Francine. The camera doesn't do her justice.

So where are the faces?

What did you say, Rob?

OH MY GOD!

New Jack, preceded by a garbage can, runs from behind and between our seats and jumps the guard rail on his way to the ring, Mustapha comes in from the other side, Dreamer and Pitbull leg it down the aisle, and the most awesome five minutes of my life take place.

Within seconds, eight large men are brawling through the crowd, sending fans running for their lives and destroying any kind of seating plan. I'm dashing from brawl to brawl, leaping from chair to chair. The Gangstas music is playing and, when you are there in person, it makes for an incredible atmosphere. There's a disturbance over by the door. I run over just in time to see Douglas and Pitbull charging back in from a brawl in the parking lot, followed by 50 hyper fans. I end up back in my seat... or rather where my seat used to be. My pile of T-shirts now has fresh blood on it, courtesy of New Jack. So what happened to him? Oh, a Samoan Gangsta Party member turned up. But I thought they weren't in this match? That doesn't make a lot of difference when he's swinging a chain six inches from my nose. Somewhere amid this chaos, both Gangstas get pinned.

At this point, that match officially begins

Apparently at some point during the brawl Eliminator Kronus was, erm, eliminated. A quick check on the old Survivor Series scoresheet showed we should now be at three on two in favour of the heels and, once the Samoans were escorted out of the building, that was indeed the number left at ringside.

The next 15 minutes or so are pretty much your regular hardcore style tag match, with one highlight being the still lovely Francine's fantastic heel expressions and cocky attitude. Unfortunately I'm enjoying the view a bit too much and miss Rob's warning of the Pitbull about to fall on my head. Ouch. A cake gets involved. Dreamer picks up half a table (broken during the pre-match fun) and, courtesy of Brian Lee, it's reduced to sawdust. The one remaining piece goes between Dreamer's head and Lee's chin, and one Diamond Cutter/Stone Cold Stunner later, the former Undertaker is back in the dressing room.

From here it's more 'regular' wrestling with the eliminations coming at rapid pace. To surmise: Tax runs in from nowhere as the referee breaks up a pagga and a Tazmission leaves Dreamer prey to a pin; Saturn is on the wrong end of a superbomb; and a Douglas belly-to-belly gets the winning pin on Pitbull 2, adding heat to the TV title match the next night.

Just in case anyone was foolish enough to think that ended the match, the Eliminators come back out and there's a brief game of Pitbull-bashing before the Gangstas come down the aisle and we're back where we started.

Watching this on video will no doubt be less impressive, and it was by no means a 'classic match', but in person it was the most incredible experience of my life.

9) Chris Jericho vs Sabu

This marked the first, and presumably the last, time these two will ever work together and to mark the occasion, the first two rows greeted them with a Korakuen Hall style barrage of streamers, earning a smile from Jericho and a grimace from security.

Not much chance of a blow-by-blow account here I'm afraid, as the experience of being in the front row (once we'd rearranged the seating after the previous match) left the match as more of a blurred whole in my memory.

The poor point of the match was a bunch of moronic fans behind us who apparently had nothing better to do than inform the crowd every time a wrestler called a spot, demand highspots and table dives after thirty seconds, and even claim Jericho had "bladed his nose" after an Arabian facebuster busted him open. There's a lot to be said against 'smart fans'. This did produce one highlight though, when Sabu used a nifty armbar reversal and acknowledged Rob's appreciation with a smile.

Highlights I can remember include a DDT through a ringside table, Sabu demanding a chair from a ringside fan, a Sabu plancha about ten feet into the crowd, Jericho landing a beautiful flying wheelkick to the groin (my groin, unfortunately) and Sabu landing the incredible triple jump for the win. Great match, harmed *only* by the two not having worked together before.

The seating arrangement was completely destroyed by the last two bouts, but I managed to identify my seat by the pile of T-shirts underneath, just at the end of a pretty crimson trail.

So that was an ECW show then. The undercard was entertaining if not fantastic, but from the moment New Jack made his entrance it was the greatest card I had ever seen. For 24 hours at least.

The trip back included the second half of the bus video, while fans swapped tales of injuries suffered during the elimination match. Just for the *Talk Radio* brigade, wrestlers injured on the shopw included Dirt Bike (leg), Sandman (knee and eye), Jericho (nose) and Sabu (back). I'd also wager that several of the men in the elimination match had a quick session with the Elastoplast.

A few fans went over to the Travelodge where the wrestlers were staying, but Rob and myself turned down the opportunity to play pool with the Samoan Gangstas among the other excitement. It seems the highlight of the fun was Mark 'pint please' Smith getting plastered, talking to the Sandman, and then running around the parking lot smashing cars with a Singapore cane...

Back in the Day's Inn hospitality room, Hack Myers was finishing off the drinks and describing the joys of Big Japan and the MEWF. Rumour has it that the 'Shah' took the opportunity to get a free night's accommodation kipping on the sofa.

I noticed that one fan seemed to be having a lot of attention, but didn't seem out of the ordinary apart from obviously being ratarsed. Then I realised it was none other than Mikey Whipwreck!

Obviously the gimmick works well as he blended right in with the other fans, except that he lacked the widespread beer gut. This made it even more bizarre when he came up to me and told me I should put on some weight!

Now those of you've who've met me will know I'm hardly Mike Awesome but still, it was a bit rich being called underweight by Mikey

Whipwreck. Still, he did give me some inspiration, exclaiming "I used to look just like you! No really!"

Save for the exclusive news that Rey Mysterio Jr still owes Mikey a tape, and Whipwreck performing a Sesame Street dance (don't ask), there's nothing else to mention before I went to bed awaiting the greatest of my 7,246 days on this earth.

Saturday 3rd August

After a late rise and stocking up on breakfast, we began getting ready in our room just in time to find *WCW Worldwide* on the TV. Fortunately there was only one match left, the thrilling main event of Arn Anderson & Chris Benoit vs Jim Powers and Joe Gomez. I won't spoil the finish...

It was then time to walk over to the Double Tree hotel (a bit like the Tokyo Dome to the Days Inn Korakuen Hall) for the Q&A session. The event was being transcribed and broadcast live on the Prodigy on-line service, which was of little interest to us but did mean the company laid on free drinks.

Tragically my shorthand teacher's repeated warning that Dictaphones can be unreliable was proved correct at the very worst time. Irony sucks. It's not quite 60 words a minute anymore, but I did get enough down for some detailed highlights. Please don't take any direct quotes as being word perfect (especially in libel cases).

First up were Shane Douglas and Francine. Whatever you agree with his views, you have to admit that Douglas can talk. First question was about Mankind, which kicked off a lengthy anti-WWF tirade. Shane's problems with Titan have been covered at length in previous interviews, though this time he found fault with Shawn Michaels' act being unrealistic within a combat atmosphere, and came to the odd conclusion that WWF rip-off gimmicks included Alex Porteau as Taz and Aldo Montoya as Sabu.

The WWF debate naturally got around to the Clique, giving the cue for a story:

"I was fighting Ramon somewhere in Germany and we'd been doing the same match for, like, 16 nights, so I thought I'd change it around a little. At the beginning, where we'd be staring down and he'd throw the toothpick at me, I gave him a hard slap to the face. I prepared myself for a punch in return... but he was crawling around on the mat looking for the toothpick!"

Douglas also revealed that the WrestleMania VI main event (Hogan vs Warrior) was practised at Titan Towers every day for two months beforehand, and announced that he would be retiring to go to medical school either next January or May. (*2005 note: Ahem.*)

Of course, what Douglas speech would be complete without a suggestion that Ric Flair retire:

"Growing up I was the biggest Ric Flair mark in the world. But I remember going to a party after a show at the Meadowlands for his 40th birthday. And that was in 1989!"

One thing Douglas said that surprised a lot of fans, but makes perfect sense, regarded the NWO angle and Hulk Hogan's heel turn:

"I hope it does work, for the sake of the business. We need the WWF and WCW to succeed, because if the business is in bad shape, it hurts all of us."

Francine was asked about women being beaten up in ECW, defending it by referring to her new heel character:

"It always looked stupid to me on television when a valet would interfere and the men would never do anything back. I deserve everything that happens to me. Let's face it, I'm the biggest bitch there is!"

A fan then asked about the superbomb through the table which she took at Heatwave:

"I didn't know anything about it. I remember the Pitbulls brought out a table for a spot they wanted to do. Just after I turned on (Pitbull 2), they came up to me and whispered that they'd just had a great idea..."

She also explained how the ECW training school had prepared her for taking painful bumps, admitting that after her first day of tutoring she went home and cried. On the subject of valets, she said that she hated the character of Sunny, to which Douglas quipped "I hear Sunny went on a special diet in Germany. Apparently it was pretty shitty!"

At this point, 100+ Internet users began looking for spare underpants as Taz and Perry Saturn walked into the room.

Fortunately they had calmed down since the last convention, and came across as pretty reasonable guys who just happened to give off an aura of toughness. Again, Perry Saturn was no giant, but still managed to frighten people without saying a word.

Taz spoke at length about the House of Hardcore, the ECW training school which the pair run. He was obviously quite frustrated at the number of unsuitable applications they receive, including 150 pound men with no athletic backgrounds. He also explained the school's tough but fair regime:

"Our students clean up, do the crappy jobs and learn respect, just like the dojos in Japan. We don't brutalise them, but if we show them how you do a hold and they mess up, they get another chance. If they get it wrong again, we show them *why* you don't do it that way."

Gulp.

He also explained that he can usually judge an applicant's potential just by speaking to them on the telephone, and that nobody is taken on unless they are suitable, whereas the WCW Power Plant allegedly charges $500 (£350) just for a tryout. When asked which wrestlers he respected for their legitimate wrestling ability, he went through the usual Severn, Shamrock and Pittman list, but added Bret & Owen Hart, Curt Hennig and Steve Austin.

Perry Saturn briefly slipped into the realms of kayfabe (on why tag teams have to rely on each other) to hint at the rumoured break-up of the Eliminators, and made a challenge to any other tag champions for a shoot match. While this no doubt impressed many of the 'smart marks' present, one has to ask what relevance this has to the business.

Unfortunately (particularly for me if he reads this), Saturn then showed a strange understanding of the magazine business, complaining at the lack of coverage and recognition in *PWI* and the like. Paul Heyman later repeated his argument, suggesting that if every fan in the room wrote in protest, Bill Apter would soon change his plans.

Excuse the diversion, but the commercial magazine business is based on profit. Of the 90,000 or so who read *PWI*, perhaps a couple of thousand are interested in ECW. I wouldn't mind betting that a good 40,000 would be happy with a picture of Shawn Michaels, the SummerSlam results, and the chance to see their name on the letters page. It's certainly not a judgment of athletic ability that *PowerSlam* always has a WWF wrestler on the front cover. It's a sad fact of life that what is good and what is popular are often two completely different things.

Back to the convention and the dastardly heels were replaced by Johnny Smith, Chris Jericho, Tod Gordon, Mike Whipwreck and, as a special treat, the Sandman! He earned a round of boos when he was spotted drinking a glass of water. He tried the pitiful excuse that he only finished drinking from the night before at 10.30 am., but fortunately a quick whip-round got him a Budweiser. Unfortunately it soon became apparent that more alcohol was the last thing he needed. If it wasn't for his character, his obvious drunkenness might have proved very embarrassing...

Mikey was still hungover and didn't say much, while Johnny Smith was displaying typical British shyness and said only that there would be people in ECW who would fit in with All Japan's style.

Jericho then gave the shocking news that his July 7th 1995 match with Ultimo Dragon was the best of his career, and that he would be entering WCW as a babyface, so wouldn't be able to team with Chris Benoit as one fan suggested.

Talking about the match the night before, Jericho admitted that the streamers had been a nice reminder of Korakuen Hall. He then addressed the 'fans' who has been so irritatingly vocal in their criticism during the Sabu match, giving a great definition:

"They were just a tiny minority, and they weren't real hardcore fans. A hardcore fan is somebody who can appreciate good wrestling, whatever the style."

The commissioner answered the inevitable questions about ECW's future, refusing to be drawn into a time line for the inevitable pay-per-view, explaining that they wouldn't run their television show in areas where they didn't plan to hold live events (doh!), and promising that whatever the expansion, ECW will always return to the Arena every three weeks. One question and answer said a lot about they way ECW is run:

"When did you cross over the line from being a fan to becoming part of the business?"

31

"Not yet."

From here on the session reverted to the conveyor belt system, so I can't be sure exactly when people arrived and left. Tommy Dreamer performed his legendary mumbling act, with the only thing of interest he had to offer being the claim that he wasn't ECW's sacrificial lamb (which disappointed those of us fully expecting him to be chokeslammed off the roof that night).

Beulah just sat there drinking a cup of tea and looking pretty, though she did say she would have a good chance against Sunny, what with her undefeated ECW record and all. The pair (and Tommy, boom boom) had to leave early "to pick up the mystery partner from the airport".

Questioning the Pitbulls was a little more sobering was there was no way of avoiding the fact that Pitbull 1 was wearing a large metal neck immobiliser, drilled into his skull after a serious injury at the last show.

The Gangstas gave the polite politically correct speech we were all expecting, highlighted by Mustapha Saed delivering an entire sentence for the first time in memory. "Smoky Mountain? Man, that was a trip. That was a triiiip!"

New Jack repeated his well-known analysis of Jim Cornette's promotional strategies (and a few less savoury tales), and discussed at length the role of blacks in the wrestling industry, making no bones about feeling that they were used as tokens everywhere they worked including ECW (this with his boss just three chairs away).

He discussed ECW's reality-based angles, including when he was announced as being in prison at the February show. ("People came up to me and asked 'Where were you then? Working in Japan?' I weren't in no Japan! I was in jail!") This type of honesty in ECW had apparently caused problems before:

"My mother is a mark. When we were in Smoky Mountain and we did stuff where we were arrested, she understood it was an angle. But when we came to ECW and did that thing where we jumped Public Enemy, the next week Joey Styles said Jerome Young and Jerome Mustapha had been arrested. My momma phones me when she sees it and she thinks I've been in jail.

"I told her it was an angle and she says 'No, they used your real names, boy. You was in jail!' I kept trying to explain, but to this day she believes I was in jail last year!"

New Jack then addressed the Brian Pillman situation. Sitting in the third row in a custom-made Pillman shirt, I have never been so frightened.

And last, but by no means least, we questioned a Mr Paul Heyman, who was quite open about the reason Sabu and Taz had yet to face off:

"How many of you would pay $100 to see that match. (Several hands went up.) Now, if I can persuade just one more person a day to pay $100 for the match, that's $3,000 a month. If I leave the match for just a few more shows, that makes $6,000 more that I've got to spend on bringing people in.

"Imagine if I were to announce that Tommy Dreamer and Raven were to have one last fight and after that, the feud would be over. You'd all want to see it, but it wouldn't make any more for us. This man (Dreamer) has waited nineteen months to pin Raven. He and you can hold on a bit longer."

Heyman went on to discuss his old pal Jim Cornette, admitting for the first time that Cornette carried their 1989 feud and, "hell, he was even a better manager than me." Paul wasn't so keen on Cornette the booker though, pointing to the TV ratings for *Raw* and *Nitro*. He explained that Chris Jericho had been acquired after he saw 'Lion Heart' on tape (no prizes for guessing which match), while the deal with All Japan to get Johnny Smith had been set up on Tommy Dreamer's advice.

The ECW bosses then had a brief argument about fan criticism, with Heyman declaring that fans could chant anything they like as long as they leave the building feeling they got value for money. Tod Gordon had a different view:

"It kind of bothers me when fans chant "You fucked up" when something goes wrong. If you're going to do that, then you should chant "You fucked up" the moment Mabel walks through the curtain and not stop until he leaves the building.

Heyman then told a great story about the infamous angle where Tommy Rich came through the canvas during the Lawler-Idol cage match in Memphis:

"We put him under the ring at three in the afternoon for an evening show. He was left there with a six pack, a large bottle of pretzels and a bottle to piss in. When he came up for the angle, he was completely slaughtered. There we were beating on Lawler with Tommy drunk and me not having a clue what I was doing. All we could say was 'Isn't this fun? Look what great heat we're getting.' We were still saying that when they had to call the police station for back-up!"

Oh, and while the Sandman fell about in intoxicated hysterics, Paul E. told the lesbian story. I won't go into detail other than to urge you to sell you grandmother, fly to the next convention, and ask him to tell it again.

The final question asked the crew for the moment that most defined ECW. Sandman chose Shane Douglas throwing down the NWA belt, Joey Styles (after a stunning moment of silence!) could only say "The whole damn show!", while Heyman launched into an incredible ten minute speech that, while quite obviously spoken honestly from the heart, sounded eerily like a TV show promo. I guess that tells you a lot about ECW's interview style.

The whole Q&A was great fun and both entertaining and informative. Just like previous sessions, the only drawback was the repeated irrelevant questions about ECW's TV timeslot on Channel 295 in Turdsville, Arizona and the like.

Following the questions, the remaining wrestlers and officials hung around to sign autographs and pose for photos. Unable to resist the unprofessional urge, I got Sandman to sign his entry in *Hulk Who?*'s spotlight feature and also the piece of cane I'd collected. Then it was over to Joey Styles for an autograph as I explained how we'd watched 44 episodes of ECW TV on the trot. "Hey, that's a hell of a shirt you've got there!" Well thanks, Joey.

One man not so impressed was *PowerSlam* photographer George Tahinos, who found the Pillman photo familiar. Perhaps that was because he had taken it. Luckily he wasn't upset enough to cancel our lift to the Arena and, after he told some classic tales about hiding under the ring during the Heavenly Bodies-Public Enemy match last December, we made a quick stop-off at the Travelodge.

Here, as well as numerous ring-rats, were several members of the crew on their way to the Arena. Johnny Smith chatting to Too Cold at the front door, Devon Storm sitting down with a beer, Buh Buh and Meanie looking utterly ridiculous in regular clothes; yes, all the excitement of wrestlers in a hotel. In just the time it took to sell somebody an international subscription to *PowerSlam*, George was ready, and we were off to the famed Arena.

The ECW Arena is a joke.

Walking from west to east in the centre of Philadelphia, you will pass across 10th Street, 9th Street, 8th... it all goes logically across to 1st Street, which overlooks the Delaware river. Like all the numbered street, walking south down 1st Street you cross the various east-west streets, including the aforementioned Samson.

As the name suggests, South Street is as far south as you can got and still describe your surroundings as Philadelphia's 'town centre'. At this point, 1st Street makes way for Swanson Street, which should sound familiar.

Swanson Street goes south through rapidly less welcoming surroundings. Remember when Public Enemy filmed those hilariously atmospheric interviews. Remember the sparsely populated, single-storey building filled, vandalised, drug-filled, bleak urban jungle which Johnny and Rocco had discovered somewhere to represent 'the hood'.

This, literally, is Swanson Street.

Ritner Street is a name given to the grey strip used to make it easier to find a particular address. The idea that ECW Arena is a converted bingo hall is a myth. The ECW Arena, or Ritner Street Community Centre to give its correct name, is a warehouse in an industrial estate in the middle of nowhere.

All that distinguishes it is a sign on the wall proclaiming "ECW Wrestling/Bingo/Philadelphia Vikings." One can only assume the Vikings are a table tennis team given the space inside.

Last autumn, ECW cancelled a planned outdoors match after complaints that the noise would disturb the neighbours. For the record, the Arena is bordered by an empty road, an 'everything a dollar' store, an empty warehouse whose forecourt is used as a car park by fans and wrestlers alike, and the American equivalent of the M1, running from New York to Florida.

As you've probably gathered, I was a little bemused by the Arena's locale. This was nothing compared with my reaction a couple of minutes later when, after saying hello to top tape trader bloke George Mayfield, and glancing at the ring-bus which was labelled as being supplied by one T. Petty (the very same), George Tahinos flashed his press pass and walked us through one of the two doors to the building (much to the annoyance of the several hundred fans already queueing).

I am not exaggerating when I say that it took me several minutes before it really clicked that this place was actually the same building I've seen so many times on television. The only comparison I can make for most British readers is that the Arena is similar in size and shape to the infamous Walthamstow Assembly Halls.

Time for a quick tour, dear reader. To my left as we walk in the door are the merchandise tables, complete with staff overjoyed to see copies of *PowerSlam* for some reason. On the wall behind them is a fire notice stating a maximum legal capacity of 1,060 people. In your dreams, Philadelphia Blue Watch. Also on the other side of the table is the door to the stairs leading up to the balcony from which Tommy Dreamer was so often chokeslammed.

The wall behind me has the two doors leading in to the Arena, the bingo numbers board covered with a black net curtain, and a payphone. The temptation to call Matt and tell him where I am is resisted on purely financial grounds.

To the right is a black plasterboard wall separating the Arena itself from the backstage area. Along the wall is the concession stand, ten feet above which lies the Eagle's Nest. The door leading up to the Nest is just by the vending machine of Kevin Sullivan/Sheik/Night the Line was Crossed fame. They still haven't fixed it.

Which leaves the final wall into which, about ten feet up, sinks the stage containing the sound equipment, stationary camera and, if you are feeling particularly gullible, Joey Styles doing commentary. Below this is a four foot raised platform which is presumably for some bingo purpose and not merely for brawling on. Steps connect all three levels. Underneath this are the doors to the gents and ladies underneath the sound stage (go on, you always wondered...)

In the middle, naturally, is the ring, surrounded on all four sides with three rows of seats and eight-row bleachers going about five feet up.

In the ring are Taz and Perry Saturn, checking that it isn't about to fall apart or anything stupid like that. Which just leaves the guard rails making an aisle down to the curtain through which the wrestlers enter and by which we are now standing after the guided tour.

Thanks to George Tahinos being an accredited photographer and needing to set up posed shots backstage, and needing a hand with his backdrop screen, we walk through this curtain.

Into the dressing room.

In the ECW Arena.

Yes, look impressed.

Impressed, though, is not the word I would choose to describe my reaction to ECW's dressing room. For a start, the word 'room' implies some sort of purpose built area. This dressing room is merely a continuation of the warehouse, blocked off by the plasterboard. To your left as you enter is a staircase leading to the stage, allowing the occasional run-in and, more importantly, letting every wrestler who so desires watch the show.

I've deliberately avoided calling this area a locker room as the entire facilities consist of half a dozen tables and twenty or so chairs. The dressing room backs on to the remainder of the warehouse, which includes a storeroom with the broken ring from Hardcore Heaven, one toilet with no door, and a large room full of sewing machines.

Steve Austin understated it: even the USWA wouldn't take a dump in this place. It is perfectly feasible that Paul and Tod use this building without the owners' knowledge.

Back in the dressing room I'm remembering the advice every wrestler receives at a young age, assuming it goes double for me, and keeping myself to myself. Around me Taz is getting his wrestling gear out of a case, Mikey's chatting to Hack, the Dudleys still look ridiculous, and Sandman arrives with 24 cans of Heineken and 24 Budweisers. Not only am I telling the truth here, but he doesn't look as if he's intending to share them.

Tod Gordon arrives, says hello to everyone, and goes over to chat to Johnny Smith and ask him what he thought of the show the night before. Johnny says he was pleasantly surprised by the great reaction he got. No trouble, mate.

George has finished setting up, so it's back to the Arena floor to ignore Sign Guy Dudley. Sandman wanders around, still intoxicated, and having missed the pile left in the dressing room, takes a copy of *PowerSlam*. We make the polite conversation you always try with a drunk, and he can't believe we've flown over from England and starts repeatedly thanking us. Like it was some kind of ordeal.

Anyone else? Oh yes, here comes Johnny Smith again. He walks over and, in a terrifyingly polite voice somewhere between Davey Boy Smith and Steve Regal, enquires "Is there anywhere in this place that I might get a cup of coffee?"

Possibly the most surreal moment I have ever experienced...

Having sent him off to the concession stand, we took our seats as people were starting to come through the doors. *Lariat* editor Dave Scherer and pals kindly let us squeeze into their row. For those watching on TV, I'm on the back row opposite the main camera, about a third of the way from the left, on the left of the bright red shirt (Rob), behind the guy with the beard who turns up on SMW Fan Week tapes and the bloke who looks like Sgt. Slaughter.

Back rows are generally a pretty bad deal, especially in the Albert Hall, but here we were all of 20 feet from the ring with a perfect view and the freedom to stand up for the entire show. Just to reinforce how small the building is, while looking at the ring you can see the walls to the left and right of you at the same time.

Once the doors are officially opened there seemed to be a never ending stream of people passing through and depositing their tickets or money in the ice cream box used to collect the gate receipts. If you will remember back to that fateful day in Walthamstow, try to imagine the same building with seven times as many people crammed inside. Cosy is one way of putting it. Once the bleachers were full, every spare inch of floor space was crammed with latecomers. Suddenly the October '95 fire incident sounded a lot more dangerous.

The next ninety minutes passed quickly with an incredible atmosphere building up. Shane Douglas, who spent the Q&A session condemning the Clique's kayfabe breaking at MSG, warmed up in the ring with previous night's opponent New Jack. Stevie Richards walked round the building complaining that the Blue Meanie forgot to wake him in time for the Q&A. Rob very kindly pointed out the queen of the ring-rats, who boasts a record of sleeping with 25 wrestlers in one weekend. No, it wasn't Missy.

Last to arrive was a middle-aged man in a Hawaiian shirt who pleased the crowd by putting on a straw hat. To everyone's surprise it was only a few minutes after the advertised 7.30 bell time when the old TV theme played, the lights came on, and the show began.

The ring announcer's first utterings were interrupted by JT Smith, who began introducing the "world's greatest rock 'n' roll band". Amid chants of "We want Kiss!" which confused those who hadn't been at the LuLu show, Stevie and company came out complete with instruments. Stevie was doing a great job of singing or miming when Sandman made an appearance and caned everything in sight. Raven turned up and a Steviekick and caneshot later the Sandman was taken, bloodied eye and all, back to the dressing room.

1) European Junior-Heavyweight title: Mikey Whipwreck vs Devon Storm

Despite the unimpressive nature of the building, it was still very strange to see the same belt I wore at Croydon being defended on an ECW show. This was a real decent opener with plenty of good action, but not enough to detract from the rest of the show. Storm showed why he is misused in a jobber role, and there were plenty of highspots to wake up the crowd. Mikey got the win with a top rope rana.

2) Johnny Smith vs Louie Spicolli

Whatever crimes Louie had been punished for by having to work with Buh Buh had obviously been forgiven. (*2005 note:* Buh Buh really wasn't getting over with me, was he?) We led the chants for Johnny again, but he took it upon himself to get over with the crowd. Another good match without the crazy brawling, with the two working a more traditional European/All Japan style. After an incredible swift German suplex, Smith got the pin with a Tiger Driver.

3) Axl Rotten vs D Von Dudley

Utter crap, with my personal highlight being to help set up the largest sign in ECW history, a bed sheet proclaiming "Buh Buh Must Die!" Three minutes of chairshots ended with the entire Dudley clan putting in an appearance. Apparently Sign Guy spoke, which was kicking off a bizarre storyline where the brothers lose their characteristics. Bad news for Big Dick when you think about it...

4) ECW Champion Raven vs Sandman

As promised, Tod Gordon insisted that Raven wrestle despite his injury. Stevie Richards somehow got himself on broad as a substitute and, complete with Kiss, Raven, Lori and Tyler at ringside, the match got underway. Sandman was in pretty bad shape, but Richards did a great job of carrying the whole affair to respectability.

A couple of minutes into the match Missy Hyatt showed up, shattering all my teenage fantasies. The years have not been kind to Missy, though up top she's getting dangerously close to Lady Blossom levels.

There was only so much they could do with Sandman's knee in bad shape, so after a few minutes the epic finishing sequence kicked in. The Meanie missed that moonsault for the billionth time, hitting Richards by mistake, Super Nova's top rope legdrop went the same way, the ref went down, Raven ran in, Missy attacked him, Lori smashed her with the loaded boot, Missy's hair extensions fell out, Sandman went after Raven, Tyler distracted him, Richards used the boot, the ref woke up, *Raven* got the pin. The usual finish.

Needless to say the crowd were less than overjoyed with the finish but, until Raven is fully fit and they tone down the ringside entourage, there promises to be much more of this in the future.

5) Chris Jericho vs Too Cold Scorpio

Now we're talking. Fantastic bout that compared favourably with even the Guerrero-Malenko classics of last summer. Jericho was going all out in his final ECW match, while Scorpio completely changed my opinion that he was overrated. Twenty minutes of flawless matwork and highspots, without a piece of furniture in sight, and Scorpio got the pin after what appeared to be the North American debut of the shooting star press.

Jericho said farewell in an obviously heartfelt speech, quite rightly calling the ECW Arena the best venue in the world to wrestle in.

Half-time began as a trip to the loos, but 1,000 plus people had the same ideas. I made it as far as the merchandise stands where I picked up a large signed photo of Beulah. A glass frame later and it was Happy Birthday Matt.

6) ECW TV Champion Shane Douglas vs Pitbull 2

After the interval, Joey Styles filmed an opening for the TV show and then interviewed the Pitbulls. Before anyone said a word, the Samoan Gangstas were hauled down the aisles in handcuffs by the cops and thrown out the front door. OK. The interview was real emotional as, quite obviously, it was nothing short of reality. Pitbull 1 explained that he's been advised to retire, but claimed he would be making a comeback. I truly hope not as it looks like he would be taking an incredible risk.

By the time the interview was over, Douglas was given a reaction you'd expect Eric Bischoff to receive. The match was based around getting heat in a believable psychology based brawl.

Something that became apparent to me over the weekend was that the basic operation of wrestling with faces and heels is exactly the same in ECW as anywhere else. The only difference is that the fans are part of the performance, willingly cheering along at the right time, arguing with Damien Kane, and so on.

In this match though, every fan in the building completely forgot the act and became a mark for fifteen minutes. There was no way that Douglas was going to get out of the building with that belt. Of course, he did. Every near fall by Pitbull 2 had us on our feet, and the blood pouring out of his forehead served its purpose perfectly, "only adding to his determination", but Douglas landed the belly-to-belly and retained the belt. They played the crowd like a fiddle and I loved every minute of it.

To make up for the disappointment of not seeing the title change, referee John Moore and timekeeper Joel Gertner (who'd been deliberately irritating throughout both shows) both rode the superbomb express.

Several men then came out with cloths and began cleaning the ring apron of blood. Only in ECW.

7) Taz & Brian Lee vs Tommy Dreamer & ?

Think back to that battle royale in Croydon. Ricco the Gladitaor. Kashmir Singh. Erik Oslo. Brixton Brawler.

The mystery man was Steve Williams.

As he wasn't announced on the microphone, it took about thirty seconds for each section of the crowd to see the man in the white hooded robe make his entrance and, at that moment at least, the crowd gave the biggest pop ever heard in the ECW Arena. Rob looked like he was about to wet himself and I dare say that I let it slip that I was quite impressed.

Again they played the crowd perfectly in leaving it for a a few minutes before Taz and Williams were in the ring together. Dreamer and Lee led a quick trip over to the stage, stopping only for Dreamer to be chokeslammed crotch-first on the guard rail. Once up by Joey Styles (ahem), Dreamer was promptly Taz-plexed off the stage and through a set of tables.

Back in the ring, after a quick Alfonso-Beulah skirmish, Taz and Williams locked up for a couple of minutes of entertaining but highly credible shoot-style grappling. Williams got the last laugh with a Doctor bomb, only for Lee to break up the pin attempt. Dreamer made the save during the ensuing double-team but, a chokeslam on a garbage can later, Lee scored the pin.

This was a very entertaining solid match with action all the way. Many fans were complaining that at barely seven minutes it was too short, but from my view this was only ever meant to be a taster to whet the appetites for future shows. That fans wanted to see more of the match was surely the whole point. It's not as if they were short-changed on the rest of the card...

8) Four Way Dance: ECW Tag Champions Eliminators vs Bruise Brothers vs Samoan Gangsta Party vs Gangstas

Martin Cox said it best when he described the atmosphere before the match as a smell of fear. 1,400 people were quite literally terrified by the prospect of these eight men brawling among them.

The Eliminators came to the ring first and, as the Bruise Brothers made their way down the aisle, I began to wonder how they would be kept apart while the other two teams entered. Foolishly I had been thinking of a *tag* match complete with corners. As the brawling began, the Samoans disappointed everyone by showing up, their offense limited somewhat by the handcuffs they were wearing.

I'll be quite honest here: I had one eye on the door behind me, looking out for New Jack and Mustapha. It was almost an anti-climax when they entered via the traditional route, though what with *Natural Born Killaz* and the two garbage cans full of weapons they brought with them, things were soon pretty lively.

The Eliminators and Bruise Brothers made their way over to the stage to allow New Jack the privilege of eliminating the Samoans via a top rope chairshot. The six remaining men then paired off and headed in our direction. They were only three rows into the bleachers when most of the back row hit the panic button and took an awesome synchronised bump to the floor!

I'm afraid a vague geographic report is all I can give for the next few minutes. The six men went back near the ring, over towards the merchandise stands, out the front door (causing a mass evacuation), back inside a few minutes later and, bizarrely enough, inside the ring. Total Elimination took care of the Bruise Brothers, but a few minutes later it all went pear-shaped when New Jack bailed out, leaving Saturn to floor Kronus. A chair from the top later and the crowd erupted for the title change.

Saturn and Kronus had the obligatory argy-bargy, broken up by the Gangstas attacking them. A young lad then came to the ring and swept the blood and weapon remnants to a chant of "Mop it up mop-boy, mop it up," Seriously.

9) Stretcher match: Rob Van Dam vs Sabu

Dave Scherer had invested his subscribers' money in the dollar store and, as Sabu's name was announced, several dozen coloured streamers were thrown in the ring. With the advantage of height to drop them this worked great, and Van Dam even wrestled the match with a piece of purple streamer stuck to his boot, perfectly matching his wrestling gear. If there's any justice, this footage will make it into the opening titles of ECW TV.

The match itself was the nearest thing to a ***** bout I'd seen in person, and was almost like watching All Japan with furniture. The pair pulled off some amazing spots with the stretchers, easing the memory of that Sid vs Gigante match at SuperBrawl I, not to mentioned that Steiners squash on *Worldwide* in '89...

Joey Styles really was on the stage for this one, complete with most of the crew. I hope they enjoyed this one as much as we did.

When it comes to every move making sense and following a storyline across a series of matches, this was right up there with Liger-Sano. For example, at Matter of Respect, Van Dam finished Sabu with a top rope fisherman buster. A month later at Hardcore Heaven, Van Dam stood up on a table during a Sabu dive, only for Sabu to land a DDT through the table.

The highlight of this match was Sabu leaping over the ropes to the table, Van Dam standing up, Sabu going for the DDT, and Van Dam reversing it into a fisherman buster through the table. Simple, huh.

After 25 minutes, Van Dam tried a somersault splash over the cornerpost onto Sabu, who leapt out of the way leaving Van Dam to crash onto the stretcher. It was almost a relief when he didn't get up before the stretcher reached the locker room, giving Sabu the win.

This was the first time I have ever left a building completely drained of emotion. Normally fans file out of a wrestling show eagerly discussing the night's events. After this card, the crowd was quite literally exhausted. The only thought in my mind was almost disgust at having paid just £10 for this four hours plus of entertainment and excitement.

I was still virtually speechless as George Tahinos drove us back to the

Travelodge hotel, informing us on the way that Beulah had somehow broken her wrist, while Pitbull 2 needed stitches for his over-enthusiastic blading. I can only shudder at the thought of the injuries that weren't so visible.

Back at the hotel we met up with George Mayfield and his entourage of Japanese followers. Sitting in his hotel room, almost passing out from exhaustion, while he displayed his collection of Hiroshi Tenzan T-shirts was another of those surreal moments.

The next hour (12.30-1.30 am) was spent across the road where we persuaded the legendary Chinese restaurant to stay open for our first food in 16 hours. George very kindly paid for us all, and the doctor says my nightmares about that never-ending plate of Chicken Lo Mein should start to fade soon.

Back at the hotel we had a quick word with Jason Harrison before calling a cab home. While we waited, Scorpio departed with his girlfriend, New Jack got ready to shoot promos all night whilst I tried to hide my Pillman shirt, and I upheld my vow to have nothing to do with anyone who was once in the Islanders.

Waiting for the cab we weren't intending to hang around with the hundred other gawking fans, but when Phil Jones mentioned that Raven was having a beer, I knew Matt would never forgive me if I didn't get a photo. He flicked through issue 22 of *Hulk Who?* before signing his appearance in the *Spotlight* profile section. He gave a couple of disapproving tuts and claimed I'd made mistakes, before taking my pen and correcting the article to fit ECW's storylines. Another classic moment.

There was just enough time left to walk over to the bar and say hello to Steve Williams and the missus. Unfortunately he was pretty busy, and I was so in awe that the only thing I could think of to say was "You're Steve Williams!" I assumed that Doctor Death already knew this information, so I left him to his beer, safe in the knowledge that in one day I had achieved everything I could ever reasonably expect out of life.

All that remained was to get the cab back to the Days Inn, find out that somebody had broken into the hospitality room and stolen a camcorder complete with the tapes of the Q&A (bastard), get five hours sleep, catch the Limelight Limousine back to JFK, go through an understandably tight security check, wait five hours for the plane, chase the sun on the journey home so it was only dark for two hours, arrive at six in the morning local time, walk through an empty security and customs area in a city that recently had its main shopping centre blown up, drive back to Leyland, laugh at the 170 tape orders waiting for Rob, drive into Preston, get my photos developed, catch the train to Euston, drop into the Kennedy Hotel to deliver Matt's T-shirts and photo, get the train back to Stevenage, and arrive back home after 35 straight hours of travelling. After 37 hours sleep in eight days, I was ready for bed.

Tuesday 6th August

I had planned to meet up with Ross at the Croydon All-Star show to end the voyage where it began. The card looked a classic:

Southern Area Title: Lee Bronson vs John Prayter
Klondkye Kate vs Pink Power Ranger
Rob Brookside vs Mighty Chang
Steve Casey vs Goldburst

Somehow, I just couldn't face it...

Hulk Who? the Extreme (February 1997)

When we're growing up, we all have ridiculous ideas for trips we'd like to make when we grow up. Some people want to visit every football ground in the English league. Others think of cycling around the coast of Britain. My dream was to spend a fortnight or so travelling around the United States watching wrestling shows wherever I could find them.

Many a rough book or notepad can be found in my loft, detailing such planned destinations as the Global Dome, Portland Sports Arena, Madison Square Garden, and even the classic London-New York-Puerto Rico-Los Angeles-Tokyo-Hamburg-London voyage. There were numerous barriers to these trips though, most significantly that I was only 13 years old and my regular income barely stretched to *Johnny Cougar's Wrestling Monthly*.

After a brief taste of wrestling across the ocean last August, the time finally came this year. I had the money (well, the Student Loans company might argue otherwise, but that's just a technicality), I had the age and experience, I could make the time, I was still young enough to have flexible and less than luxurious travel plans, and most importantly I had a best friend foolish enough to come along for the ride.

The aforementioned flexibility proved vital in the months after I woke up one morning, read the latest *Torch*, saw a group of WWF tapings in Tennessee the week before the ECW convention, and let my imagination run. At various times our schedule included a WWF pay-per-view in Memphis, a Superstars taping in Knoxville, WCW in Atlanta, Southern States Wrestling in Fall Branch, Tennessee, and the Eddie Gilbert memorial show in Louisville, Kentucky. Fortunately, with a little luck, and despite numerous changes of venue, our final voyage proved near-perfect, with even the inevitable low-points proving memorable.

I've heard of many fans going over to WWF pay-per-views as part of a holiday in the States, there've been several British representatives at the ECW Arena, and I even know somebody who went to a Global show, but as far as we can tell, this is the first time anyone from our fair shores has attempted such an undertaking, including a serious go at Bill Apter's infamous `seven shows in seven nights' challenge.

Far more so than the Philadelphia experience of *Hulk Who? Goes*

Extreme, this trip was a journey through a foreign land as much as a group of wrestling shows. For this reason, I make no apologies for deviating my account away from the squared circle wherever appropriate. I certainly hope you agree this makes for an entertaining and informative read, and if anyone is inspired to embark on a similar voyage... we take no responsibility.

Build-up:

The weeks and months before our departure provided a few memorable moments amid the panic of organisation and the ever hilarious "no, please let me have two weeks off university and a coursework extension, it's erm, like a serious journalistic trip. I'll be writing about it in the national press and everything."

Perhaps the highlight, however, came with our attempts to get details for the Eddie Gilbert Memorial Show, with a scheduled Terry Funk vs Doug Gilbert chain match. Knowing only that it was likely to be in Louisville, we remembered that a Rotten brother was organising it, but unfortunately thought of Axl rather than Ian.

This led to several confusing calls to what we believed was the Axl Rotten information line, having taken the number from the trusty old Internet.

"Hello?"

"Oh, er hello. Is this the, erm, Axl Rotten phoneline?"

"Axl what?"

"Axl Rotten. I'm looking for the Axl Rotten Hardcore Info line."

"Hardcore what?! You messin' me about boy? Get outta here!"

Tuesday 11th February

After bumping into a confused lecturer at Preston railway station the previous evening ("Where are you off to then?" "Chicago."), and a mere three hours sleep (Matt's cunning but flawed plan to combat jet-lag), we went through the traditional early start process before catching a 10 am. flight. Obscure wrestling sighting number one came already, with the audio tapes on sale at the airport including the classic *Hancock's*

Half Hour - The Grappling Game ("All I gotta do is tell Crusher that Strangler called his mum a bit of old brass - and it's followed by fifteen rounds of sheer murder.")

The plane was exactly what you deserve when you get a student discount fare, with the main amusement coming when Matt, unaware of airline complimentary drink policies, realised he'd missed out on a free beer. The in-flight entertainment brought us Terry Funk's ECW music as the airline's theme, and a man watching an Undertaker squash on television during the movie. Unfortunately it is my duty to warn all cinema-goers about this theatrical travesty. *Fly Away Home* is *Free Willy* with geese, and ranks below *Suburban Commando*. Avoid at all costs.

Thanks to a short delay and ridiculously brief connection time, we made it through Newark Airport's immigration and customs (as intimidating as last year), and literally walked on to the connecting flight with a minute to spare. Sitting there in our shirt-sleeves, we remarked on how white Chicago looked from the air...

All our cunning plans of running a Dutch auction among local hotels fell apart when we realised we didn't have any quarters for the phone so, with our bodyclocks set to 10pm, we got on the 40 minute train into Chicago itself. Bizarrely we passed such stations as Harlem and California, while the LOD-skit style scenery included a slightly out of place branch of student favourite Netto. Meanwhile a quick ruffle through the local rag revealed that our plans to catch *Beavis & Butthead Do America* were out of the window, though we could always go and see *Fly Away Home* at most cinemas.

Trying to get our bearings in a darkened Chicago centre was highlighted by our pitiful attempts to do anything other than stand on a street corner looking at a guidebook. We eventually made it over to the nation's busiest railway station, Union Station which resembled a luxury hotel; a far cry from the Euston Station experience. After validating our rail passes and booking seats for the following evening's train to New Orleans, we trotted off to the less impressive Greyhound station.

Greyhound had a special deal where if you booked three days in advance, a second person could accompany you for free. We thus presented a simple list of routes, times and prices to the man at the desk to get all the relevant tickets for our Tennessee experience. Simple enough for you?

Apparently not. We were being served by a Mexican gentleman who lived up to every stereotype Bobby Heenan has put forward. Call me racist, but I'd argue that the ability to speak English was a requirement for the service industry. Eventually our money went back and forth a half-dozen times, with my name checked on every occasion, and we wandered off muttering the words "God, that was hard work."

We thought we'd pretty much got the hang of the road layout by now, so wandered off, reflecting on the merits of walking about in downtown Chicago on a darkened evening. Two things stood out on our trek: the irony of homeless people sleeping less than a hundred yards from the most amazing skyscraper architecture you can imagine; and the fact that it was abso-fucking-lutely freezing. It was with blue noses that we arrived at the guidebook's recommended Avenue Motel.

And it was with blue language that we reacted to the fact that the Avenue Motel was closed for refurbishment. Giving up on the wandering about plan, we returned to the Hilton Hotel and amused ourselves by mingling with Chicago's wealthy classes in the queue for taxis. Naturally a smarmy bellboy opened the door and then held out his hand, and naturally we replied "Don't bet on the horses." Thank you, Mr. Dangerously.

So, off to get stiffed £50 by the Days Inn, catch *The Simpsons* and the basketball return of Dennis Rodman on the gogglebox, brave the blizzards to find a fast-food chain (Arby's, whose gimmick was corkscrew shaped fries) and back to bed after a knackering 24 hours of travelling.

Wednesday 12th February

Waking up just in time to miss the free breakfast, I turned on the television to find a forecast wind-chill temperature of -11°. That's -11°Fahrenheit. Elsewhere in the state it was as low as -39°. And we had ten hours to kill.

Despite the chill, Chicago proved a decent enough city to combine sightseeing with store-browsing. Searching toy stores for the new

Mankind figure (it was a national holiday, so there were bloody kids everywhere) and playing the superb Mario 64 filled in the gaps between such tourist attractions as a radio station with a variety of fragments from famous landmarks (Berlin Wall, Westminster Abbey, the Pyramids). Outside the tower stood a colourful bunch of protesters who initially earned our respect for braving the snow. Then we discovered they were opposing British policy over Rwanda: "The Queen is a whore: stop her racist wars." We were this close to coming to blows with the blaspheming scoundrels.

After other cultural landmarks including a Hard Rock Cafe style McDonald's (imagine four life-size statues of the Beatles in your local branch), we hit the important shops, namely music and video. Avoiding the endless piles of *WWF Full Metal - The Album* and the video release of *Fly A-bloody-way Home*, Matt stumbled across the ultimate toy. A Beavis and Butthead keyring, it featured four buttons which activated the duo's voices. "Whoa... cool!", "This sucks!", "Hey baby!" and "I AM CORNHOLIO! Are you threatening me?" What else is there to say. You'd be amazed how many situations Matt found where the new toy proved appropriate.

Last port of call was the Sears Tower, otherwise known as the tallest building in the world (depending on who you believe.) What with views spreading out for ten miles, allowing us to play the old `spot the pay-per-view venue' game, superb central heating and no time limit in the viewing gallery, we soon wished we'd gone up there a bit earlier. As well as using the world's highest urinal, we did the old standing on the guardrail to get a little higher up (which will only make sense if you've seen *Ferris Beuller's Day Off.*)

After our second Big Mac meal of the day, it was on to the "City Of New Orleans" to, um, New Orleans. It was pretty obvious that an Amtrak train was better than your average Network South East commuter train, particularly as our seats were on the top of two floors. With reclining armchair seats, plenty of legroom and acres of space to walk about, we were in for a comfortable night.

Thursday 13th February

After drifting off to sleep I awoke shortly after 1 am. to find Matt had disappeared. After he failed to return in the next hour and I couldn't find him in the lounges, panic truly set in. I was utterly convinced that he had got out at a station for a cigarette break and been left behind in deepest darkest Indiana.

Instead, I eventually found him in a previously unseen smoking lounge where, true to form, he had met up with society's strangest. I'd missed out on a psychiatrist's tales of shooting her husband on numerous occasions, but one character was still recovering from an earlier experience. Apparently a guard had inspected the carriage and mentioned that nobody should be worried if sniffer dogs were brought on board to search for drugs as it was quite common. Shortly after the guard left, the white-faced traveller revealed that his luggage contained marijuana and magic mushrooms.

He kindly offered us a sample of the latter, but we timidly decided that the middle of the night, on a train, in a foreign country might not be the best place to try such a new experience. Instead we bid him farewell as he left the train at 3.30 am. in the trailer park of Fulton, Kentucky. No wonder he needed hallucinogens.

This only left a young man with his own reason to fear the presence of authority. This Florida resident had recently gone up to Wisconsin for a party (kind of puts Preston-Manchester in perspective) and, like all good piss-ups it had ended in assault charges. Unfortunately a condition of his bail was that he spend the next 12 months within Wisconsin's borders, which presumably must have made it a bit hard to get to work each day. After two months, he was missing his beloved car so much that he was now on a clandestine journey from Milwaukee to Chicago to New Orleans to Miami to collect the vehicle and then drive back before the probation officer noticed. Now that is what I call a student story.

Another hour's dozing and we arrived at Memphis station at the somewhat unwelcome hour of 6 am. Perhaps we should have noticed something amiss when, instead of a platform, the departing passengers were expected to walk along the track to the station itself. Remember that little village near you with the really crap railway station? That is what Memphis, the biggest city in several hundred miles, has to welcome its visitors.

Considering the early hour and yet another snowstorm, we decided to wait around in the station for a couple of hours, allowing us to really soak up the atmosphere. Despite its size, Memphis is visited by just one train a day, so its station is understandably spartan. We could just feel the 1950s in the air.

Eventually hunger took control and we began what we thought would be an epic trek into the city centre, with the station nowhere to be seen on our map. Instead it was just a hundred yards before we caught a tram into the bustling metropolis.

Yes, I am being sarcastic here. Maybe it was just the snow, but it soon became apparent that Memphis was empty, and it would be at least noon before anywhere was going to open. The term ghost town seems a cliché, but quite frankly this so-called lively city made Stevenage look impressive.

After braving the language barrier at the Greyhound station (we invented the language, so obviously it was they who couldn't speak English properly), and finding ourselves paying 60 pence for two rashers of bacon which resembled small scabs, among other rip-off prices, we finally found the visitors centre open.

One of the three charming old ladies staffing the desk, genuinely using the expression "gee, whizz" kindly broke the news to us: the Big One Expo Centre, site of Thursday's USWA shows, was eight miles away. And the last bus back was an hour before the show started. And the nearest hotel was almost three miles further down the road. In lieu of a cunning plan, we eventually settled on the old standby of going to that hotel, getting a taxi to the show and then taking it from there.

With the `city centre' about five hundred yards square, and nothing of any consequence open, we spent the next few hours playing that favourite student game, wandering about in the cold while snow seeped in through our trainers, and then waiting 40 minutes for a bus. The only interesting moments came when Matt was interviewed by a resourceful reporter from the local news crew about the freak blizzard, proving our abilities at choosing just the wrong day to visit, and walking past the positively underwhelming Pyramid Arena, laughing to ourselves at just how easy it would have been to get to whereas, thanks to Uncle Eric's shenanigans, we'd had to rearrange our journey to take in Chattanooga.

Arriving at our hotel more by luck than judgement, we discovered what "miles from anywhere" really meant. Skipping lunch with the plan of eating at the infamous Big One food hall, we phoned out for a taxi at about 5.30. Come 6.15 we realised just how reliable local taxis were and decided to start walking, with the map giving us the clear instructions of going down James Street (an expressway rather than a residential area) and turning left at Hollywood Street.

After half an hour it started to sink in just what a ridiculous thing we were doing. We were in a foreign country and walking in the mud at the side of the equivalent of an A road in near pitch-blackness, with no idea of where we actually were. After an hour's walking, highlighted by a great choice between a road tunnel with no pavement (US readers: that means sidewalk) or crossing an electrified railtrack, this holiday was really taking the piss. When we finally came across Hollywood Street, after 75 minutes' walking, I truly believed there was a God. Fifty yards down the road, and there it was, the Big One Expo Centre, and we were dead on bell-time.

"John, just a thought. Why is the car-park empty?"

And why were the doors locked?

And shouldn't there be a bit more noise from inside?

Arse.

Pondering the true meaning of "All dates subject to change", we went across to the nearest gas station and politely asked if they had the number of a taxi firm. "I'll call one for you," the attendant offered, "but it won't come. Ain't no taxi gonna come up here."

Of course, there was a happy ending, with a customer named Harry offering us a lift back, along with the six cans of Coke Matt had just picked up for 60 pence. Somewhat frustratingly the journey back took less than five minutes, with us conceding that we might just have been slowed by traipsing through continuous puddles of melting snow and mud.

With cringe-worthy offerings of thanks we returned to our hotel room and began wringing out or socks just in time for the USA special, *Thursday Raw Thursday*. Having just been baffled by the cancellation of a USWA Memphis show, we were not best pleased to tune into the live broadcast from Lowell, Massachusetts and be welcomed by one Jerry Lawler...

The show opened with the news of Shawn Michaels vacating the world title. Erm, OK. Then Rocky Maivia won the Intercontinental title from Hunter Hearst Helmsley.

At this point we wondered if somebody was trying to tell us something.

The Headbangers then squashed Montoya and Holly while Ross, McMahon and Lawler discussed Michaels having a knee injury. Following the bout, Michaels made his infamous 'lost smile' speech as we discussed the eternal question "shoot or angle?" As always, it was a little of both.

Undertaker pinned Vega. Yawn. Sid and Austin went to a 3:44 no-contest when Bret Hart ran in. Monsoon announced the winner of the Final Four match would get the world title which, as we later realised, guaranteed us the Triple Crown of live title changes (after Davey Boy-Bret at SummerSlam '92 and the MOM-Quebecers fiasco at the Albert Hall).

With lack of sleep and our earlier stroll catching up, I'm ashamed to admit I fell asleep during Farooq and Crush's challenge for the tag titles. I'm even more ashamed to say that when I woke up and heard them announced as winners I nearly died of fright. Thank heavens for screwjobs. Oh yeah, Davey and Owen showed signs of dissent... again.

And in your main event, Bret Hart pinned Vader despite the interference of Steve Austin. So far, so pedestrian.

After the show we were too exhausted to go out to eat, meaning our only food since a meagre breakfast was a moon pie (sort of a mutant Wagon Wheel). Once the novelty of watching UFC, In Your House and SuperBrawl promos on the pay-per-view preview channel, and laughing at the adverts for hubcap sales in the Memphis paper wore off, it was again time for sleep.

Friday 14<u>th</u> February

One advantage to being the only guests at hotels during the quiet season is our soon to be favourite words, "complimentary continental breakfast." I'm not exactly which continent chooses unlimited doughnuts and Danish pastries to start the day, but we certainly weren't complaining. The snow had finally disappeared to be replaced by glorious sunshine, and it was a far more pleasant Memphis that we caught the bus back to (passing a shop named "The King's Court" and an "NWO Mail" van.)

We couldn't possibly miss out on Gracelands, so the morning was spent with every amusing Honky Tonk Man, Colonel Parker and Flash Funk reference you could imagine. The house itself wasn't quite the mammoth mansion you'd imagine, and the tour managed to stay just the right side of tackiness. Unfortunately we'd arrived on Valentine's Day, meaning the floral tributes at Elvis' grave were at ridiculous levels. Even worse, I think a few devotees took offence as we glanced through the King's collection of jump-suits, eagerly speculating "wasn't that the one he wore at SummerSlam '89?"

Cleverly leaving too little time for lunch, we caught the Greyhound bus across the river into Arkansas, heading for Forrest City. We greeted West Memphis (looking like a Wild West-style dust strip rather than an actual town) with the boos its native Sid Eudy deserved, before arriving at our destination a little over an hour later.

Underwhelmed is barely the word. We pulled in next to a liquor store between two motels and, assuming it was just a rest stop for the driver, began moaning that this would have been the perfect place to get off. Then we spotted a rusty Greyhound sign hanging from the side of the store. We were in the city centre.

Assuming we'd missed something, we checked in to the Comfort Inn where we were greeted by a noticeboard proclaiming, and I swear I'm not making this up,: "Y'ALL COME BACK REAL SOON, Y'HEAR." We should have realised something was amiss when it became apparent that the elderly lady on the desk was totally thrown at the concept of a long-haired male.

Glancing through the visitor's information in our (pleasantly spacious) room, we soon found that aside from a Chinese restaurant, a branch of Wendy's and two (count 'em) banks, we had already seen most of Forrest City. The brochure also included a What's On guide. Craft Fair, August. That was it. For the year.

The literature also included a town history which, from memory, ran along these lines:

1872 - Bunch of people building a railway sit down for lunch and can't be arsed to move.

1873 - The boss decides to establish a town.

Nothing to do then but phone up the USWA hotline. This consisted solely of Randy Hales reading out the dates and venues of a week's shows in a manner aimed directly at cretins. Admittedly it was for dates a fortnight earlier, but that may just have been Arkansas. We also called the UTC Arena in Chattanooga, where staff refused to accept Matt's credit card without a US phone number, but told us there'd be additional tickets released on the day.

Then it was a quick flick through the telly stations, where we soon found former USWA announcer Dave Brown presenting the weather! He somehow manager to resist the temptation to say "rain tomorrow, Sunday will be brighter, and on Monday, Jerry 'the King' Lawler takes on Austin Idol," so we grabbed a meal at Wendy's (yup, another hamburger and fries). Listening and observing, we soon realised we were right in the middle of Henry Godwinn country, right down to a framed photo of a pig captioned "Soooeeey!" Honestly. Meanwhile, out in the car park, a quick survey revealed just under half the vehicles on hand were pick-up trucks.

With about thirty-five minutes until the show was meant to start, we began walking to the community centre which, we were informed, was "just up the road." Repeating the mud/dark/fast cars experience, we soon realised where the phrase 'a country mile' originated. It was more by accident than design that, forty minutes later, we arrived at a meagre village hall and paid our $8 for ringside seats, and walked in midway through the opening match.

After all the troubles we'd faced over the last three days, we truly learned to appreciate wrestling. The ring was abysmal, there were no crowd barriers, there was no ring music, the ring announcer was sat on the stage, the faces and heels came out of different dressing rooms, Downtown Bruno was reffing, and we were watching Ken Wayne fight Tony Myers. This was wrestling at its most basic and pure.

The heel Wayne took the win with a handful of tights, but we were too busy getting into the atmosphere to pass judgement on the match. The crowd of about 300 made more noise than I've ever experienced at a wrestling show, and it's worth bearing in mind that it probably consisted of about 10% of the town's population, a proportion no other promotion today could match. One word of advice: don't joke about inbred people and funny looking eyes until you've actually sat in a crowd of them. One man in particular had chosen to sit next to us and spend his evening dressed in overalls, punching the air and repeatedly chanting "Go (insert face's name) go" for the entire evening. Arkansas is weird.

So, I think we've pretty much established this was a million miles away from a WWF tour at, for example, Wembley Arena. So we couldn't believe who walked out next...

2) Brooklyn Brawler vs Bobby Bolton

I guess you can never beat the mystery of just who will appear on an independent show. Believe it or not, this proved a greatly entertaining match. Steve Lombardi might be a nobody, but you don't job for a decade without getting the hang of selling and taking bumps, and this was anything but a Tatanka squash. Fast paced exchanges, no horrible restholds, the odd highspot; this sure beat the hell out of the WrestleMania main event. After a great series of close falls, Bolton got the win with a reversed small package.

3) Super Hysteria vs Steven Dunn

It's quite a bizarre sight to see 300 people cheering in unison for somebody who used to be in Well Dunn. I won't try and pretend this was Misawa vs Kobashi, but it was all good fun, with Dunn initially getting a top rope disqualification win but then demanding the match continue and winning with a sunset flip.

During the interval I took a walk over to the concession stand where they seemed to have all bases covered. There was everything from a USWA sweatshirt to a Brian Christopher photo album, with an incredible amount of photographs for sale. It's all very well the WWF turning up once a year and taking $10 for a piece of foam, but when you're visiting a venue anything up to once a week, and your audience is largely farmers, you have to play to the market, and with dozens of pictures sold at $2 a time you can see how the USWA stays in business.

Meanwhile Matt picked up the main snack on offer, a giant pickle. I repeat, Arkansas is weird.

4) PG-13 vs Flash Flannagan & Bill Dundee

It's worth pointing out here that the previous evening PG-13 (and Lawler) had appeared in Massachusetts, around 1,000 miles away, and had travelled to appear on an Arkansas spot show. That says something to me about the dedication some of the guys in the business possess. This was by far the match of the night, with over 20 minutes of constant action spanning the spectrum from dastardly double-teaming to hilarious comedy. Ice and D, complete with Nation of Domination hubcaps, put on one of the most entertaining performances I've seen.

The main storyline had Dundee trying to get hold of his son (with the inevitable spanking getting a great crowd reaction), while the comeuppances of the heels had us in tears. What with Wolfie selling a low blow by announcing in a squeak that he had to nip to the toilets, and Jamie Dundee threatening to tell his mother of Bill hitting him (think about it), there wasn't a quiet moment. Taking the inevitable style differences into account, I don't think it would be an exaggeration to call PG-13 the new Eddy Guerrero and Love Machine. Of course, in the best heel tradition, they lost the non-title match when Curt Hennig look-a-like Flannagan pinned Wolfie with a cross-body.

5) Billy Travis vs Brian Christopher

Being a spot show, this led to a confusing situation with the USWA title. Christopher had actually lost the title to the NOD's Elijah the previous Sunday in Memphis, but the switch hadn't aired yet. This somehow led to him appearing without the belt, conveniently making this a non-title match. Confused? Well, this is the USWA remember.

Quite simply, Brian Christopher will be atop the USWA for decades to come. As well as inheriting every ounce of crowd-working ability his father possessed, Christopher has developed a 1990's ring style. With his cocky babyface role he is reminiscent of the 1994 model Shawn Michaels, with astounding charisma. The merest hint of a superkick had us all shouting ourselves stupid.

One sign of how the USWA protects its territory came during this match when a group of children started discussing a rumour that Christopher was actually Lawler's son. I don't think anyone here will be picking up on wrestling being worked any time soon.

After snatching victory from fellow babyface Travis with a handful of tights (very sneaky, but he's a nice lad really), Christopher signed autographs for a good twenty minutes. McMahon and Bischoff can only dream of having people this over.

6) Unified Champion Jerry Lawler vs Mike Samples

An amusing pre-match angle had Steve Lombardi announcing that he had been personally sent by Vince McMahon to take care of Jerry Lawler and that his expert guidance would help Sample destroy `the King'. Yeah, right.

This main event consisted solely of Samples digging out every variation on the heel cheating behind the ref's back routine, with everything from brass knuckles to pulling the hair, to Lombardi laying in the chair shots. The difference is that this was so well done it was enthralling. The best piece of crowd manipulation came when somebody realised there was no back entrance to the building and Lawler had to work a spot to distract the crowd from seeing PG-13 sneaking out the front door. Meanwhile, I'm not ashamed to say we popped like never before when Lawler pulled down his strap. It sure as hell beats the Hulk-up. The Brawler's interference finally backfired and Lawler took the win with a roll-up.

After the show we hung around in the crowd waiting for autographs and tried not to crack up when Brian Christopher had to ask his dad for the keys to the car. Lawler chatted with the fans, with one little toddler telling him that Samples had been holding a chain: "Was he? I'm glad you didn't tell me or I'd have run!" `The King' then posed for a photo but not without taking the piss out of my accent and asking "Are you guys from Mississippi?" And like a fool I answered.

You'll hear a lot of tales of how abysmal the USWA's product is. This show saw a crowd heavily into the storylines and creating immense heat, yet never threatening actual unrest. The matches were all entertaining, without a resthold or deadspot in sight. Everything that happened meant something. Everybody took bumps, even referee Bruno. Nothing stretched credibility and none of the spots required suspension of disbelief. At just £5 for nearly three hours of action and fun, I'll take this `crap' any day.

It's also worth making clear that, despite my account, Forrest City was in some ways a perfect town. It literally had nothing to offer besides somewhere to sleep, somewhere to eat and somewhere to watch wrestling. So that's retirement sorted out.

Saturday 15th February

So, we're sitting there in a deserted breakfast room in Forrest City at six-thirty in the morning. The silence is overwhelming. A squirrel running in the road outside has been the major excitement so far. And then we see it. A WWF ring-truck drives down Forrest City high street. You couldn't make this stuff up.

After bidding a fond farewell to the 1950s, we took the Greyhound back to Memphis, only to find we had been blessed with a comedian driver. "Well, we're just approaching Memphis. Everybody gets off here. If you're going on to Dallas, you wait for the next bus. Unless it's already gone, in which case you're in trouble. Don't worry about your luggage as you'll be going back on the same bus. Unless they switch buses. I don't know. You'd better move it yourself then, because they sure won't. So, let's just run through this again. This bus ends here, but the next bus to Dallas might be this bus. You all get off here and either get on a different bus or back on the same one. Your luggage stays here, but if it's a different bus you'd better move it. I don't care, because I'm going home now."

With local buses not running in Memphis on Saturdays, and the distance being uncertain (don't ever trust an American map), we hailed a cab and found yet another eccentric talkative driver.

"Where to, boys?"

"Channel 5 studios please."

"You boys going to the rassling show?"

"Yes! Do you watch the USWA TV?"

"Every week when I'm not working. Everyone watches. I tell you boys, that J.C. Ice, he ain't welcome in the Dundee home yet. I got eight boys of my own back home, and if they acted like that PG-13 I'd have them over my knee..."

The conversation continued with a discussion of the previous evening's show, the relative ages of Lawler and Dundee, and the ring style of Brian Christopher. "He'll rassle clean, but if the other guy starts rassling dirty, he'll get dirty as well." For once a driver truly earned his tip.

Even at a little after nine in the morning, there were about thirty or so already milling in the Channel 5 parking lot. Some people find religion at Lourdes, others are awestruck by Bethlehem, but we were almost shivering with the knowledge that we were standing on wrestling's most famous section of concrete, site of countless legendary brawls, and the greatest hit and run incident of all time.

Among the crowd were several small children, quite naturally playing wrestling. You may remember this from your own school. "I'm Jake the Snake," you'd inform your mates. "You're the Million Dollar Man."

One of these children, perhaps five years old, was vigorously arguing that, "I'm Sir Mo. It's my turn to be Sir Mo"...

As we stood reminiscing, a USWA official began asking the crowd for their tickets. Gulp. Panic. No problem though as, the moment we explained where we had travelled from, he revealed he was Olivia Newton-John's brother in law (not quite sure what that had to do with anything) and said we could come in as his guests and... they might even use us in the show!

With about twenty-five minutes before the show went on air, the crowd were allowed to file into the studio, but not before the aforementioned gentleman checked for signs and demanded that nobody be wearing WCW merchandise. Quite right too.

After passing through a storeroom (which you can see on the various brawls if you dig out your Memphis tapes), and pretending we hadn't just walked past Steve Lombardi, we were escorted into the studio. This was a pretty basic set-up, with Matt and myself sat on the middle corner of the two sets of benches (two rows in each) around the back and right of the studio. The ring was just a couple of feet away in the centre of the floor (well, duh!), with a stationery camera on the far-side and two handheld operators walking around.

The wrestlers would enter from the same entrance to ourselves (on the left as we sat), and from a door behind the stationary camera. Yup, even in a tiny television studio, the faces and heels came out of different doors. Finally, over in the far right sat an announcer's desk and a dubious looking throne.

Ms. Newton-John's relative took care of the warm-up as well as directing the action, and ran through the card before introducing Bundy the Gorilla, the USWA's mascot, who sat a couple of seats down from us. Also mentioned was the floor manager, in charge of the TV production, who was celebrating his 2000th show at the station. Sadly our immediate cake-related thoughts didn't come to fruition.

After checking Matt and myself were in focus, and checking our names and hometowns (by amazing coincidence, a cameraman originally came from one of the many other Prestons across England), the producer introduced Lance Russell who got the standing ovation a legend deserves. Luckily he didn't start telling the Brian Pillman story.

The producer then made a final countdown and we went live to air. A monitor at the back of the room showed the feed from the studio, while a second screen was tuned to Channel 5 itself, which meant Lance and company could keep track of the adverts.

After tape of new USWA champion Elijah showing off his scars from the title win against Brian Christopher in Memphis the past week (keeping track of the title?), and the opening credits, Lance ran down the card. Then, as the director cut to a close-up of our fine selves, the man who has introduced every great name from Jackie Fargo to Tatanka (ahem) said that the opening match was so important, "we've got a couple of special guests who've come all the way from England. John Lister from Preston (ha, take that Stevenage, I've turned my back on you) and Michael (doh!) Brannigan from Manchester. Let's give them a warm welcome!"

So, let's recap here. Lance Russell, that's LANCE RUSSELL has just introduced us by name on Memphis television, and 100 fans are giving us a standing ovation. Forget Fin's editing in *PowerSlam*, I don't care if this does make me sound unprofessional: this was truly the greatest moment in my entire life.

First up was an interview with Reggie B. Fine, now the NOD's King Reginald. (In the weeks before our trip, Reg caught on to the remarkable success of Jerry Lawler, and was thus copying the King gimmick, dropped strap and all, in a hilarious failed attempt to become invincible!) Lawler quickly interrupted, had a go at Reggie's valet "Queenie", and introduced a special co-host for the day.

Sunny.

Hello.

There's us, sitting there, and ten yards away there's Lance Russell and Sunny. Life is good.

1) Jerry Lawler & Bill Dundee vs USWA Tag champions PG-13

Despite the distraction, this proved a pretty entertaining bout. The taxi-driver's fantasies came true as Dundee whipped his son, PG-13 took loads of hilarious bumps, Lawler dropped his strap, we marked out big time, King Reginald ran in with a chain, the heels won and Lance told them off. Great stuff.

2) Steven Dunn & Super Hysteria vs Truth Commission

Perhaps in your weirdest dreams you might have seen four Colonel DeBeers lookalikes. Well, that's what we were faced with here. Fortunately the joys of masks meant we were spared the knowledge that we were watching the man formerly known as Mantaur. The leader of this motley crew gave the predictably politically incorrect speech in an accent so utterly atrocious it turned out to be genuine. *(2005 note: Another member of the squad went on to 'fame' as Bull Buchanan.)*

Super 'teaming with the guy I faced yesterday' Hysteria was smashed to the floor, so naturally Bill Dundee got to replace him mid-match, and the Commission were counted out while continuing the destruction of

Mr. Hysteria. They complained, and Lance told them off. Great stuff.

They then announced the next Memphis Big One line-up, namely:
Dunn vs Truth Commission Tank
Dundee vs Truth Commission Recon
Mike Samples vs Bobby Bolton
Tag Champs PG-13 vs Flannagan & Travis
Unified Champ Lawler vs King Reginald
USWA Champ Christopher vs Elijah

Sounded fun, and it would have been interesting to see Christopher headlining above his father, but alas the show was for the following weekend. Instead we were treated to a great King Reginald interview where he denied the earlier run-in, while Sunny sarcastically yawned. It all turned a bit nasty with Sunny and Queenie nearly coming to blows (with the encouragement of the entire male section of the audience) and Queenie making a disgraceful allegation about Sunny's chest. Lance told her off. Lawler then came and encouraged the fight, with all of the crowd behind him until he suggested Reggie "go back to the project." Cue hilarious black man behind us telling Reggie that "you don't have to take that, boy."

Up next was a Flash Flannagan and Billy Travis promo which, to be honest, didn't sound like a barrel of laughs. Fortunately they cut to a pre-recorded PG-13 interview with plenty of dubious drug allegations. Boy, was Lance upset!

3) Flash Flannagan & Billy Travis vs Ken Wayne & Mike Samples

Nothing great, nothing awful, but a good laugh when Bundy the Gorilla decided to spray Samples with silly-string. Bet he wishes Championship Wrestling from Indiana had lasted a bit longer now, eh? Sunny rambled on about the Nightmares (like she's old enough to remember), and PG-13 ran in with the hubcap for the DQ. A superb four-on-two kick-in ensued before Lawler and Dundee made the save.

Lance then ran down the USWA's spot show schedule for the following month, including Jonesboro, Arkansas and Humboldt, Tennessee. Don't you just love independent wrestling?

Mike Samples came out next for an interview, telling Sunny she was "not too bad looking" and he could pull a few strings in Hollywood for her. It should be pointed out that Samples' gimmick is not a million miles away from a certain nWo figurehead. The rest of the Bobby Bolton targeted interview saw Sunny ripping the piss behind his back, ending with a sarcastic bow. And when Sunny bends over, people notice. Heh heh heh.

The ensuing Bobby Bolton interview was memorable only for the fact that Lance was distracted on his headset by a "backstage incident." Angle alert!

4) Bobby Bolton vs King Reginald

Basically a parody of a Lawler match, this was progressing nicely until Bundy the Gorilla, who'd spent the whole show cheerleading and throwing out some very tasty sweets, walked over to Bolton, patted him on the back... and DDTed him on the floor! After Reginald got the pin, Bundy unmasked as Mike Samples. The fiend! OK, OK, I admit it - we marked out for this one.

After the next commercial break (during which the director offered a Sunny T-shirt to whichever fan made the most noise, causing one poor lad behind us to have what appeared to be an epileptic fit, demanding that Sunny hug him before he leave), they cut to a backstage shot of the Truth Commission beating Steven Dunn to a bloody pulp. Well, you gotta laugh.

Brian Christopher then came out for the pop of the day, giving a dirty look to two fans who'd foolishly come along in their home-made NOD T-shirts. He went on to explain that, though he'd lost the USWA title to Elijah (ahem), he'd got revenge by cutting open his arm and head. Cut to close-up of Elijah's wounds. Lovely.

5) Brian Christopher vs Brooklyn Brawler

Steve Lombardi in main event shocker. Actually this wasn't bad at all, with Christopher's teasing of the superkick the main story. Eventually he hit it and, shock, horror, just as he went for the pin PG-13 ran in for the DQ. Elijah joined the action before a mysterious fellow made the save. A couple of minutes later it suddenly dawned on us. Doug Gilbert was back in Memphis. Cool.

As Lance wrapped up, Gilbert grabbed the NOD fans' T-shirt and tore it up on camera while Christopher cackled and the fans went crazy. Cue closing credits.

Walking back out to the world's most dangerous car park, I think I spoke for both of us in saying that the USWA's TV show was one of the highlights of our wrestling lives. To sit in that studio watching Lance Russell host the proceedings. To literally follow in the footsteps of all those parking lot brawls. To be perhaps two feet from the gorilla angle, an angle that follows a tradition of over twenty years of angles in the same place. To be an actual part of the same show where perhaps hundreds of young wrestlers have made their live television debut.

Where a young photographer named Jim Cornette announced his plans to enter management. Where Eddie Gilbert gave that interview on the 900th show. Where the Moondogs massacred that jobber. Where Terry Funk issued the challenge for the empty arena match.

All of these memories were part of the experience that, with the demise of the territories and the traditional house show circuits, probably has to rank as the most historic thing a wrestling fan can do today.

This isn't to say the USWA's TV show is out of touch or dated. The talent on display was, with only a few exceptions, fresh and youthful, and the wrestling was far from dull. With ninety minutes of constant action, angles, interviews and hype it was soon obvious where the inspiration for RAW and Nitro comes from. In just an hour and a half we had become totally familiar with every ongoing angle and the history of every storyline that would be part of the imminent house shows, while being entertained throughout.

In *Hulk Who Goes Extreme?* I recounted the tale of how, to pass the time, we took great amusement in playing the roles of marks at

Croydon to the full, getting right into cheering the faces and booing the heels. In the USWA we didn't even have to make the effort; it just came naturally. The director and cameramen, obviously through great practice, managed to fine-tune the crowd's reactions with gestures and bribery, yet it never came across as patronising or artificial.

I can't say enough about that fascinating, exhilarating Saturday morning in the Channel 5 studio, except that anyone who cares about the history of this business should make it their life's ambition to become part of decades of history.

Anyway, time was pressing and, with blazing sunshine the climate problem this time, the so-called "two mile" stroll back to the station ended in a sprint to catch the bus. We fortunately arrived just in time to catch the driver coming out of the gents to board the bus and off we went.

There's not that much one can say about a four hour coach trip, with the main highlights being the man sat next to Matt wearing a cap with the word "Jarrett", and passing by a location known as Bucksnort, Tennessee (though strangely it didn't say "Population: Jimmy Golden and his dog.")

Arriving in Nashville we noticed a huge looking arena just yards from the station, meaning Monday was under control. A minor panic followed when we discovered there were in fact three branches of Shoney's Inn in the town but, more by luck than planning, we guessed our rendezvous point correctly and wandered half a mile down the road where we were greeted by Ross Hutchinson and Kenny McBride.

A trip over to, you guessed it, McDonald's occupied the next couple of hours with that ever-hilarious American game of human Frogger the main challenge on the six lane expressways. Then it was back to the hotel to ask for a taxi to the Fairgrounds Arena. And wait. And wait. And wait.

The time passed with the manager of the hotel explaining that he too followed the wrestling, warning us that the Fairgrounds would be full of fat old women, and recalling the last live USWA show he'd been to, on which Cactus Jack won a battle royale.

When the driver eventually came it turned out that `just down the road' actually involved a ten mile journey at double the offered price.

Still, he did give us his card, telling us to "give me a call when you want picking up."

Ha ha ha ha ha ha ha.

Eight bucks later we were standing inside what appeared suspiciously reminiscent of a cattle shed. The arena was pretty similar in size and layout to the ECW Arena, though had the territorial trademark of two different entrances for the faces and heels. Unfortunately, seeing Wolfie D arrive with young daughter in his arms kind of spoiled the evil heel facade.

The crowd was perhaps pushing 400 which, in this day, is certainly nothing to complain about for a venue you run every week. Remembering that Brian Dixon struggles to get a crowd of that size once a month, it's difficult to criticise the USWA.

Any time you go to a show with Ross Hutchinson, bugging the crap out of wrestlers is going to be on the agenda, and this was no different. Ignoring our advice that trying to `kayfabe' the greatest con artists of them all is a bit of a loser, it all ended up with a conversation with Bill Dundee, who gave permission for Ross to film the show for that, erm, documentary for local television. You know the one...

With Ross and Kenny on hand, the talk soon turned round to Dundee's heritage (his `real' voice has a broad Scots accent), ending with the hilarious sight of a thoroughly bemused Flash Flannagan trying to work out what a `Sassenach' was.

Come eight o'clock and we had to stand for the national anthem (like we're really proud of that Star Spangled Banner) before Frank `King Kong Bundy's granddad' Morell came out to ref.

1) Bobby Bolton & Steven Dunn vs Mike Samples & Steve Lombardi

Lombardi replaced the amusingly named Terry 'Oscar' Golden (continuing the Hogan theme) in this decent opener. As always, the emphasis was on winding up the crowd, and this one needed it the least. I've seen some avid fans at Croydon, but I'd have to say that Nashville is the only place I've been to where it seemed everyone on hand literally believed the action was 100% legit.

Best spot of the match saw Samples go for the cover and complain of a slow count, only for the referee to drastically speed up when Samples was in danger of being pinned, reminding him that "you asked for it!" (Ironically, a month or so later I was at a small show just outside Wigan and saw the exact same spot with Johnny Kidd and Blondie Barratt, which I guess is what they mean by wrestling being an international language.)

Bolton, to quote Mick Foley, showed plenty of "fire! pizazz!", but it wasn't enough to save him from a dastardly double-team and pin at 6:22 by... Lombardi. That's Steve Lombardi, with a pin. Don't get many of them to the pound.

2) Jerry Lawler & Bill Dundee vs Truth Commission

Lawler and Dundee are obviously still over with the crowd, but the days of deafening screams seem long gone. This bout was clearly there to establish the new heels and I guess the old hands were the best bet for getting sympathy as those dastardly 'South Africans' had their evil way. Plenty of good old-fashioned fun trying to get Frank Morell to see the double-teaming, and it ended at 16:10 when the nameless fourth member of the squad ran in for the DQ.

Intermission was as always designed solely to allow the fans to buy their merchandise and cough up for a Polaroid picture with the stars. I'd have to say that, dollar for dollar, the USWA really does have the best marketing department. It's all well and good laughing at the Memphis crew, but seeing people pay good money for a Billy Travis keyring really puts things into perspective.

3) Tag Champions PG-13 vs Flash Flannagan & Billy Travis

Another shockingly decent match, well and truly putting paid to the stereotype of Memphis shows being all ten minute headlocks and stalling. We joined the few fans giving the Nation of Domination salute, only for J.C. Ice to inform us that "we don't want you." Charming. The fun and games ended at 14:46 when the champions stole a victory.

4) USWA Champion (ahem) Brian Christopher vs Elijah (Pinfalls only)

Just to put this title thing into context, there is virtually no risk of fans getting suspicious over the titles changing all over the place (as long as they don't read the PWI almanac). The 90 minute live TV show in Memphis is cut to an hour for syndication, so all confusing references are cut out. The main cities on the circuit (Memphis, Nashville, Louisville, Evansville) are all a couple of hundred miles apart and, in any case, with a show in each town every week, there's little likelihood of fans going to more than one venue.

This was a short but spirited brawl, with highlights including the astounding fan reaction to Christopher, the ever-present teasing of the superkick, and the traditional confusion as the referee tried to count wrestlers out and reprimand them despite the stipulations. At 7:13, the former Spellbinder somehow made an extending cane appear literally out of the air, and a swift blow up the bracket earned him the title.

The second money-spinning interval provided another great moment when we discovered that Mabel had no-showed, meaning his scheduled `King vs King' bout with Reginald had been cancelled. Thank you, somebody.

5) Loser Leaves Town: Jerry Lawler, Brian Christopher, Flash Flannagan, Billy Travis & Bill Dundee vs Elijah, King Reginald, PG-13 and Gravedigger

Just for information, Gravedigger (a poor man's Mark Calaway) had been unmasked the previous week in Memphis and revealed to be... nobody anyone had ever heard of.

With Doug Gilbert returning as referee this proved the perfect example of why the USWA was so much better than we'd expected. Among the countless highlights were the pants-wettingly funny kung-fu display by Jamie Dundee (ending when Christopher, who'd been casually watching, landed a swift kick to the chops); Gilbert confiscating a gas lighter and every so often checking it worked, teasing a heel turn; and

Bill Dundee spanking his son, only for Dundee Jr. to run away crying "I'm gonna tell my mama on you!"

Oh yes, and halfway through the bout, PG-13 ran to the dressing room claiming they were going to get the Honky Tonk Man to referee, at which point Wayne Farris looked through the curtain before disappearing. Of course, it all went pearshaped for the heels when Gravedigger tasted his own shovel at 14:46 and earned a one-way trip to the dole office.

Three thousand miles from home, it seemed a shame not to mark out at the back of the arena, and we were soon chatting away to the Honky Tonk Man... as you do. Sitting there trying to be polite, we didn't know where to look as Ross asked the question on everybody's lips:

"How did it feel to job to the Ultimate Warrior in 31 seconds?"

Honky looked hurt for a minute before explaining "the way I look at it, I got $22,000 for thirty seconds work. I can live with that."

After tutting at Jerry Lawler pushing himself throughout the official programme, the longest reigning Intercontinental champion of all-time explained that he was scheduled to come to the ring that evening, but the company hadn't come through with the money. He also asked if we remembered the UK Honky Hotline; "It was advertised in that, er, *PowerSlam* magazine", and discussed his complete lack of knowledge over who his mystery protégé would be, explaining the utter lack of planning and communication that is the backstage of RAW. After `Rockabilly' I'd say it was for the best...

After embarrassing two girls by declaring them "rats" and offering to share them with Wolfie D, Honky then left, followed by the still masked Gravedigger, prompting our mature quartet to break into a rendition of "Na na na na, na na na na.." You had to be there.

Back round the front we remembered calling for the taxi and talked our way back inside the arena where Brian Christopher discussed his WWF dealings before showing us his laser pen for signing autographs and telling the dimmer fans that it was in invisible ink. We then got talking about the Eddie Gilbert memorial show, prompting him to tell one of the sicker jokes of the fortnight:

"Oh yeah, I hear loads of independent promoters are still booking

Eddie. Apparently he's working real stiff..."

Next in the queue to be hassled was Jerry Lawler who ran down Nitro, said Steve Austin was overrated, and answered the question as to why they hadn't brought the Jake Roberts feud to Memphis:

"Oh, we tried to get him down here a couple of times. But he kept showing up drunk and couldn't work!"

With a four-hour drive home pressing, the last of the workers left, with Bobby Bolton calling us over, recognising us from the television show, inviting us to go to Louisville on Tuesday night, and almost wetting himself at the fact that we'd come all the way from England.

As our cab was now half an hour late, he offered us a lift back to the hotel, only to be overruled by passenger Brian Christopher:

"We got this thing in Tennessee when you need a ride, boys. You go like this (extends thumb in air and waves hand). Usually, what'll happen is this (drops thumb, extends middle finger, cackles, car drives off)."

Cocky bastard.

Come midnight, and three calls to taxi firms later, it soon became apparent that no-one was going to arrive, leaving us stranded. Fortunately the last security guard decided he wanted to go home and persuaded a night worker to give us a lift.

Rather worryingly, we could only give the hotel's location as "just by the topless dancing bar." Even more worryingly, he didn't have any trouble finding the place.

One overpriced pizza delivery later and I nodded off after what would have to be one of the better days in my wrestling life.

Sunday 16th February

After a ridiculously early visit to the Shoney's restaurant (the U.S. equivalent of Harvesters perhaps) and making them regret the words "all you can eat breakfast bar", only the well-organised, punctual packing machine that is Ross Hutchinson stood in the way of another four hour coach journey. Despite the young Scot's efforts, we were soon on our way and, a couple of hours of sunshine and Smoky Mountains later, we were passing through Kenny's beloved Shelbyville, the town where he spent 1995-6 on exchange.

There's not exactly a great deal to say about Shelbyville, except that Gypsy Joe promotes All-State Wrestling every Thursday night at the back of the Greyhound station. Seeing the marquee outside we could guess at the excitement that would be caused by a `championship match', All-State not having its own titles. Oh, and there's a "Bagwell's Repair Centre".

The first real excitement of the trip came when, ignoring the no smoking rules, Kenny sneaked a quick ciggie in the toilet. One flashing light later and a raging driver decided young McBride was being thrown off at the next stop, a town not quite as notable as Shelbyville.

O.K., we thought, not to worry. He can get the next bus and catch us up. Unfortunately the next bus was in 24 hours, meaning Kenny was facing a night on the side of the road.

A change of underwear later, some humiliating begging and pleading, and the ever-classic "He's a diabetic and there'll be no insulin in this place, so if he dies it's all your fault", saved our party from disaster.

"That does it," Kenny informed us. "I'm giving up smoking!"

Upon arriving at Chattanooga, having put our watches forward an hour, we noticed a slight con. The Greyhound station, traditionally in the downtown area of each city, was not actually in Chattanooga, more a distant field. About twenty quid taxi fare distant. While we worked on a cunning scheme involving a taxi to the airport and then the complimentary shuttle bus to the hotel, our fellow passengers provided the traditional Tennessee welcome with a bodybuilder overhearing the word "wrestling" and telling us all about his old buddy Tony Atlas.

Getting in the taxi, we wondered why the driver was so keen to check we knew about the $6 minimum fare. Forty-five seconds and two turns later we realised why as he pulled up into the airport.

Waiting for the shuttle to arrive, we took a stroll around Chattanooga airport, which had to be one of the most impressive sights of the trip. Perhaps because nobody ever uses it, the airport resembles a more upmarket version of the London Hilton, with plush green carpet and gleamingly clean marble steps. It also has a bookshop where the 1996 PWI Almanac is number nine in its best-sellers display.

The surprise of the airport was nothing compared with the Chattanooga Choo-Choo hotel. Far from the hundreds of identical Travelodges or

Comfort Inns, the Choo-Choo is a converted railway station, home of the engine from the song we had to ban Matt from singing to any Chattanoogans. The waiting area is now the lobby, the ticket desk has become the reception, you can stay in converted carriages on the track and there's even a rail service to take you around the hotel. It was almost mindboggling that with over 3,000 rooms, the hotel was bigger than the entire population of Forrest City, where we had been just two days earlier.

Of course, we were in the cheapest, half a mile from the check-out, let's get four people in but only pay for two so Matt and Kenny have to keep hiding, backpackers room, but it still beat the crap out of anywhere else we stayed.

Still, no sooner had we checked in than we had to begin the complicated walk ("You haven't got a car? You need a car.") to the UTC Arena. Knowing the vague direction and that it was past a hill proved enough for us top orienteering types, and we were soon following a passer-by's directions through a set of tennis courts and out into...

Into a rampway going under the arena with Barry Horowitz wondering what we were doing there, and an Ultimate Solution style security guard waving an offensive weapon at us.

A few dozen hearty apologies later and we'd been escorted from the artists entrance security zone and made our way over to the box office where Chief Jay Strongbow's nephew tried to score a couple of freebies. Once he'd been dealt with, with just an hour before showtime, Matt initiated perhaps my favourite conversation of all time:

"Hi, have you got a couple of $17 tickets left?"
"Yes, here you go. Second row from the ring."

Keeping tickets back until the day of the show to encourage a walk-up crowd is cool. Ross and Kenny swore a bit at the trouble they'd gone to with international phone calls, bought the two seats next to us, and went off to scalp their tickets for the stands. Between that and spotting a ridiculous number of bWo and ECW shirts, we were soon inside and watching our cash disappear at the merchandise stands. The range was surprisingly limited, with only Bret Hart, Michaels, Sid, Austin, Mero and Marlena having T-shirts, and no official event programme. I picked up a Marlena shirt (Janet Jackson album cover pose, now a popular fashion item in Preston), while Matt managed to get one of the last Austin 3:16 shirts before they became by far the quickest item to sell-out.

Inside the 10,000 arena itself (which, by the way, is the equivalent of your local University's sports hall), the crowd of 6,399 (about 85% of capacity considering seats sectioned off for the cameras) looked on jealously as we discovered that our second row seats were on the aisle, facing the camera. The memories of blizzard Chicago and early-morning abandoned Memphis were finally beginning to fade.

The ring announcer then ran down the card, explaining that Maivia vs Helmsley had been added, Bart Gunn would replace Maivia in the six-man, and the Final Four winner would immediately defend against Sid.

With little excitement in the remaining minutes except for putting Lance Wright off his job with "Hype Central" chants, Perfect Strangers playing on the sound system, and Jerry Lawler saying hello on his way to the broadcast booth, it was soon 6:30 and time for Doc Hendrix to hit the ring for the Free For All.

With no possible way to ignore the overwhelming Freebird chants, he had to admit "I'm Doc Hendrix and some people say I fly free as a bird."

Next up was Steve Austin who worked the crowd, including a personal verbal attack on a lad in the front row with a 3:16 shirt and sign, arguing that "making a crappy little sign don't make you as good as Stone Cold."

Unfortunately it was then time for the darkest of dark matches:

1) Godwinns vs Headbangers

The only real stinker of the entire fortnight, this featured two guys working their butts off, selling perfectly, and showing innovative offense and great charisma. Then they jobbed to the Godwinns.

After an in-ring Vader interview, during which we strained our necks trying to read the floor manager's format sheets, it was time for the countdown and the show to go live on air.

2) Marc Mero vs Leif Cassidy

Special mention has to go to Sable for keeping in her costume up top, and managing to walk in perhaps the longest heeled boots in the history of wrestling. This was a real decent opener, but with Mero's highspots limited by a knee injury, the crowd reaction to the fine matwork was disappointing; as Ross pointed out, a Japanese crowd would have been going insane for some of the submissions and escapes on display. The turning point came with Sable slapping Cassidy on the outside, and Cassidy grabbing her only to be hit with a Mero topé. The 'Wildman' followed quickly with the shooting star press for the win at 9:27.

The Shawn Michaels situation aired on the live broadcast at this point, while the live crowd were entertained by our new mate (who recognised us on the way to the ring), the Honky Tonk Man.

3) Flash Funk, Goldust & Bart Gunn vs Farooq, Crush & Savio Vega

Flash and the Funkettes danced their way down the aisle as the world (and unfortunately Kevin Dunn) read Ross' "WWF fears ECF'nW" sign. Little did we know how well-timed it was. Goldust's entrance saw the traditional golden shower (as it were), with the tragic sight of grown men trying to grab pieces of gold foil from the air (I got two!) Bart Gunn's entrance was highlighted by a bloke dropping a pin. The Nation chose to enter through the crowd as we reflected on the genius of a gimmick where Ron Simmons, Crush and Kwang can be considered top heels.

The match was an unspectacular brawl, but Funk's one man show kept it entertaining. Predictably it ended with some dastardly cheating as Crush broke up a Gunn cover and put Farooq on top for the pin at 6:42. Oh yeah, and Jamie Dundee gave us a wink on his way back down the aisle.

4) Intercontinental champion Rocky Maivia vs Hunter Hearst Helmsley

A very pleasant surprise, this proved far better than it looked on paper, with the relatively inexperienced Maivia keeping up well. The general storyline was Helmsley dominating but failing to get the cover, with a nice spot being a repeat of the Maivia small package that won him the title, only with Helmsley escaping this time. The finish saw Goldust come to ringside and distract Helmsley, allowing Maivia to hook a reverse rolling cradle at 12:28 to retain the title.

After the match came the angle where `spectator' Chyna grabbed Marlena and choked her out before being arrested. From our vantage point this came across as extremely legitimate, explaining the `correct' audience response. Of course, on television it was handled as to obviously be an angle - but I guess that's wrestling for you.

5) Tag champs Owen Hart & Davey Boy Smith vs Phil LaFon & Doug Furnas

Yet another match vastly underrated by most viewers, this was every bit as good as we expected. By far the best regular WWF tag match of the last two years (like that's any kind of compliment), this had constant, fluid, dare I say Japanese quality action throughout. Excuse the continual namedropping, but Davey Boy acknowledged our "Stampede rules!" chants.

Live this was ****, and it doesn't lose much on tape. Just as the rest of the crowd started to get into the action, and things were getting really exciting, the screwjob finish kicked in. Don't you love American wrestling?

Davey Boy went for the powerslam, Owen ran in and nailed LaFon with his Slammy trophy, and the champions were disqualified. The pair then argued, including Smith accidentally breaking the trophy, but eventually Clarence Mason sorted it out. Stay tuned.

6) Final Four for WWF World title: Bret Hart vs Steve Austin vs Undertaker vs Vader

It's extremely rare in today's frantic week by week wrestling world that a match can seem like a major event. I'd say that in the WWF and WCW last year, just four bouts (Hart vs Michaels, Hart vs Austin, WCW vs Outsiders & ? and Hogan vs Piper) seemed to have that real big match status. Sitting in a pumped UTC Arena, it was clear this match fitted that category.

There's no argument that it didn't live up to its status. Outside ECW, this is the only match I've ever witnessed live that could arguably be considered *****. On film this was excellent, and being there live only increased the atmosphere inherent with four guys fighting at the same time.

Within a couple of minutes a misplaced chair to the head busted Vader wide open. I wouldn't stake my life on it, but live it seemed almost certain that a blade wasn't involved. The extent of the injury and the obvious pain it caused created a performance from Vader that will be long remembered and even earned him a standing ovation after his elimination. We were actually hoping the win wouldn't be his, just for the fear that he would have to risk a match with the professional worker that is Sid.

Amid constant action and incredible heat, a personal highlight saw Vader and Hart brawl over the guardrail and literally into our seats. Ticket stubs went in the resulting puddles of blood (that one never fails to earn you a dirty look from other fans), while Matt literally had to wipe himself clean after being splattered with crimson.

Back in the ring, Austin was the first eliminated over the top rope after a legitimate strain to an existing knee injury necessitated an unplanned early exit, while Vader went the same way a few minutes later (though not until after pulling off a missed moonsault). Finally Steve Austin's backfired interference allowed Hart to eliminate Undertaker to take the title at 24:04.

This was a truly classic match, and the intensity of the four competitors only added some much needed prestige to the vacant title. Unfortunately, as the broadcast went off air, Sid arrived.

7) WWF Champion Bret Hart vs Sid

It'll probably take longer to write about this match than it took to happen, so I'll cut straight to Steve Austin running in for the disqualification and everyone going home.

Being thousands of miles from home, there was again nothing better to do than risk the wrath of security guards and watch everyone leaving. Highlights included Flash Funk departing with the Funkettes in a Scooby Doo style van immediately christened the Funkmobile, persuading the Spanish commentators to burst into "rudos, rudos, ruuuudoooos!", watching as only Ross took any notice of the Nation of Domination's anonymous henchmen, and seeing Mankind leave with a delirious Dewey Foley holding his hand. (*2005 note: Ross also chatted to a wannabe wrestler who was considering a trip to WCW's PowerPlant. He intended to use the name 'Horshu'. Yup, seven years before he appeared on the national stage, it was Luther Reigns.*)

Of course, just because everyone had left didn't seem a good enough reason to begin the walk home, so we amused ourselves by taking the piss out of two girls auditioning to be Ahmed Johnson's ring rats, and pretending to show interest in a group of 'hardcores' whose knowledge extended to having once seen the word "jobber" on the Internet. Ho hum.

The end became inevitable as a garbage man began tossing sacks of litter into a large open bin, earning himself chants of "Droese, Droese", and a round of cheers as each sack hit the spot, with Kenny suggesting he enter the Royal Rumble. Unfortunately for the gallant refuse worker, the last sack bounced off the rim and back to the flaw, making one phrase inevitable:

"You fucked up! You fucked up!"

Just as we began wetting ourselves, the remaining security officer lifted up his gun and decided now was the point we were going home. Looking at the pistol we agree. A half-hour later I tired of Ross calling reception to ask for a free sample of the adult channels in our room and, as the surreal conversation turned to who would win a fight between *Scooby Doo* and the dad from *Button Moon*, I fell asleep.

Monday 17th February

It seemed the only thing I missed while asleep was an episode of WCW Worldwide at 1:30 am. The excitement included Jim Powers jobbing and a Horsemen vs Dungeon of Doom main event. No contest in case you're wondering.

With another early coach to catch, there was no time for breakfast (like we could have afforded anything in that place), and we only had a few minutes to flick through the dozen or so channels on offer. In this brief period, however, we managed to find cult film *Bad News Bears Go To Japan*, which started off like an episode of *Champ Forum*, and led at one point to the young baseball team's manager putting on a mask and fighting Antonio Inoki. You wouldn't believe the pop in our room when Inoki jobbed.

The return trip proved slightly less interesting the second time, so we passed the time (which seemed shorter once we put our clocks back) with a complicated series of calculations to see if we could afford to drop the plans to head south to Birmingham, Alabama for a WWF show, and instead head up to Louisville. With the WWF show being reminiscent of another Birmingham visit I could mention (the card turned out to be Mosh vs Freddie Joe Floyd, Thrasher vs Horowitz, Godwinns vs Blackjacks, Bracchus vs X, Diesel vs Hopper, Goldust vs Vega and Undertaker vs Farooq in a cage), it seems fortunate with hindsight that we chose the Louisville option.

Then we argued for about two hours as Ross tried to claim Al Snow was the lowest thief of all for the Avatar/Hayabusa gimmick copy, while we kept on winding him up until everyone on the bus was about to get involved.

Once in Nashville, we were an hour early for checking back into Shoney's, so we walked over to the arena wondering where the wrestlers would go in. Just as we were about to ask a security guard, a familiar voice asked the same question from his window. Chauffeur Jim Cornette received directions and continued driving while passenger Vince McMahon carried on shaving.

Barry Horowitz and Tracey Smothers went past next, causing Kenny great distress when "Freddie Joe" failed to recognise the Scot with his new King Kong Bundy hairdo.

Round the entrance to the underground car park it was a beautiful sunny afternoon, and there seemed nothing better to do than hassle arriving wrestlers. First up was Downtown Bruno and Steve Lombardi who discussed our journey, with Bruno pointing out "So you're following round all the territories. I guess that's what we do, except we get paid." Everyone concerned tried not to recall exactly how much they got paid.

After Bruno answered the eternal question (yes, he was the rogue cameraman that cost Hogan the belt at King of the Ring '93), Lombardi challenged us to name all the characters he had portrayed. Three and a half hours later...

Unfortunately he seemed a little embarrassed that we knew about his day as the Bushwhackers' kangaroo, so the pair went off for a stroll, asking us to point Bill Dundee in their direction if he turned up (?!)

At this point we were joined by an ugly fat woman in a bWo shirt, carrying a variety of signs declaring her love for Phinneous Godwinn. It turned out that Tennessee had produced the first ECW 100% mark, proven when the lady thereafter referred to as "Fat Minger" saw Chris Candido arrive and began berating him for hitting her beloved Tommy Dreamer with a garbage can.

Despite the distraction, and despite the obvious frustration at having just lost their mobile phone, Candido and the charming young lady on his arm proved more than willing to chat, sign autographs and pose for pics. Sunny/Tammy was a pleasant surprise; not only just as beautiful as she appears on TV, she was perfectly pleasant and polite even in the middle of a near tantrum. As well as discussing the pictures of herself in Matt's *Weekly Pro Wrestling* ("I love that outfit! I made it myself!"), she also talked about the complete lack of organisation that Honky had described at RAW tapings, and modelled the ECW Candido 'No Gimmicks Necessary' shirt.

Just to recap, all my course pals are sitting in Preston on a rainy February day learning about Economics of the Media Industry, while we're standing in T-shirts in blazing heat helping Chris Candido and Sunny look for their phone. Heh heh heh.

The autograph hunters began gathering in hordes not long after so, stopping only to talk to Bret Hart, and lean into the car driven by Farooq and taunt a poor little girl with the accusation "You see that Ron Simmons? That's your dad that is. Your mum's had him.", we checked into the hotel and got the day's meal... at McDonald's.

Here we sat next to a group of men with WWF identification tags so, within five minutes, discovered which hotel the crew was staying at. Hey, you travel 3,000 miles, you're gonna act like a mark.

Back at the arena we took the intricate "pick up your pre-ordered tickets" challenge and made our way to our seats, stopping only to consider the less pleasant medical effects of eating at McDonald's for seven straight days. (Hey, I told you this account would be detailed. At least I haven't mentioned the phrase "Did anyone leave a gherkin in the toilet?" yet.)

The great ironies of international travel raised their ugly heads again as we found that the seventh row seats we'd braved cross-Atlantic phone calls and Tennessee accents to get turned out to be the worst of all eight shows we went to. If you remember when you were a kid and got bored with your `Jack in the box', imagine just how dull it is when you are Jack for over four hours.

For the trivia buffs, the crowd was 5,876, with the $85,000 gate the highest in the town since 1989. Being at least a 10,000 seater building, the fact that it looked so full on television only shows why the WWF is considered the master of television production. Another pointless rendition of the national anthem by a Nashville `celebrity' and it was time for the dark match:

1) Jackie Fulton vs Ed Rock

I guess it wouldn't be a TV taping without a nobody receiving a tryout, but this proved a bit of a rarity with the crowd actually reacting to the newcomer and getting into the match. Fulton won of course.

RAW went live on air with Sid and Bret Hart entering the ring, only for Steve Austin to run in and work over Sid's knee, delaying the match until later in the show. Did anyone say "ratings ploy"?

2) Savio Vega vs Marc Mero

Nothing special here, though highlights included Sable kicking the crap out of PG-13, with the finish coming when she was chased into the ring and Mero was disqualified (answers on a postcard...) Ahmed Johnson then ran into the ring in a pair of pink pyjamas laying everyone out with the largest 2x4 you've ever seen. I guess this counts as playing to a worker's strong points.

Between matches the live show went to interviews backstage, with the live broadcast being shown on monitors around the arena and on the giant screen. Bret Hart rambled. Sunny came to ringside with the flimsy excuse of being a timekeeper and with a flimsier hot pink outfit.

3) Intercontinental champion Rocky Maivia vs Leif Cassidy

Pretty much your usual Cassidy match, i.e. he does all the work and gets toss-all reward apart from the chance to lie down for three seconds. The highlight for television viewers was Jerry Lawler grabbing an ECW sign (which we'd already noticed as being suspiciously prominent) and setting off the now infamous angle. Unfortunately we couldn't see the monitors, so were instead entertained by Maivia's wide range of flawlessly-executed progressive offence. (Don't worry, he's American, so he won't understand irony.) One deadly shoulderbreaker later and he retained the title at 9:32.

Next up was the usual family values in-ring interview with Goldust and Marlena (announced from Hollywood, causing one wit to pronounce "Bullshit, you're from Texas boy!"; thanks for that great inside info), ending with Helmsley distracting and the woman soon to be known as Chyna repeating her run-in from the night before.

4) Headbangers vs Matt & Jeff Hardy

The Hardy boys were fortunate enough to get matching outfits, presumably establishing them as a `real' jobber team. One fan spoke everyone's mind, asking "where's Nancy Drew?" Obviously this was a serious, important, relevant match and not just filling time until the second hour kicked off, which is why it lasted all of 3:58 before the jobbers, erm, did their job.

Just as everyone turned over their TVs to avoid Nick Patrick vs Randy Anderson, the second hour of *RAW* started with the delayed World title match. Again, Austin attacked Hart (this time backstage), Monsoon announced the match would end the show, and Eric Bischoff frantically rearranged the *Nitro* line-up.

5) Flash Funk vs Owen Hart

Cool. Naturally they couldn't let something this good get over on TV, so it was at this point that Paul Heyman phoned Lawler. Meanwhile we relaxed and watched a New Japan calibre bout complete with the smoothest plancha of the fortnight by the former Scorpio. Hart got the win at 11:43 after Davey Boy hit Funk with the Slammy trophy.

6) Bart Gunn vs Hunter Hearst Helmsley

Probably the only highlight of this one was the way at least half the crowd went to the toilet as soon as they heard the word "Gunn". It ended at 4:40 when Goldust took Helmsley on an arena tour for no apparent reason causing everyone to turn around and look for any top stars hanging around the broadcast booth. As only Henry Godwinn was there, everyone turned back to the ring. Gunn got the countout win and the respect of the crowd. Well, that's half true.

The monitors then went to Dr. James Andrews announcing that Michaels could return in four to six weeks, receiving shockingly little response.

7) World Champion Bret Hart vs Sid

Look, Sid was in it. What else do you need to know about the match quality. Austin ran in and whacked Hart with a chair, giving Sid an easy powerbomb for the title at 14:14. Nothing like hard work and professionalism being rewarded. And this was nothing like...

The live show went off the air with Sid and Undertaker nose to nose in the ring, while all the fans suddenly realised what the WrestleMania main event was going to be and began making plans to spend the $29.95 they'd save by not buying the show.

8) Bob Holly vs Freddie Joe Floyd

I've got absolutely no idea what happened in this one as everyone was far more interested in watching the production crew take down the *RAW* signs and replace them with *Superstars* banners. Maybe I'm being harsh, but seeing Lawler and Ross walk out didn't exactly inspire us to watch this one. According to the Torch, Holly won.

9) Davey Boy Smith vs Crush

After a two hour, high energy, live broadcast, this wasn't exactly enticing. Crush got a dodgy victory and Clarence Mason got the sack.

10) Goldust vs T.L. Hopper

Can't comment on this one really, as I went to the loo just for the juvenile, immature gag of pulling the chain in synch with Hopper's `music.'

11) Headbangers vs Godwinns

No improvement on the previous night, the Godwinns were accompanied by a Nashville `celebrity' who at least gives me the inspiration to use the word `twat' in this magazine for the only time. It ended quickly with the appearance of two blokes we'd assumed to be jobbers when they entered the arena earlier in the afternoon, but turned out to be Barry Windham and Justin Bradshaw under the `New

Blackjacks' gimmick.

12) Blackjacks vs Headbangers

This ended quickly when the Godwinns ran in. This whole scenario was just as bad as you're probably imagining.

Sid then gave an interview. The ring announcers kept reminding us of the `main event' in a desperate attempt to stop everyone going home.

13) Undertaker vs Vader

This is the match where Ross' "Sabu" sign got on screen. Mankind ran in and accidentally hit Vader before Undertaker picked him up for the tombstone, accidentally dropped him, and everyone concerned tried to pretend Vader hadn't just nearly broken his neck.

I've probably been a little overly cynical with the individual matches here, but the show overall was great fun. It was quite surprising just how easily the two hours of the live broadcast were filled without the promotion being spread thin. The only criticism I'd make is that the *Superstars* taping would have been far better before the live show as it came across as obviously second rate, with little incentive for fans to stay on.

With the epic show finally over it was off to the hotel lobby to watch a valet driver asking various 300lb men for their keys (asking very politely, one should add). First to arrive was Goldust who signed his appearance in HW?'s `Spotlight', discussed the merits of chewing tobacco and offered the critique "Dusty Rhodes is fat."

Over the next couple of hours, dozens of wrestlers were subjected to the UK Clique school of harassment, so I can only recall a fraction of the many bizarre conversations. For starters there was the Headbangers who admitted they'd prefer to work for ECW, "but we need the money you get here." Jamie Dundee recognised us from the Memphis TV, explaining "I wanted to come out and call you "pommie bastards", but they wouldn't let me say "pommie"." Leif Cassidy turned up and reminded Ross that "I didn't even get a chance with the Avatar gimmick, so it was a bit hard to steal anything."

Kevin Dunn came past and discussed the fine art of sign confiscating, Kevin Kelly explained the ECW angle, Lance Wright did an edition of Hype Central for the camera, the Godwinns failed to understand sarcasm, and an anonymous bloke vigorously denied being a referee, earning a surreal chant of "You slap mats! You slap mats!"

Rocky Maivia flicked through *Hulk Who?*, said he was 24, and denied being the most over-pushed wrestler in WWF history, though strangely changed the subject when asked to name somebody with a bigger push.

Vader, sporting a truly gorgeous scab above his eye, politely excused himself with "excuse me gentleman, I have a date with Coors Light", while Tony Anthony looked miserable. Tom Prichard gave a dejected sigh when we mentioned Mark Henry.

Then came Clarence Mason who, on hearing Matt was a lawyer, offered him a job with the firm! Chancing our luck, we asked to join the Nation, to which he replied "You'll have to check with our honourable leader Farooq. He's off at the titty bars!"

It getting a bit chilly, we played the old "we're guests, honest, I mean don't you get loads of people staying here in ECW shirts?" and headed up to the bar, only to find the sucky side of American licensing laws and have to hover outside. This was not made any more amusing by the aforementioned Fat Minger (who'd been sat front row, on the aisle) sitting with the likes of Vader.

After chatting to the Funkettes, Tracey and Nadine (first name basis, see?), and watching Ross confuse Ahmed Johnson ("You're asking me the difference between working for Global and the WWF? I'd have thought that was pretty self-evident!"), it only took a little more of the Hutchinson charm before Kevin Kelly came over and started choking out Ross, earning the pop of the night.

And finally, it was time to go over to the lobby and chat with the lonely bloke sitting on his own, one Lance Wright, who didn't want to be drinking with his boss. Lance was a real nice guy, and told us all about working for ECW and the WWF, and put to rest Sky's claims that the WWF edit their own material:

"They make us cut it to shreds - we're fighting it all the time. It's bad enough that you can't see everything, but the really annoying thing is that it costs us huge amounts of money because we have to edit everything together twice."

The much-feared production manager then came over to Lance, attempting to put us off the scent with a whispered, "Lance, come here. Kayfabe." While we sad little smart marks began cracking up at having heard an insider term, Lance was persuaded to go out on the town with the Funkettes. Doh!

Oh, and T.L. Hopper went to the toilet, which was really funny at the time.

So, stopping only at a gas station for supplies, and a drink named "Samoan Splash", it was time for bed again.

Tuesday 18th February

With the old "all you can eat" deal at Shoney's, it was another rush job in the morning, with only thirty seconds of television viewing time. And in that thirty seconds we saw an advert for Sunny appearing on that evening's Entertainment Tonight.

Another day, another Greyhound trip, another time zone change. This time we entertained ourselves by adopting an underage girl returning home from prison, buying her cigarettes at every stop, and wondering why she kept laughing at wrestling jokes she so obviously didn't understand. With no smoking on the four hour journey, and a special offer at one of the gas stations, Louisville's residents were greeted with the sight of Ross and Kenny frantically smoking the largest cigar in living memory outside their Greyhound station.

Louisville seemed a pretty welcoming sight as we simply turned out of the station and walked two hundred yards down the road and found the historic Louisville Gardens, home of the evening's card. Quite a change from "just down the road." Even better, our planned home for the night, a basic but cheap Travelodge (just by Skip's Auto Sales), was just two hundred yards further down. With the fine weather continuing, Louisville was starting to rock.

The *Rough Guide to the USA* contains many useful travelling tips.

Not among them is the fact is that you have to be 21 to rent a room in Kentucky.

Louisville suddenly seemed to suck.

The only option remaining was to spend the night at the Greyhound station and take through-the-night buses and/or trains. With a couple of hours to kill, and nowhere to stay, we chose to forget our impending poverty and go to a well-hidden, empty Chinese restaurant and get some real food for once.

Down at the arena, we took a trip round the back so we could laugh at Ross trying to get refereeing work, and then went in the paying entrance, failing to get Ross' huge rucksacks kept safely.

About 200 were on hand for the USWA weekly show, which was quite a depressing sight in the 7,000 seater building. Designed perhaps for basketball, with stands on the two long sides of the ring, the arena would obviously have been perfect for wrestling... 20 years ago. Today it is simply embarrassing, especially as those with the cheapest tickets are sat up in the stands, rather than creating an atmosphere on the floor. Oh, and separate dressing rooms again.

However, the few fans that remained were clearly among the most loyal, and one thing that stood out was that, despite being pretty much the same basic show as in Nashville (and presumably the rest of the circuit), the workers recognised the subtle differences between the two audiences, tailoring the action to their demands. I'll try to mention a few examples throughout, but it was amazing just how different the two crowds really were.

Before the show started we got chatting to perhaps the sweetest middle-aged "old lady" (if that makes sense), who was as dedicated a fan as you could find, and probably the nicest person we met in the States. She asked us to explain Matt's 3:16 shirt (which took all our talents to avoid committing blasphemy), showed us her photo collection (I'd say she keeps Brian Christopher in food based on the number she had of him), and described just how popular Doug Gilbert would be, pointing out that "I'm being serious, nobody disses Eddie here."

She also proved just how effective the USWA characters are, explaining that her sons were "just like them. All that baggy pants, and rap music. I sure hope Bill Dundee puts his boy over his knee again."

Incidentally, although we didn't realise it at the time, we were in Eddie Gilbert's hometown on the second anniversary of his death, which is kind of cool. We were also in the Louisville Gardens a year to the day from In Your House VI getting a sell-out crowd in the building.

1) Steve Lombardi & Mike Samples vs Bobby Bolton & Kip Morris

That's Kip Morris as in "Smoky Mountain jobber" in case you'd forgotten. As we'd basically seen this one before, we amused ourselves by winding up our new mate Lombardi with a chant of "You're a kangaroo! You're a kangaroo!" He seemed to be enjoying it, so we continued with "You were Doink! You were Doink!", and once we ran out of gimmicks at 16:36, they went to the finish with our man pinning Bolton.

2) Truth Commission vs Todd Morton & Bill Dundee

Yup, SMW jobber Todd Morton. Nothing new, but still reasonably entertaining, and interesting to see most of the crowd recognising the masked men as Punisher and Smoky Mountain Massacre. At 8:33, Morton did what he's paid for.

First interval, Dundee sells pictures, Ross talks to him, the USWA doesn't hire a new referee. The same old story.

3) USWA Champion Brian Christopher (double ahem) vs Elijah

Well, many British wrestling fans can claim to have seen a title change, but how many of us have seen the same title change twice?! More of a brawling style than in the Nashville match, the main change came when a fan threw a chain to Brian Christopher. This seemed a little outlandish to us, but it was explained by the man behind us that he throws the chain every week, and it seems they always incorporate it into the match. Now that's interactive! Unfortunately for Shawn, I mean Brian, the chain couldn't overcome the still-impressive magic cane, and the title changed hand again.

4) USWA Tag Champions PG-13 vs Billy Travis & Flash Flannagan

Very cool entrance here as Jamie Dundee came to the ring smoking a cigarette, his loutishness upsetting all the mums in attendance. Whereas one didn't get the impression the Nashville crowd would watch other promotions, the Louisvillians (is that a real word?) were on the case, taunting Dundee with the charge "Sable kicked your ass! Sable kicked your ass!", causing a great crybaby tantrum, ending with him refusing to wrestle and suck his thumb.

The match was completely different from Nashville, with PG-13 being chased literally around the building, and even brawling atop the tables that sectioned off the floor seating. There was also plenty of fun with the heels making Lawler style references to Travis' apparent drug and alcohol problems. It ended at 21:13 with Travis falling victim to the world's greatest hubcap.

Second interval, more photos, Ross gets chatting, Frank Morell keeps his job.

5) Loser Leaves Town: Brian Christopher, Billy Travis, Flash Flannagan, Bobby Bolton & Bill Dundee vs Elijah, Gravedigger, PG-13 & King Reginald

Doug Gilbert was again the referee, and the phrase `hero's welcome' doesn't suffice. The man responsible for so many dastardly turns in the USWA got the loudest cheer of the night, celebrating from atop the tables and milking every minute of it.

In the match itself, though, he put on a completely different performance to Nashville, clearly favouring the heels, and having more than a couple of cross words with Brian Christopher. What with a photographer appearing at ringside for the first time, we were convinced that this was the night that the `Dangerous' one would be turning. Again we were wrong.

After another excellent bout, albeit far more brawling orientated and with less comedy spots than Nashville, poor old Gravedigger stared at the ceiling again, leading to the comedy quote of the night from a man just behind us:

"I guess Tony Falk'll be back next week then."

Just to wrap things off, Brian Christopher wished Gravedigger farewell with a chant of "Na na na na..." Wonder where he got that idea?

While we're talking about the show, it's worth mentioning that the booking compared with Forrest City perfectly fit the entire basis of a wrestling territory. The spot show saw the heel win the opener to get the crowd into the action, but all the faces going over in the remaining matches so that the fans all remember the good time they had when the show returns in a couple of months. The weekly venue show saw all heel victories on the undercard to keep the heat on those moving up the card, but the main event saw the heroic babyfaces win to give a sense of hope and justice to the loyal fans. Sometimes the simplest things work best.

Well, with nothing to rush off to, it was round the back of the arena (which consists of nothing more than a wide alley between the Gardens and a multi-storey car park) to hang out with all the ring rats. I would say this was another historic site, but fortunately we don't know of any stories about ring rats and the Louisville Gardens. Or witness harassment.

While Jamie Dundee cadged a couple of cigarettes from Kenny, and Matt listened to Bobby Bolton's stories of the late Bulldog Bob Brown, Ross and myself found Doug Gilbert willing to be interviewed. Once through the tight security, through the deluxe dressing room and into an empty arena floor, the former Freddie Krueger asked where we wanted to film the interview. There was only one place that would do...

Well, the argument that I've never even stepped in a wrestling ring finally fell as I made my way through the ropes. As we started setting up the interview questions, trying desperately not to break into old `Hot Stuff' interviews, Doug said he had to pop back to the dressing room for a moment.

We amused ourselves in the meantime by running the ropes, practising the patented Bret Hart chest-first to the turnbuckles bump, and realising why you don't see many highspots in Louisville. The USWA's gate receipts might be fairly low, but it's not like they've got a whole lot of money tied up in wrestling rings.

While we were having the time of our life filming a remake of the classic Funk vs Lawler Mid-South Coliseum angle, a little girl came over and spoke in a worried, apologetic voice:

"Uh, there's kinda been a problem... Doug went to the car for something, and the guy giving him a lift thought he was ready to go, so they drove off..."

All of three seconds later it dawned on us that we had been diddled. Of all the shitty things that have happened in our life, it has to be said that being no-showed by a Gilbert is perhaps the only one to be perversely proud of. With cries of "He lied to everybody! Oh yeah, he liiiiiieed to everybody!", we returned to the back of the arena where Brian Christopher was getting a little upset.

It seemed young Flash Flannagan had somehow ended up with Christopher's keys... and was now halfway back to wherever the Flannagan clan calls home. Searching desperately for his spare set, Christopher opened up his luggage, revealing a rogues gallery of foreign objects! After giving Kenny an old pair of brass knuckles as a souvenir, he asked us to leave while he got his emergency keys from a secret location (we saw where they are, so highest bidder gets the details). Remembering the gags of Nashville, there was only one way to say farewell:

"Hey Brian! We have this thing in England for when your car breaks down. What you do, is you go like this (extend thumb)...."

Wednesday 19<u>th</u> February

With the USWA circuit finally over, it was off for four hours entertainment in a Greyhound station. I have to admit this wasn't the most welcoming of places, especially when, like Ross, you are carrying over £1,000 of camcorder equipment.

While Kenny slept, Matt kept watch, and I phoned to arrange the new train journey and a hotel for Washington (it didn't seem the best of ideas to be wandering around the nation's murder capital late at night), Ross found the games arcade where time became irrelevant. Among the choices was a strange variation on *Tekken Fighter*, with unusual animals as the characters.

Imagine my position. I'd been on the road for a week. It was 3 am. in a Louisville Greyhound station. Nobody else seemed to speak English. And I was watching a polar bear perform a huracanrana.

We soon bid farewell to Ross and Kenny (we'll catch up on them later), and finally slept for a couple of hours on the bus to Cincinnati. (The 'creatures of the night' are not the Undertaker's followers. They are the people who sit next to you on a Greyhound at 5 am.) A disappointing arrival with Brian Pillman not greeting us led to a hurried cross-town taxi journey to the railway station to arrive just in time... to find the train was an hour behind schedule.

Picking up our tickets from another station with just one train (the "Cardinal") a day, calling at 6 am., we found the world's most dedicated ticket clerk. Apparently still hailing from the 1920s, he gave us a ten minute lecture on why the train was late, what the problem was with the engine, and how the train worked. Second only to the weirdos in Games Workshop, this was a man who truly loved his work.

So, onto the train at 6 am., and there's not much else to say. The journey became more and more behind schedule as rumours spread that it had been inspected in Chicago, causing the delay (not that anyone would tell you officially). Food was too expensive to consider, so we only had a packet of pretzels all day. And then the entertainment began.

First came a presumably insane gentlemen named Fuzzy Davis (honest) who took over the public address system and gave us a running commentary on the scenery throughout Virginia (which was admittedly impressive, except for the strange moment when we ended up going down the middle of some town's high street). A few hours later came the punchline when he told us to write to our local representatives to ensure the route continued to be subsidised by the government. I'm sure my MP would love to help.

Then came the passenger lounge complete with movies. And the first showing of the day? *Fly A-Fucking-Way Home.*

The fun finally came to an end at 10pm when we arrived at Washington DC's Union Station, grabbed a meal at (I'll let you guess), and called for the complimentary shuttle bus which had been the main reason we'd chosen our hotel. Interestingly they'd overlooked mentioning that the bus only ran three times a day.

A "me no speeka da Inglese" taxi ride got us there and we watched another $56 disappear before collapsing into a real bed at last. Matt watched *Animal Instincts II* and I slept.

Thursday 20th February

Waking up at 10:45 would normally have been a great relief, but unfortunately we had to check out by 11. A cheapest-on-the-menu breakfast followed while we eavesdropped on the hotel inspectors sitting next to us and began the old *Fawlty Towers* routines.

Quite cleverly we had now missed the last shuttle bus into the city, so it was off to the regular bus "just to the Armory stop." Of course, nothing on the bus route told you where the Armory stop was, so a long walk back over ground we'd already covered and we were standing by the D.C. Armory, reminiscing about that great Midnights-Pillman/Zenk match at Capitol Combat '90.

A trip on the Washington equivalent of the underground took us to the Capitol Building, where we found from the newspaper stands that the Chinese leader had died. This wouldn't normally merit mention, but it did make us realise that this was our first contact with the `real world' for a week. The joys of working the Memphis circuit week after week became more apparent.

Once we'd hijacked a school trip round the Senate and Congress (which wasn't sitting), and given up searching for Senator John McCarthy's office (Dear Senator McCarthy, Anytime, Tank Abbot,) we went off to the Supreme Court. Here we laughed at the ignorance of most American's regarding their legal system (though, admittedly, two US History A level holders, one of whom is studying law, do have an advantage), and wondered where Clarence Mason sat.

We then carried on up Washington's Mall (the city is built around a central strip of parkland, with everything within walking distance), looked at the National Archives (holding everything from the Declaration of Independence, through Cassius Clay's draft forms, to the Magna Carta, which technically is ours, but the security guards had large guns, so we let them off), passed the Internal Revenue Service ("Irwin, Irwin!") and reached the FBI.

Unfortunately it was now 4 pm. and JT and pals had all gone home so, stopping only for a quick "Fly Me To The Moon", we took a quick detour to Ford's Theatre and soaked up the gruesome atmosphere of Abraham Lincoln's assassination.

Next was a quick look at the White House (causing another minor security alert by walking in the wrong place), and over to the Vietnam Memorial. This is a genuinely moving exhibit, listing every US solider who died in the war. It starts off just a couple of inches high above the ground, but then the path gradually dips down until the list of casualties reaches to two feet above your head.

Following the Lincoln Memorial, where it seemed we weren't the only ones who'd seen that episode of *The Simpsons*, we crossed the Potomac to the Arlington National Cemetery in search of the Pedro Morales grave from that Sgt Slaughter skit. Unfortunately it had just closed for the evening so we took the Metro back to Union Station. For sheer accessibility and historic value, Washington has to rate as one of the best tourist cities, and I'd certainly recommend it for a day's visit.

Unfortunately Amtrak had another little surprise for us, revealing that our `all inclusive' rail pass didn't cover most trains in the Northeast, so we either had to wait two hours, or pay an extra £30 each. Two hours later we set off.

Arriving in Philadelphia proved less hassle than most places as I remembered the drill from last year, even if the ticket machine did give me $15 change in 25c coins. A local train got us over to the airport where we called the shuttle bus, taking only four attempts to make our accent understood and get us picked up at the correct terminal. We were then rushed to the Travelodge, arriving at midnight... just in time to miss the latest ECW TV show.

Stopping only to chat to somebody who seemed to know us, and we didn't recognise (it turned out to be James Cheevers, who knew us from Ultra Kaos), and say hello to Tom Misnik, who explained that the Manhattan Center RAW on Monday was totally sold out (ECW received 250 calls asking how to get tickets the day after the Lawler angle), it was a hopeless search for food that led us to bed.

Friday 21<u>st</u> February

With the infamous diner across the road shut, and the surrounding area not too welcoming (you can actually watch the crack dealers from your hotel window), we grabbed breakfast in the hotel bar before trotting up to the convention room. Those buying the official video of the convention will see the opening scene in which Matt and myself enjoy our first beer for a fortnight. Even American crap tasted good after ten days.

The convention room was actually the penthouse of the hotel, and was instantly recognisable as the site for many ECW interviews, most notably Steve Austin's Monday Nyquil sketch. Apparently the stairs of the hotel were the site for the Gangstas numerous `punched out lightbulbs' promos.

After a few hours of chatting with fellow fans on everything from Michinoku to the MEWF, and putting up with the infamous Kathy, we met up with fellow Brits Martin Cox, Phil Jones, Mark Smith and Scott Farrell, who brings us up to date on events so far in Philly...

Perhaps being overtaken by a 'Bischoff Courier Service' employee whilst travelling up to Manchester Airport was the first indication that this trip was going to be something special. If not, the second soon arrived when the Viz character Victorian Dad sat opposite Mark & I for our flight. Laughs galore were evoked by viewing both him and his unfortunate looking family.

They say things come in threes... the entrance of Liu Kang as the flight attendant for our Continental flight to Newark, New York was also mildly humorous.

Despite a worryingly leaky plane, we arrived at Newark only to be stopped by customs and for Mark's Chicken Salad Sandwiches to be legitimately checked for explosives. While we were waiting for the internal transfer to Philadelphia we bumped into two other UK conventioneers who unluckily were from Liverpool, one of whom thought it was particularly clever to be wearing a Shawn Michaels T-shirt..."I'll ask Shane Douglas to wipe his ass on it" was the reply to the obvious.

We eventually got to our Travelodge at 6:30 and rushed in to see whether the WWF Wrestlefest *arcade game was still in operation. Joy quickly turned to sorrow when the elevator opened and the infamous Kathy appeared and invited Mark and myself to a local non-league hockey game. Instead, offering (insincere) apologies we rushed upstairs to meet American room-mate Pat before I dished out the first of many beatings on* PowerMove Wrestling *on the Playstation to anyone and everyone.*

The next part of the evening was spent chatting to Phil & Martin from Wrestling Insight *and the pleasant Tod Gordon who was pleased to see that we had travelled all the way from the UK..."You guys know* PowerSlam?*" was one of the questions he asked us before he left with the promise that we would definitely enjoy ourselves. How correct he was.*

The trip then brightened up when gorgeous strangers Amy & Shannon joined Mark and myself at the hotel bar (The reason being we were the only two normal looking people... sorry guys!!) which is where we stayed for the next few hours. By the time the ECW TV show started, Kathy had returned and yes, her three volume scrapbook was out. For those who have never had the pleasure, let me explain... Kathy has these scrapbooks which are full of the most pathetic and pointless wrestling pictures ever. Photos will be taken from the back of a hall and there is no legible way of making out the individuals in the ring... but she names them. `Why?' springs to mind.

The best quote of the evening was delivered by Kathy during the aforementioned show...

Joey Styles: "After the break, Taz takes on Scott Taylor"
Kathy: "I've got his autograph"
Us: "Who, Taz?"
Kathy: "No, Scott Taylor"

(2005 note: Kathy had the last laugh when he became WrestleMania superstar Scotty 2 Hotty.)

To be fair, my attention was focused on Amy and Shannon and so when the two girls from Alabama and myself went off for a three-in-the-bed romp, my trip was already complete. Actually, we all disappeared back to our rooms, but in the end Amy and Shannon joined the convergence in our room for another few hours of mindless chat.

After the arrival of Tom 'I know what's happening at ....(Insert ECW Event Here) but I can't tell you' Misnik in our room because he couldn't sleep (Translation: I know the girls are here), the time was already 03:00...hell I'd been awake for 27 hours.

Eventually at around 3:30 the thought of bed was too strong and luckily it was in the girls room... even if it was on the floor in sleeping bags due to the 'party' in our room.

Two hours' sleep seemed fine as I got up, kicked ass again on the Play Station and then five of us headed down to South Street in the worst taxi ever. This was just a shopping excuse and also a chance to pass Raven's house somewhere on South Street. One shop that caught everyone's attention was Condom Kingdom. Just imagine is all I can say. However, the book shop next door brought one of the many delights of the short-trip... the top-shelf Japanese magazine which completely knocks the pants off any other magazine you may have seen in your life ('Unbelievable' to quote Vinnie Mac)

With all the Brits except Ross and Kenny (more on that later) together, we were off on a three and a half hour bus trip to Queens, most of which involved circling Manhattan repeatedly after our second viewing of Newark Airport of the trip. The trip was made a lot more enjoyable by watching the last few episodes of ECW TV, a personal favourite being the emotional ceremony surrounding the announcement of the pay-per-view.

We were a couple of hours early for the show, so after introducing ourselves to the infamous Amy and Shannon (basically two hot looking chicks into wrestling and devil-worshipping, which is always a winner in my book), we braved the language barrier at McDonald's for the umpteenth time. Spotting a promotional poster on a lamppost, I naturally did my bit to harm the walk-up crowd by taking it as a souvenir.

Back inside the venue, Elks Lodge 878, we began to worry at just how posh the building looked. It turned out that the Elks are a real-life equivalent of the Water Buffaloes in *The Flintstones*, perhaps equivalent to ECW visiting your local Masonic temple.

With front row tickets guaranteeing our seats, we took our time examining the merchandise stands. Beating both the USWA and WWF, there seemed to be T-shirts for everybody and everything, with other items including Perry Saturn trading cards, and a barrage of Francine posters including some innovative uses for cut out hearts. Tommy Dreamer was walking about signing autographs, but fortunately we managed to keep Matt from seeing him. Matt spent the rest of his money on merchandise, while Mark Smith broke all existing records with the largest t-shirt order in history.

Just outside the hall itself was Rob `7-11 what?' Feinstein, the man who vowed never to darken ECW's door again in 1995, selling tapes with the full permission of ECW. You gotta love this business.

When we casually walked upstairs into the grand hall (similar in layout to the Manhattan Centre), we couldn't immediately find Section C, Row 1, Seats 1 & 2. In fact, there didn't seem to be any seat numbering. Or empty seats. But there were over 800 people (and a ring) in a 650 capacity building.

Yes, nobody had actually bothered informing the Lodge's security that any seats were reserved, meaning we ended up sat with several other disgruntled Brits in a crowded corner, continually standing on our seats just to see the ring. For this we were charged $35, while those with $15 tickets were among those barging their way to ringside seats. Considering ECW has now run a successful pay-per-view event, is a little organisation really too much to ask?

Oh, and things weren't helped by an overactive spastic sitting in front of us. But more on him later.

Being ECW, the show started late, and the crowd took an instant dislike to the ring announcer.

1) Balls Mahoney vs Chris `The Rookie' Chetti

This was a bit of a weird one as it took a while before everyone realised that it was a proper match and not just an excuse for a Sandman run-in. By this time the traditional `tough guy vs young challenger' storyline was lost on everyone, so the crowd simply revived the old "shah/sh*t" days, with innovative cries of "balls" and "nuts". Mahoney won with a second rope elbowdrop at 7:32.

2) Shane Douglas & Brian Lee vs Pitbulls

Douglas was out with a knee injury, which he slyly blamed as a groin strain, pointing to Francine and grinning all the while. Anyway, he announced Candido as his replacement, Back In Black began playing, and the old entrance music/mass brawl began, giving the usual feeling of being in a live version of ECW's fine music videos.

I was in a clear minority here, but I didn't care much for this match. It was far better on tape, which suggests the inadequate view and still-present resentment over the ticket situation may have clouded my view. That said, it was far from a classic, and consisted mainly of a quick walk around ringside followed by some unimpressive spots in the ring.

It picked up for the finish, which saw Lee superbombed, but Douglas interfering, and Lee using his crutch to floor and pin Pitbull 1 at 12:29.

3) Buh Buh Ray Dudley vs Spike Dudley

Another limited affair, this didn't involve much more than Spike Dudley being thrown about a bit, and then Axl Rotten shoving him from the top rope straight into the Dudley Death Drop at 6:34. The best point of the match was undoubtedly Sign Guy Dudley's new heel tie-dye suit! Damage Control helped Spike out (with the blonde woman earning a "Show your tits!" chant), while the FanCam operator zoomed in for a classic shot of a "Brotherly Love" motto carved by the Elks members.

Being ECW, the ring then needed repairing (can you imagine that happening halfway through *RAW*?), so I trotted off to the toilets where *Lariat* editor Dave Scherer revealed that Ross and Kenny hadn't turned up, and then passed the bWo on my way back.

4) Raven & Steve Richards vs Sandman & Tommy Dreamer

A simple storyline match, this saw Richards and Raven arguing throughout. Sandman was in a pretty poor state, meaning his only contribution was a clearly drunken topé, leaving Tommy Dreamer to carry the match. The main highlight from our seats was Raven wearing the same T-shirt as Matt. Eventually Richards superkicked everyone in sight and walked out, leaving Dreamer to DDT Raven but mysteriously allow Sandman to get the 13:51 pin. Brian Lee ran-in, but Terry Funk made the save to huge applause.

Despite having just had a break, they then took another interval during which nothing particularly interesting happened except for Mikey Whipwreck grassing up some people who'd caused trouble in the crowd.

5) Gangstas vs Axl Rotten & D Von Dudley

Even more than last year's Four Way Dance, just the thought of this one was terrifying. With the crowd more than a little overpacked, the usual Gangstas fun would have resulted in lawsuits Jim Cornette would be proud of. The match stayed in and by the ring then, the gist of it being lots of blading and New Jack using a suitcase full of weapons, and then using the suitcase. Gangstas got the pin at 6:31. Joel Gertner shoved the ring announcer aside (pointing out that we deserved "a TV star, not a TV repair man"), announced D Von & Axl as winning on points, the Gangstas started to beat him, Buh Buh turned up, and it all ended in tears.

On a second trip to the bathroom I tried to pretend I couldn't see Jason (of 'Sexiest Man Alive' fame) hanging around, presumably looking for work.

6) Taz vs Little Guido

Big pop for the word "Brooklyn" in Taz's ring intro. Suplex. Suplex. Suplex. Choke. 4:52.

7) Tables & Ladders are legal: ECW Tag Champs Eliminators vs Sabu & Van Dam

You'll often hear critics saying that a WWF show was below expectations, but the main event saved it; well, this was certainly the case at Queens. This was one of those matches that is an amazing performance and display, yet is so different that it's almost impossible to rate on the traditional star system.

The first five minutes saw, for the first time on the show other than Taz vs Guido, some excellent chain wrestling on the mat. Unfortunately the more vocal fans were too obsessed with furniture to appreciate it, earning verbal abuse from myself and (slightly more authoritatively) John Kronus.

From here on it evolved into an extensive arena tour covering most sections of the building, and an incredible series of innovative spots, most of which were simply there for brutality's sake. Just as the challengers took control, a 'missed' move led to them colliding, with Total Elimination finishing Van Dam. Van Dam refused to shake hands, which was part of an ongoing storyline that concluded at Barely Legal.

This had to rate among the most exciting 21:42 of my life, being equivalent perhaps to last year's Sabu-Van Dam stretcher match multiplied by the legendary Doc Dean-Rob Brookside ladder bout.

Despite the stunning main event, this was almost certainly the show I was most disappointed in. The undercard seemed rushed and unsatisfying, relying more on the novelty of seeing the characters live to provide the entertainment, while the action simply lived up to all the negative points against ECW. It may be that the novelty factor only works once, and I had my introduction last year, or it may be that the letters ECW automatically entail overly ambitious expectations. Either way, it was more than made up for the following evening...

After a video of past conventions on the bus back, we went to the bar and met up with our Tennessee travelmates, with Kenny McBride filling in the gaps:

A couple of hours after John & Matt left Louisville we got on the

bus, drove to Nashville, and hung about for another few hours until the daily service to Shelbyville arrived. We hopped on that, and it was only a little over an hour before we arrived back in my old stomping ground of Shelbyville, Tennessee. The Greyhound stop is actually the offices of a taxi company, which is owned and run by two twin brothers, Ben and Glen Mullins. The offices have a kind of warehouse attached to the back, from where All State (which means All Shelbyville) Wrestling is run.

We walked 'home' to the house of Lyle and Patricia Hampton, my host parents of the previous year. They hadn't changed a bit, and were overjoyed to see me; that is, after Pat remembered who I was. Pat is 72, and Lyle is 66, and Ross was worried. Lyle is, to use a wrestling analogy, the kind of guy that Goldust would really like. Pat is, well, senile.

We immediately headed down to my school, Shelbyville Central High School, to visit some of my friends there. Turns out one of my friends is in jail (for drug offences, but no-one would tell me exactly), and my favourite teacher is pregnant. We stayed on for soccer training, at which Ross impressed everyone with his vast knowledge and expertise. Not that he's a great player; it's just that Americans know fuck all about football.

That night (Wednesday), there was a girls' basketball game. "Not a big deal," you might say. You've obviously never been to Shelbyville. The Eaglettes are one of the best high school basketball teams in America. In the last 8 seasons they have been national champions twice, State champions four times, and State runners-up twice. The hopes of an entire town rest upon them, and they carry it admirably. This was the regional play-offs. They had to win this game to get into the State play-offs. The whole audience was on a knife-edge all night. They shouted, they cheered, they booed the referee when he judged against their girls, and they went wild when the SCHS Eaglettes went home victorious by 72-60.

The next day was Thursday. In Shelbyville (for me anyway) Thursday means just one thing - wrestling day. Lyle, of course, had other things on his mind. We went along to the Jack Daniel's distillery, some 15 miles away in Lynchburg. We didn't have time to take the tour, but we did look round the grounds, and get really pissed off by the thousands of midges that seem inhabit the area. We also did a little souvenir hunting, with me purchasing the Jack Daniel's Beer T-shirt I would wear to the Arena later that week. Yes, that's right, Jack Daniel's Beer. You haven't heard of it, because it's only sold in about 10 counties in Middle Tennessee. Shame, because it's the only American beer I've ever tasted that wasn't "sex in a canoe" - i.e. fucking close to water.

After seeing the sights of Lynchburg, and drinking a real milkshake from a real metal tumbler in a real small-town American drugstore, we returned to Shelbyville for what we really wanted to see: rasslin'.

Ben, Shelbyville's top babyface, recognised me immediately and gave me a hearty welcome. His brother Glen, the promoter and, since Gypsy Joe's move to South Carolina, booker (cue lots of heel comments about nepotism) also remembered me and gave me a warm welcome too. Strangely though, their children, whom I spent every show last year baby-sitting, ignored me completely. Ah well...

The show was a slight let down. Ben was injured, so he didn't wrestle. Jason Vaughn, a local boy a year younger than me with only around two years experience, and a wrestler in the "Sean Waltman if he'd lived in Tennessee" mode, was not at the top of his game, which can be quite high. The Morton brothers who are, unknown to almost everyone, Rick's younger cousins, were decent, but not outstanding. I wonder if they should get down from their high moral stance, and just let Rick get them a few bookings? CHRISTOPHER (Meltzer take note) Ashford-Smith, better known as Chris Champion, even better known as Yoshi Kwan, was slick, but turning babyface has all but killed his character. Slicing up Gypsy Joe's face with a sword and blowing fire in Glen's face are cool things to do. High-fiving fans and wrestling by the rules are not.

The highlight of the show, for us though, was "Hot Chocolate" Cory Williams - the greatest black wrestler in Middle Tennessee (which, believe me, is not saying much - although he is a very good worker). He entered the ring to the strains of Dr. Dre and Ice Cube's "Natural Born Killa", which you know better as the Gangsta's entrance music. Preparing ourselves for the trip north to Philadelphia, we began making the "X" sign, to which Cory did not respond with the expected heel reaction of "I don't need your support", but rather grinned at us, and

"ECW cannot exist full-time. I'd say three nights a week was the maximum because, unlike the WWF, every night we're giving 185%."

On sponsorship: "What I can't understand is... our target audience, which is 20-35 year olds, spends more money than every other demographic. I can't see why people wouldn't want to sponsor us."

Everyone kissed the Eliminators' butts for a couple of minutes before Perry Saturn described his favourite type of match ("I'd rather just do a wrestling match, with no ropes on a mat, but none of you guys would pay to see it.") and Kronus named his dream opponents ("I'd like to wrestle a couple of swimsuit models!").

Sandman then addressed the subject of "You fucked up!" chants: "You have no idea for how many months that bothered me that the Arena crowd would do that to me (after his knee injury at A Matter of Respect). That's why it's the toughest crowd in the world to work for - but also the best crowd."

Steve Richards then suggested "Think back to that show the WWF gave you at the Philadelphia Spectrum or wherever, then you won't think we fucked up so much," while Axl Rotten slagged off the Memphis workrate. "There's no-one in our locker room that I wouldn't lay down for, because they've all earned their spots here."

On wrestlers "selling out" by joining the WWF, Sandman said he could earn up to $125,000 a year and "I sleep in my own bed every night. But you gotta understand something. Scorpio's got nine kids at home. He made the right decision for him business wise. Scorpio's one of the top five workers on the planet." And the others? "Benoit, Steve Austin, right now for the whole package of ringwork, interviews, everything."

Axl Rotten then described the difference between the companies: "There (in the WWF) you're a company whore. Here you're your own man."

With the subject of putting ECW TV on in Britain, Sandman was somewhat floored by the combined accents of James Cheevers and Ross ("What the fuck is £500? I know the Meanie's about 490lbs..."), so didn't really grasp the concept that you actually get paid for TV shows in our country.

After a long account of the political problems ECW face getting into new venues, Saturn pointed out that, "As much as we're Team Extreme, you guys are part of Team Extreme too. You've got to speak up and help get us into those buildings."

Next up was the bi-annual slagging of the sheet writers with the usual "not stepped in the ring" argument (Saturn: "I'm not going to tell you the pilot's shit. I can't fly a plane."), which still doesn't address the fact that the majority of ECW fans wouldn't have heard of the company without newsletters and, arguably, wouldn't be in a position to appreciate the workrate on offer.

Just as predictably the Revere, Massachusetts incident came up, with the Eliminators arguing that Eric Kulas had no business being in the ring if he couldn't take punishment. That Saturn saying "I wish the kid would have fucking died because he makes what I do look bad," got a round of applause was one of the more worrying events of our trip.

Back on the WWF invasion, Sandman pointed out that "You'd be stupid to think Paul E. would put WWF stars in the ring against ECW stars," while Retard jumped up and down shouting "You'd kill them!" over and over again. Hello, Retard. It's a work...

Asked who they most respected in the business, everyone picked Terry Funk. Sandman: "He was doing what we're doing today, twenty years ago. The guy is God to me. Him and Flair."

Saturn: "The difference between Funk and Flair is that Funk has moved with the times."

The next question concerned Memphis, with Axl Rotten calling the crew a "bunch of asskissers", while Sandman said Lawler taught him how not to blow up in matches. Saturn had strong memories of the territory:

"We had a lot of good times, a lot of shitty times, but we learnt a lot and paid our dues. I kind of miss doing the loop once in a while, Memphis to Nashville to Louisville (Sandman: "And Evansville in front of 38 people!"). It's a great place to learn how to work."

Sandman compared the drop in wrestling business to fashions, predicting it would come back to another peak. He also missed the territories: "It's so hard for guys breaking into the business right now. You have no idea how many wrestlers in America are working for $20 a night. With the territories you'd go to Missouri, bang, you'd get run out by the Mauler, go to Florida where you main event with Dusty, he runs you out of town, you go up to Portland, get another angle going."

Saturn picked up, "You'd spend nine months in California, go to New York. That way you stayed fresh and you don't have to set yourself on fire to get people's attention."

After Sandman went back to bed, Axl Rotten condemned the variety of gimmick matches he'd fought, and the extreme style practised by `brother' Ian with Insane Championship Wrestling. "[The thumbtacks] looked good, it was a total gimmick, but it meant nothing. When the history of wrestling's written, do you think they're going to say, `oh yeah, by the way, Kojo Yakataki stuck his head in a piranha filled pool?' They're taking it in the wrong direction."

"Everyone thought this was going to be such a big deal, but he didn't have the money he claimed he had, so it went straight downhill. He didn't have the talent to put those guys on TV everyday." No prizes for guessing which Dallas based promotion Axl was slagging off.

Back on gimmick matches, Saturn pointed out that, "It all comes back to the lack of territories. Guys don't have anywhere to learn to wrestle, so they make up for it with bullshit gimmicks. I don't use chairs: I'll jump off of anything, but I'm secure in my talent. All these guys (in ECW) that do gimmicks can wrestle, but you demand these gimmicks. It's not just the violence that makes ECW popular, it's the guys that work hard. From the bWo and the stuff they do, which is very entertaining, to violence and wrestling. I can do the comedy with Stevie, but he can wrestle with me. The violence is just a small piece of it."

On the training school: "We have an amateur wrestling mat and you train on it for months. You don't even get in a ring until you learn how to wrestle. I'm an airborne ranger, I grew up in a ghetto, a real ghetto, and wrestling's the hardest thing I've ever done. I guarantee you, it takes weeks just to learn how to tie up correctly. Terry Funk was saying last night that there's not enough guys today who know how to wrestle. They look good but... I don't even know if Lex Luger can apply a hammerlock."

Talking about amateur backgrounds, Axl said he saw a sign for wrestling at his junior high school. "I didn't know there was a difference, and I'd be rolling around on a mat. I thought I'd be hitting guys with chairs and the Grand Wizard would be coming out to the ring with me. But wrestling is wrestling."

With that the first half wound up and the autograph collecting began. So far so interesting, but a combination of lack of preparation on the fans part, and a definite tendency towards self-congratulation on the part of some panel members meant the session wasn't as good as on previous expectations. Still, after saying hi to Power Slam photographer George Tahinos, it was soon time for the second half of the afternoon. Guests included the Pitbulls, Tommy Dreamer, Beulah, New Jack and Jim Molineaux.

Once Tommy `mumble' Dreamer had been told what happened to the microphone (Sandman shorted it out by throwing water at Tom Misnik), and he'd explained the trouble the New York commission gave them (prompting suggestions that ECW hold cards on Indian reservations, EFC style), Dreamer turned to Pitbull 1's neck injury:

"After the match (where the injury happened) we were doing interviews. He had a towel around his neck and said `I don't know man, my neck hurts.' He went to the chiropractor and had his broken neck adjusted... and then he went to the hospital on the Monday."

On accusations that Dreamer tried to hard to be hardcore: "Anyone who accuses me of working too hard, I say fuck them. We all work hard... though I'm probably one of the stupider guys."

Asked about the moonsault she performed in a mixed tag, Beulah revealed "That was terrifying. I landed on my face. I can honestly say it was worth it, though."

Dreamer: "We went to the training school and she hit it 14 times in a row with mats. In the ring, I told her `when you go up, count to three and go.'"

Beulah: "I counted to three three times!"

As the conversation turned to independent groups copying ECW, New Jack referred to Insane Championship Wrestling as "I Can't Wrestle", before the word `Revere' reared its ugly head.

"That turned into some legal shit, so if I gotta go anywhere near there, I drive right around Massachusetts!" He played dumb over the incident, described by Dreamer as an "unfortunate situation", before explaining that he was legally bound from speaking about the case.

To cut a long, expletive-filled story short, New Jack isn't a sheet reader, calling them the "*National Enquirer* of wrestling." He pointed out that out of the ring events were far more scandalous in the WWF and WCW, but the larger corporations could cover them up:

"I ain't slept with no 12 year old. I ain't been caught in no hotel room, drugged out of my mind, not knowing my ass from a hole in the ground. But if they want to build a star, they can sweep that shit under the carpet."

Arguing that his personal life was irrelevant, as long as "people still pay to see me", New Jack turned his attention to the Internet, recalling watching a friend read a rumour on his computer:

"(It says) I'm in jail. I'm sitting in his house! I'm like, `Goddamn, if this is jail, I'll stay right here!'"

Dreamer pointed out that the sheets tend to "create the news. You shouldn't rip people up because you don't like them, you should rip them up because they had a bad match."

Continuing on the theme, New Jack referred to Dave Meltzer claiming the Gangstas couldn't work longer than five minutes. "Has anyone seen Smoky Mountain. I can work twenty minutes with no music. I get in there, I do what I'm told, I get the fuck out."

At this point an overweight balding man ran into the room and started chucking bagels at everyone's head. But it was Paul Heyman, so that's all right.

After a fan asked the Pitbulls if "it's now a game of oneupmanship with the Triple Threat?", and several fans referred to some guy called Mark, Paul E. was asked what would happen on Monday:

"I don't know what the hell's going down. I don't know what's going down tonight yet. I'm not even thinking about Monday... Let me ask you a question: Who in this room ain't gonna watch *RAW*? (One foolish hand rises.) OK, how many of you usually watch it anyway? (Few hands raised.) Of their audience, how many of them know we've got a pay-per-view on April 13th. Knowing what we have ahead of us, and knowing that I'll be damn sure to say it a few times, after this Monday they're gonna realise...

What's going down Monday is that at least an extra 80 people are going to watch RAW, and an extra two million people are going to know ECW has a pay-per-view on Sunday April 13th."

After pointing out the basics of opportunity cost ("every decision should turn on more people than it turns off"), Heyman addressed the idea that Wade Keller might have tried to get ECW thrown off pay-per-view:

"Let's go under the assumption that he has it in for us. If Wade Keller can take us down to that extent, we're dead against Eric Bischoff or Ted Turner. They know the business better and they know how to play the dirty tricks even better."

The good word of Heyman was briefly interrupted by the Pitbulls revealing they'd met after a fight in the third grade ("we used chairs!"), Paul E explained ECW's difficult position:

"We're still too small to be big, but we're too big to be small. We can run this building which holds 900 people and have 150 people outside on the street, or we can run this other building which holds 15,000, which we're not ready for."

The predictable barrage of specific arena questions was interrupted by Retard asking if Tommy Dreamer was going to have any tag matches with Terry Funk (duh, that night!), and New Jack muttering "Flashbacks..." while slashing a paper cup to ribbons. Ho ho ho. Heyman then returned to answering anything and everything.

On ECW's position in three years: "I hope we're bigger. I hope we're better. I hope we're more talented. I hope we're better educated. But most of all I hope we're alive."

On toning down the product to ease expansion: "ECW gets hit by a torpedo and goes out of business... it could happen. ECW is banned by a state... it's a possibility. ECW changes it's product... Not while I'm alive."

On TV shows: "If you give me an hour a week, I hope to entertain you and to entice you to buy more of our merchandise and come to the arenas. The Monday Night War is a war for egos and a war for bragging rights. It's detrimental to both companies."

On the PPV bombing: "If not one person buys the pay-per-view, there's still an ECW on Monday April 14th. We'll have to recover...

There's nothing that's worth risking this whole thing for. If you told me to bet everything that is ECW and if the sun rises tomorrow you'll double it, I won't take that bet."

The rest of the crew got the message at this point and said farewell, leaving Paul to argue that the 'big two' were lousy at following up angles, and discussing the phone calls that set up the WWF angle ("Any time anybody in this industry takes the time to call, I'd be a fool not to listen.") He explained that discussions usually follower both parties putting out feelers, and admitted the Holiday Hell tour was part of an angle he pulled out of because he didn't like the planned follow-up.

The Triple Threat then arrived, with most of the room confused as Kenny asked Candido if they'd found the missing phone ("No, never. They mailed me a new one at Buddy Landell's house yesterday.") Ross got the follow-up, asking about... you guessed it.

Heyman said he wanted to keep the Michinoku wrestlers within their own element in ECW, similar to the treatment of AAA workers. "Taka Michinoku is the hottest new superstar in Japan. He's absolutely phenomenal. There's lots of interesting mixes with the Michinoku wrestlers, but you can only bring in so much talent at one time."

Joey Styles arrived, Douglas compared Francine to Sherri Martel ("Younger, faster, prettier, better in bed!"), and Candido explained that he didn't hold the Body Donna gimmick against the WWF:

"It was a good spot for a 22 year old kid. You've gotta do what you're told. There's only so long you can work in one territory. (When I leave ECW) I'd rather go back there than back to Memphis."

While Heyman explained that he wouldn't risk Shane Douglas being injured before Barely Legal, somebody got out a felt tip and created Ox Bagel. But you had to be there.

Paul E.: "If Bischoff would keep his dick in his pants, he might learn how to do an entertaining nWo pay-per-view instead of copping a feel from an 80 year old toothless woman." OK. And we won't get into the wife-swapping allegations.

Next, Heyman picked his five dream talent acquisitions (Benoit, Misterio, Austin, Taka Michinoku and either Shawn Michaels or Ric Flair to reward Douglas.)

Brian Lee can do a moonsault. OK.

Matt mentioned the Michaels word to Shane Douglas and, among the stories you surely know by know, the `Franchise' described him as "An incredible performer, but his head is swelled five times bigger than his body. His attitude supersedes his ability in the ring."

Heyman said he'd spend an imaginary extra $1million on TV production and local promotion, and then praised the loyalty of existing workers:

"Chris Candido could have sat out the rest of his contract with the WWF and then called Atlanta and said, `I'm right off of Monday Night Raw: how much?' They'd have thrown a contract his way just like that."

Candido: "They would?"

Paul E. awarded Matt first prize in the Spike Dudley lookalike contest, while Joey Styles detailed the pay-per-view advertising campaign: "It's a marketer's dream. We know exactly where our audience is and when: Monday nights, watching cable."

Heyman said he wouldn't show up on the Philadelphia *Nitro* the day after the pay-per-view ("I don't even think I'll be awake on Monday April 14th."), and then told the story of how he'd offered to give Bobby Eaton work to help Chris Chetti improve, but WCW rejected him out of hand:

"Wasted talent is the biggest crime in wrestling today. It's a waste of goddamn resources. Put (Eaton) in the ring with Alex Wright for 20 minutes every night and watch Alex Wright become a star. Put him in with Konnan for 1:15 (referring to a recent Nitro) and what do you get? Nothing but Konnan's hand raised in the air."

James Cheevers brought up the subject of ECW coming to Britain: "I'd love to do an episode from London. I'd love the World title to be defended in England. It's hard to get on TV without a distributor. They have *PowerSlam* magazine there, which is cool and it has a decent readership. Maybe we'll start a love triangle with Princess Di and get on the front page of *The Sun*. I'd love to go to London. In fact, maybe I'll go there on April 14th just to get away!"

After we described Channel 4's content (Joey Styles: "Sounds like my kind of TV!"), Heyman turned to the subject of programme content: "If you've got Cablevision and your kid comes home at 1:45 in the afternoon, they can pop on a porno film. Deep Penetrators or whatever. But they said to us we're not the right image for Cablevision."

James suggested that might be where they were going wrong, and Douglas glanced at Francine and raised his hand while grinning.

Heyman discussed at length the departures of Missy Hyatt ("There's no place here for her attitude."), Kimona ("Missy got to her."), Woman ("I don't think there's room for Nancy here anymore. In fact, I don't think there's room for Nancy to fit in through the door any more.") and the Mexicans ("I don't have any ill-feeling towards Konnan.")

He was also asked about bringing in Dallas Page: "I'd love to bring him in if he brings his wife. In fact, he doesn't even have to come along with her!"

Candido explained the effects of the WWF's schedule ("You're on the road so much... We just found out that Elvis is dead. You don't know what the fuck's going on."), while Joey Styles said McMahon and Ross were his ideal play-by-play men ("Vince can be very excited about the match despite not knowing what's going on. Jim is very analytical and knows the names of the holds.")

And finally, on the subject of his greatest inspiration, we'll leave the traditional heartfelt promo to Paul E.:

"It's both a positive and a negative. I have, in one way or another, been involved in this business since I was 13 years old. I'm 31 now. 18 years I've been in and around this business. It's all I know. It's all I wanna do.

I love this fucking business. I love everything about it... I've seen how shittily people I know, and myself, were treated. I love this business and I think it can be run a different way. I think you can do your job and take pride in it.

I think this business needs a crew like this. I think this business needs more people like those who are sat at this table or like Tommy Dreamer, or like Taz, or like any of the guys in this company who play hurt, who work with pain and bust their ass, and turn down better money for the chance to look in the mirror and say `I'm proud of what I do and I'm proud of what I've accomplished.'

The positive side of my biggest influence... This is a dream. This is a fucking dream and it's a dream that everybody has together. Rick Rude once said to me, `You know what the fucking problem is? If I was a garbage man I'd want to throw the most garbage into the truck so I could be the best fucking garbage man there is. That's the way Rick Rude is."

And we have a crew of people like that. They want the chance to build something, to look at a wrestling company and say `I built that, with my tears, with my sweat, with my sacrifice.' The whole dressing room has the right to say that. When they see a packed house tonight, they have the right to say `I built this. From a bingo hall into this. Where people fly in from England, from across the country, from all the way around the world. To where we're able to do a pay-per-view. From nothing to something. No matter how big or how small, everybody can take credit for it. We built it with pride, with honour, with dignity and never by fucking anybody else over.

That's my inspiration. It's a fucking dream, it's a dream come true, and I do it with a group of people I admire. Every night of my life I go to bed and I thank God for this opportunity. I wake up in the morning in tears because I'm so unbelievably overwhelmed by how much I admire the guys in the dressing room. That's my inspiration.

It's an inspiration any man in my position should have, because it will drive you, it will drive you so fucking hard because that dressing room has earned the right for you to work that hard for them, because they work that hard for you and for this company."

If I ever have a few hours to live, I want to be locked in a room with Paul Heyman and Jim Cornette and just talk wrestling.

Once all the necessary photographs had been taken, and Ross had given Paul E. the "I wanna be a referee" speech, it was soon time to make the trip to the ECW Arena. Not only did we get to go in a traditional yellow school bus, but we passed Beulah Street on the way! Arriving back at Ritner Street Community Centre was another special moment, if only to be reminded of just what a joke the place is. The concept that the greatest wrestling in the Western world is based in a run-down warehouse with no apparent amenities is astounding enough, but simply trying to imagine the concept of holding a pay-per-view there is enough to blow your mind.

George Tahinos having gone on ahead, we had the best part of an hour to kill before going in, which was spent entertainingly enough chatting to Amy and Shannon, and trying to ignore the locals' friendly banter, including sentences ending "twenty bucks a gram."

Being ECW, various workers had to make their way through the crowd to walk in the same entrance everyone else used, with the opportunity to personally harass Tommy Rich coming as one of those truly great events in one's life. Meanwhile a bloke came up to Matt and intuitively pointed out, "You look just like Raven." It took all of Matt's self-restraint to avoid punching Tommy Dreamer.

Once inside the famed hall we found our reserved ringside seats to be most agreeable (third row, opposite the stage, just past the far left ringpost as you watch on TV), and the time soon passed as Beard Dude read his copy of the *Torch*, Hat Guy collected tickets, and we suddenly realised the bloke sitting next to us wrote an article on Jushin Liger that we ripped off in *Hulk Who?* once. Twenty minute past bell-time (another no-no if they want to really make it big), the chants of "Start the show!" paid off and the Eliminators hit the ring.

1) Tag Champs Eliminators vs Sabu & Rob Van Dam

Perry Saturn grabbed the microphone and decided he wanted to prove who was the best tag team in the world, and announced a return tables and ladder match. OK, fine with us. This was miraculously better than the night before, with less of the asshole contingent during the opening matwork, and even crazier spots with the ladders. The only thing lacking in this match was a coherent storyline, but given that I grew up on Pat Patterson booking, and the first rule of wrestling is to play to your target audience, that's hardly a major criticism. Van Dam again fell to the Eliminators, this time tasting two Total Eliminations at 20:18, and again refused to give a handshake.

Quite simply, this was the best opening match in ECW history.

Next up, Joey Styles taped a TV opening ("So, is anyone going to watch *RAW* on Monday?"), the Pitbulls came out, Douglas challenged them to come up to the stage, Lee and Candido jumped them, and the

Pitbulls went out on stretchers. Not what you'd call a challenging night's work for the `Mad Dogs of War.'

2) Chris Chetti vs Little Guido

This had a hilarious comedy opening, with Tommy Rich deciding his grandfather had been a Mafia boss in Philadelphia (he's now being announced "from Nashville, Italy"!), followed by a perfectly passable match for Chetti's Arena debut. Once everyone got tired of chastising Rich, Chetti took the `upset' win with a 5:07 roll-up.

3) Balls Mahoney vs Steve Richards

A pure comedy match, from the bWo's entrance, through Mahoney's impression of Razor Ramon, this was again perfectly passable, with Richards getting the win with a Steviekick when the novelty started wearing off. After the match a woman in a bWo shirt (who'd been sitting behind us the night before) ran into the ring but was `arrested'.

4) Axl Rotten vs Spike Dudley

After his comments at the Q&A, Axl decided to make this a great technical display, with fans eagerly judging it on an Olympic points system. Yeah, right. He kicked the living crap out of Spike before pinning him with a variation of Farooq's finisher. The rest of the Dudley clan began beating on Spike, and Natural Born Killaz began to play...

5) Gangstas vs D Von & Buh Buh Ray Dudley

Obviously this was your usual crazy brawl (certainly too extreme for Barely Legal), with notable points including: a guitar and radio being used as weapons; Buh Buh busting his nose; D Von coughing up blood; Buh Buh taking the stiffest chairshot ever, with the metal chair literally snapping in two; both Gangstas bleeding profusely, with New Jack looking remarkably like one Eric Kulas; the Buh Buh lookalike just by us crapping himself the moment New Jack's vision was blurred; and

Axl Rotten selling so well that Tom Misnik had to check he wasn't dead. The highlight, though, saw D Von put on a table by the ring barrier, and New Jack performing a running leap about ten feet from the balcony straight through the table. Oh My God!

Just when everyone thought the surprises couldn't get any wilder, New Jack went for the top rope chairshot finish, only to be caught in a Dudley Death Drop and pinned by Buh Buh at 14:22.

As Matt put it, this was the best Gangstas match ever.

The interval was spent queuing for cold pizza and making `telephone' hand signals to Sunny on the sound stage. Unfortunately she was too busy holding her cat and wondering why people were making "pussy" based jokes. Meanwhile Mop Boy made an appearance to clean the blood from the mat. "Mop it up, Mop Boy, Mop it up!"

6) Taz vs Lance Storm

Storm had missed his flight, so we were in for a mystery replacement, who turned out to be one Tracey Smothers. 1,199 people shrugged their shoulders while Kenny marked out. The routine this time was mule kick, mule kick, jawjacker, suplex, suplex, choke. 3:30.

7) Raven & Brian Lee vs Terry Funk & Tommy Dreamer

Once again, Raven and Matt wore the same shirt... The stipulation here was that if Funk pinned Raven he'd get the title shot at Barely Legal (which was slightly confusing as everyone knew about the Three Way Dance already.) Raven offered to let Dreamer pin him, causing a "moral dilemma" on the TV broadcast, and more confusion in the arena.

A couple of minutes later, four huge men jumped over the guard rail and took mine and Matt's seats to be the best route to the bleachers. The TV footage here is priceless as, while everyone else runs for their lives, I am standing my ground trying to get a decent photograph, whilst Matt is literally frozen as a bloodied Raven falls at his feet.

Once the action returned back to the ring (and I'd found my chair again), Lee repeatedly hit Funk with a garbage can, causing more than a little difficulty when a piece of Funk's ear went flying off. The heels noticeably backed off, and everyone panicked for a couple of moments before Funk was helped back to the dressing room.

Being that this was a Raven bout, they coped well by simply accelerating the scheduled chaotic finish. Richards ran out and got chokeslammed; Lori came out in bWo gear but got DDTed; Sandman and Tyler reunited; Sandman DDTed Raven and got the pin (?!); and Dreamer and Richards shook hands. It's really helpful to have Joey Styles on television to explain this kind of stuff.

8) Sabu vs Chris Candido

There have been very few truly emotional moments in my years following wrestling (Randy and Liz at WrestleMania VII was about the lot as a mark), but seeing Chris Candido main eventing was enough to bring the proverbial lump to my throat. Suddenly it came home just how ridiculous, how insipid, how downright offensive the entire character and use of `Body Donna Skip' really had been. Candido more than proved my gut reaction right here, thoroughly deserving top billing, while Sabu... was Sabu.

After Candido worked the crowd on the microphone, complaining that the opener had been designed to take away from his main event status, they performed a simply flawless bout. Arguably this was nothing more than a `regular' Sabu singles match, but that cannot be the slightest criticism.

Following 16 minutes of everything from missed table dives to top rope ranas, Sabu took the win with a seemingly impossible variation on the triple jump. Sabu may have won but, as the two shook hands, it was Candido's name being chanted by the crowd.

Being a hardcore fan is inherently masochistic, but moments like this make it all worthwhile.

There was only one thing wrong with CyberSlam '97. It wasn't The Doctor Is In. Apart from that, it gave us two classic matches, two solid brawls, and an entertaining rag-bag of supporting bouts. Not at all bad for £16. And Sandman signed Matt's cigarette packet.

Back at the hotel the UK Clique went over to get the first food of the day at the infamous Chinese restaurant, at which we literally didn't get a word in edgeways as we 'ordered': "Ah yes, you come late, we just closing soon, much food left, you pay for two, get food for four. Ah, chicken left, you get plenty chicken lo mein, and what else, yes? Shrimp, oh, you have shrimp. Thank you very much."

Fine with us. After stuffing ourselves stupid for the equivalent of £4 each, Matt opened his fortune cookie to be told that he was "a great believer in the success of Mankind."

One more trip across the road of death and post-Arena exhaustion caught up with me, so I collapsed into bed. For many conventioneers, though, there was far more excitement to come. Scott Farrell picks up the story:

Back at the hotel we found out that due to some previous problems all the wrestlers were staying at another hotel except for Spike Dudley who was ignored when checking in. However when I reached my room I found that the video of Bill Alfonso's escapades from the previous night had been tracked down and was about to be played.. .It was certainly very interesting.

It started off with Bill driving around Philly with the camera on the dashboard. Next up was a chest exposing Alfonso in the hotel lift chatting to women and asking them if he could film their breasts whilst asking them personal questions. Following that he went up to The Sandman's room where we were able to see two women laid on the bed obviously waiting for some excitement (Now we know why he was pissed off at the Q&A!) The film ended after this but at least from my perspective Amy & Shannon weren't involved!!!

As for Amy & Shannon, well, when Saturn turned up at around 2:00 Shannon once again disappeared to once again 'check the finances'

Up in the Florida Dudes' room, the beer was flowing (Matt apparently breaking all records), while Ross managed to almost get himself assaulted by saying Tommy Dreamer couldn't work. Then somebody lost their pay-per-view ticket, entailing a full search of everyone's room. For some reason, John seemed a little surprised to be woken by two strange men ransacking his room...

I was in desperate need of some sleep and so at 7:00 a dream come true as I slept in Amy's bed... even if she was downstairs at the time. Still it was something and I enjoyed rolling in the area where she had been only hours previously.

Just ninety minutes sleep was possible until Shannon woke me up wanting to come into her room. With the smile on her face it was apparent something had happened but all she would say was that 'Saturn's a loud snorer'

Eventually she asked if I wanted to know and the full details came out. Yes she had slept with Saturn and Amy turned Kronus down after he forgot her name the previous evening. Ha!

Sunday 23rd February

After trying to spot myself on Superstars, and finally waking Matt up (he having rolled into bed at 9 am.), there was just enough time to check out and catch the shuttle bus to the airport with all the fellow Brits. Laughing as they contemplated carrying their huge suitcases around Philadelphia (with them realising why we'd only brought one small bag each), and watching Ross and Kenny argue over the fact that they now literally couldn't afford to eat, we declined to join the final trip to Philadelphia's Centre City and bid farewell. Once again, Scott has the closing details:

It was then time for a trip to Toys 'R' Us, or not as we were soon to find out as the minibus driver refused to take us unless we could offer a specific address. Remembering that it was near the ECW Arena we asked for Swanson & Ritner street only to be told that there was no such place. Even our combined efforts with the Toys 'R' Us theme song were unsuccessful and so we ended up back on South Street. After another trip to see that Japanese mag, Mark, Martin & I were left in total agony after spotting one of the funniest T-shirts ever. Based entirely around the F word, Mark continued to laugh all the way home even saying it out aloud on the plane. I believe he's still laughing at it now up in Carlisle.

We managed to get hold of a taxi driver who knew how to get to Toys 'R' Us and despite just 1 hour being left until our flight it was a necessity. The immediate fight was between Phil, Martin and myself for the last two WWF Mankind figures on offer. After grabbing the first one it was a laugh to see the guys run to where the other one was left. While that battle was taking place I picked up the greatest toy of all time... Tickle Me Ernie. For those who have never had the pleasure this involves the Sesame Street *character and after squeezing his chest he starts laughing and vibrating. Rated for kids ages 1 1/2 and upwards it was a definite purchase.*

One final laugh came when Ross threw a tantrum after being unable to re-enter the building to buy a 50 cents plastic Karate toy from a dispenser... amusement was offered through his obvious unhappiness!

And so ended the trip to Philly for what was the greatest weekend of my life.. .it contained so many high spots it was unforgettable.

We, on the other hand, still had two days left on our voyage, even if the live wrestling was over. A two hour train journey took us into the Manhattan area for the third time on the trip, and we arrived at Penn Street station. Once we'd found the elevator where Hunter Hearst Helmsley had recently been tombstoned, we checked out the newsagents where, whilst not so innocently flicking through *Playboy Celebrity Nudes '97*, we came across (so to speak) an interesting section on Kimberly Page. Unfortunately DDP also appeared in some pictures...

As well as the New York Times, I picked up the 1997 *PWI Almanac*, which again comes highly recommended. We then went out into the street and paid homage to Madison Square Garden, trying to ignore the fact that it was playing host to Sesame Street Live.

With a couple of hours until our connection, we wandered around the streets of Manhattan, realising we couldn't afford to even go into most of the designer brand stores, and instead visiting those centres of ethnic culture, HMV (finding several albums by Marti Jones) and Toys 'R' Us (they'd sold out of Mankind figures).

At 5 pm., we walked out of Toys 'R' Us, we realised that, thanks to oversleeping, we didn't have time to go up the Empire State Building, literally 100 yards away.

At 5:05 pm., a crazed gunman opened fire at the top of the Empire State Building, killing one tourist and seriously wounding several others.

Holy shit.

Of course, we didn't find out about this until the next day, instead moving on to a bargain basement video store, which boasted Hulkamania Volume *1* and a great compilation, *WWF Presents the Country Boys* (including Uncle Elmer vs John Studd, Elmer vs Tiger Chung Lee, Hillbilly Jim vs Rene Goulet and Hillbilly Jim on Piper's Pit and the Body Shop). We also met a bloke in the street selling Ding Dongs chocolates.

After another quick visit to Wendy's hamburgers (see, we had a balanced diet, it wasn't McDonald's every night), we hopped on the 6:30 "Lake Shore Limited" to Chicago. An hour or two later we made a stop to connect with an ongoing service at Albany, New York, and many a "Whoo!" was uttered.

After reading through the New York Times (which, even with most of it skimmed through, took more than four hours), I joined Matt in the land of the sleeping.

Monday 24th February

With nothing interesting like breakfast to break the journey (we were now living off Matt's credit card), it was soon midday and a return to Chicago's Union Station (the biggest railway station in the U.S.) Booking ourselves into the nearest Days Inn to the airport, we had lunch and performed the old 40 minute train journey/shuttle bus trick to arrive at a vastly overpriced hotel offering rooms the size of most student flats, with two double beds, sofa, tables, armchairs, luxury bathroom, television...

and no USA Network.

Realising *RAW* was off the agenda, Matt continued making up sleep from the long Saturday night while I sampled the fitness room for about three minutes before sinking into the jacuzzi. As we were the only people staying at the hotel, this proved a relaxing way to spend the afternoon, even if we couldn't afford to eat any more.

Come 6:57 and we tuned in to TNT for our first experience of the two hour *Monday Nitro*. Whether you think it good or bad, this had pretty much everything you'd usually associate with Nitro. Public Enemy beat Jarrett & McMichael at 4:47 after shenanigans involving the briefcase. Schiavone ran down SuperBrawl highlights, including Randy Savage's turn. Duggan pinned Galaxy in 3:05. Hugh Morrus beat Joe Gomez at 3:20. Ice Train beat La Parka (travesty of the decade). Meng & Barbarian beat Jericho & Guerrero at 7:30. Misterio beat Juventud Guerrera in a whopping 5:26. Prince Iaukea pinned Pat Tanaka in 2:20. Ultimo Dragon bt Dean Malenko by DQ at 8:40 (the only storyline development of the night, with Malenko having snapped). In the main event, Dallas Page fought a ridiculously clad 'Squire' David Taylor to a no-contest when the nWo hit the ring. And, naturally, the last 10 minutes saw an nWo interview, concluding with Bischoff stripping Luger & Giant of the tag belts, and Sting so blatantly joining the nWo that it was obvious he hadn't joined.

I know I'm naturally biased, and I know that money's the bottom line, but how people can say this meaningless, attention deficit crap is better than RAW really does baffle me.

As Zebedee once said, time for bed.

Tuesday 25<u>th</u> February

Being the only people in a hotel does have its advantages when there's a full continental buffet laid on for free. With no money left for tips we had to make a quick exit from the shuttle bus, leaving plenty of time for our connecting flight. Aside from the continuing horror of reading about the Empire State Building tragedy, we saw a televised hockey game where the Philadelphia Flyers' offensive line was referred to as the Legion of Doom.

Once in Newark, we'd somehow ended up with a four hour wait until the flight home, so we went to find what you can buy with $5 in a major airport. The answer is a cup of tea, a packet of cigarettes and literally nothing else.

Boring flight home, no decent film (though at least it wasn't you-know-what), and we were soon ready for our final wrestling sighting, the Kendal-Windermere train (think about it.)

A farewell at Piccadilly, a 40 minute journey to Preston, a ten minute walk into University, and I was just in time for an Economics lecture.

Of course, being Preston, it was pissing it down.

Life was crap again...

Hulk Who? Final **Frontier (September 1997)**

I really did mean it when I said "never again".

After all, I spent the summer working and was returning to my final year at university, which meant no more fortnights off. After that it was a lifetime of work without a break, or a spell on the dole. Either way, I wasn't going anywhere.

But then came that once in a lifetime opportunity. You know the one: the Beatles reform, a new coronation, your local team playing at Wembley. When I found out that Terry Funk was having his retirement show, facing Bret Hart, nonetheless, I had to go.

Of course, it was never going to happen. Too far away, too much money, too little time. But it was a nice little idea, planning routes around the States to take in the WWF pay-per-view and perhaps Memphis TV. Hell, I could even make it to the Sportatorium. But it wasn't going to happen.

Then Kenny McBride called to say "I've had this crazy idea..."

Friday 5th September

Why do all these trips have to start at 5am?

Unfortunately a five minute delay at Stevenage station was magnified along the trip to Gatwick (highlighted by a billboard for the Museum of Mankind) and I checked in just late enough to get the seat from hell. There's nothing quite like sitting next to a hyperactive five-year-old for 10 hours.

The in-flight entertainment was wrestling central, kicking off with a half hour documentary on Jeep Swenson (The Ultimate Solution). Sorry, my mistake, a look behind the scenes of *Batman and Robin*. Then came *Liar Liar* which, although having no signs of the heavily rumoured Sting-Giant scenes, did mention Randy Savage and Rick Rude. And Jim Carrey's first unavoidably true answer concerned our beloved sport: "The Olympics is real, but the stuff on Channel 12 is fake." The highlight, however, was *Murder at 1600*. A Presidential conspiracy thriller, its lead villain was the Secretary of State, played by none other than Billionaire Ted!

Once I'd survived 10 hours of annoying kid syndrome, all that remained was immigration. "Yes, I'm very responsible, officer. I'm a student, but I do work as a journalist, but I won't be working here... I know I'm here in Dallas, but for 'address of residence for first night' I've put Cincinnati. No, not today, Sunday. Yes, I know that's in two days... Oh yes, I do know people in America. There's, erm, Terry Funk in Amarillo... No, no I'm not travelling alone, I'm meeting a friend who's flying out tomorrow. I'm meeting him in Nashville. Or Louisville. Or Cincinnati. No, I don't know exactly when we're meeting up... Thank you very much, sir."

The wonders of free enterprise meant I was soon on a minibus to downtown Dallas, eight miles away. My particular vehicle had drop-offs at the Radisson Hotel, the Marriot Hotel, the Embassy Suites, and the Greyhound bus station. No prizes for guessing...

The first thing I learned about Dallas is that you don't want to hang around near the Greyhound station, so it was offer for a wander in the 90 degrees plus haze. Downtown Dallas seemed pleasant enough, with an offbeat mall highlighted by a hologram store, including one 3D picture that recreated Jack Ruby shooting Lee Harvey Oswald.

Talking of which, I couldn't miss out on the Sixth Floor Museum of the Kennedy assassination. Housed in the old Texas Schoolbook Depository, tells the whole story, culminating at the window where Oswald reportedly fired the fatal shots. Looking out as the traffic continues driving down the route taken by JFK's motorcade is a truly chilling sight.

Outside, I made a stop at the conspiracy theorists' favourite haunt, the 'grassy knoll'. Though rumoured to be the site for one of the most infamous inside killings in world history, on a warm summer's afternoon it is arguably the most peaceful place on the earth.

Still, time was pressing and I had another Dallas landmark to visit. Getting to the Dallas Sportatorium is easy. Just turn out of the bus station, down the road, through the Convention Centre, out the other side and... oh... it's not so nice any more. In fact, it's Pisshead Central. Never mind though, as a quick trip through an underpass so full of empties that the winos have left, and you're at the great building itself. The Sportatorium is like the ECW Arena in every aspect (size, location, facilities) except that the crowds are a little smaller to say the least. I'd managed to turn up an hour and a half before the show started, so amused myself watching wrestlers arrive and trying to spot anyone famous. I failed. The highlight was when one wrestler arranged with one of the corporate suits (well, T-shirts) to spend the night at the liquor store, as lone as he was back by nine for his match.

Hanging about outside in the car park I found myself joined by a large muscular blank man. Pause for innuendo. I got chatting and, once the Princess Diana queries were out of the way, I discovered he was soon to become the first graduate of the Al Jackson wrestling school. Eventually my new pal gave me a world exclusive: his ring name was going to be the Atomic Dog, a JYD for the nineties gimmick with the 'Atomic Driver' finisher. Mr Dog was scheduled to do a month's work for the USWA, starting out on TV on September 20th. Tragically, when the big day came, the company was rapidly going down the pan and the taping was cancelled. And so ended the career of the Atomic Dog.

(2005 note: For several years I was under the impression that Atomic Dog went on to be the hotly tipped Superstar Steve who ended up working for Pro Wrestling NOAH. Astute readers will recall that Superstar Steve is, in fact, white.)

Back at the Sportatorium, complete with 'Home of Wrestling' banner and a painted out Global sign, I paid my $5 general admission (ringside was $8 and the 'boxes' $6) and received a small piece of paper with the word 'TICKET' printed on it. The building is purpose-built, with banked benching on the three sides of the ring and a stage on the other. The arena, which has been hosting wrestling since being built in 1953 (a previous arena on the same site hosted shows back in the thirties) could easily hold 3,000 by my reckoning (the official capacity is nearer 5,000) which made my visit all the more depressing.

I made a head count and found a total of 108 fans at the show. With the building rent apparently $1,000 a week, I'll let you do the maths. I'm told the usual gate is between $1,500 and $2,400 with pay-offs ranging from $25 to $125. Whatever the exact figures are, nobody's getting rich here.

On my side of the ring, the bleachers held a mere four people. This didn't stop the elderly jobsworth security guard on my section insisting

I remain in my seat at all times, despite being fifty yards from the ring.

As the sun set outside and the building fell into darkness, watching the scattered gathering proudly saluting the Stars and Stripes during the national anthem was a truly tragic sight. Fortunately nobody ever bothered to clean up after Global left town, so I was able to stand and face the British flag.

As the first wrestler came to the ring, *More Human Than Human* began playing. But it wasn't the Dirtbike Kid. It was a bloke with yellow facepaint...

1) Luminous vs Black Bart

You start the day waking up in your bed in Stevenage. You end it in the Global Dome watching Black Bart. Something has gone wrong.

It turns out that the Bartster, as well as working full-time installing telegraph poles, runs a training school at the Sportatorium on Saturday mornings. This bout showed the effects of a small crowd, with Bart's heckling done on a strictly one-to-one basis. It wasn't exactly a *****classic but, thankfully, after 13:04 of fascinating stalling, Luminous got the pin with the old sunset-flip/heel holds ropes/ref kicks arms away business.

2) Iceman King Parsons vs Kurt Von Hess

1983: Iceman Parsons wrestles on sold out shows at the Sportatorium for one of the hottest promotions on the planet, World Class. 1997: Iceman Parsons wrestles at the Sportatorium for one of the least successful promotions in the world, the Confederate Wrestling Alliance. How times change.

If you know your wrestling, you'll know your stereotypes. Parsons was black, and consequently could paralyse a man with a flick of his solid skull. He got the pin at 11:08 after a... erm... I don't know exactly what it's called but it basically involved Parson's shoving his arse in the other bloke's face.

A moment of excitement followed when Black Bart and Bill Irwin (the very same Goon) ran in for some extra-curricular activity, prompting Al and Action Jackson to make the save, before challenges were made for a future six-man tag.

3) Mark Von Erich vs Nick Golden

Mark Von Erich. OK. Whatever you say. The highlight of this one was Golden's manager Brandon Baxter, who completely stole the show. Only 20 years old, he worked the crowd like a pro and did a great job of distracting them from the action in the ring, which closely resembled a remake of *Secrets of Wrestling* in terms of smooth execution. Golden helps out at the training school, which makes you wonder about his opponent. A 'Von Erich' in the ring before he's ready? Never. Naturally Von Erich won at 11:37 with, what else, the Von Erich claw.

The first interval gave me a chance to flick through the programme, which appeared to be a fair piece of work for such a small audience. There was a profile of Black Bart (his favourite food is peas), a fan of the week who claimed to have been coming to the Sportatorium every week since 1968, the line-up, a full page preview of the main event, a poster of Luminous, the previous week's results, birthdays and a Do You Remember? feature.

Out in the lobby, I passed up the opportunity to get a picture taken with Terrence Garvin, and caught up with the Atomic Dog, who kindly let me hide behind him as we passed security so I could sit in the front row without paying. If Dallas wrestling ever goes bankrupt for the sake of $3, I'm going to feel awfully guilty.

4) The Dogs of War vs the Blackbirds

Or Brian Adias and Mike 'Promoter and, wouldn't you know, tag champion as well' Blackheart vs Al and Action Jackson. Yes, Adias is the same one from the early eighties and, yes, Al Jackson is the bloke who fought Jerry Lawler in the *Superstars* squash where Lawler did in-ring commentary. Meanwhile Iceman Parsons got the boot for not having a legitimate CWA manager's licence. I'd love to see what one of those looks like.

This turned out to be the match of the night, with the Blackbirds providing some real energy and playing the hot tag for all it was worth. The highlight came from Adias becoming 'punch drunk', wobbling around the ring, and attempting to tag in Action Jackson! In the end, though, the tag champs won the non-title match when Blackheart pinned Action at the 17:30 mark.

Before the main event, there was a quick interval to allow for a coin toss to determine the next challengers to the tag titles. This pitted the Blackbirds against Bart and Irwin, and High Voltage (not the WCW 'stars'), who were represented in their absence by the bizarrely-named referee 'Speedbump'. As it was a three way affair, the CWA commissioner (who appeared to have been a random customer from the liquor store) announced that the odd one out would be the winner, prompting some wit to point out that "Bill Irwin's pretty odd!" Luck was on the side of the Jacksons, though, meaning that the team who lost a non-title match to the champions were now the top contenders. I'm sure Giant Baba would be proud of the booking logic.

5) Title for Title: CWA Champion Terry Garvin vs CWA Light-Heavyweight Champion Treach Phillips

The dastardly heel entered the Sportatorium to the sounds of *Freebird*. Unfortunately the dastardly heel was Terry Garvin. (No relation to the WWF executive of a greater fame.)
Despite its unlikely status as a main event, this was perfectly bearable, with Garvin demonstrating some competent matwork. He even inspired one Dallas regular to start a chant of "Fuck him up, Terry, Fuck him up!". Charming. (*2005 note: Believe it or not, such behaviour was not commonplace at wrestling shows in 1997.*) Brandon Baxter, managing Garvin, continued a fine evening's work.
Naturally the title vs title stipulation means the only suspense was about how the screwjob would come about, and in the end some middle-aged bloke (who had earlier tried to steal the belt) ran in and started beating up Phillips at 14:49. It transpired the man in question was former light-heavyweight champion Chuck Singer. He proceeded

to slightly overdo the destruction and apparently legitimately bust open Phillips with a kneedrop using the belt.

Most of the crowd filed off peacefully, with a couple of entertaining exceptions. A gentleman who had been extremely vocal in his disapproval of the heels was quite literally frozen in shock, while a young girl burst uncontrollably in tears and had to be carried from the building. Cool.

It now being past 10pm and pitch darkness, I didn't fancy a walk back through the abandoned winoland, so talked my way into catching a lift with the Atomic Dog and Al Jackson, who, rather amusingly, decided to play the big star all the way home and ignore me. The pair discussed plans for the Atomic one to work in Dallas ("I'm telling ya, there ain't no way I'm gonna take that iron claw. I don't want no part of that shit.") before concluding that if Tom Brandi (Salvatore Sincere) didn't offer them work, Al Jackson would return to boxing.

Back at the Greyhound station I once again experienced the joys of the midnight crowd, only to find that everyone in the building wanted to head north and it was almost an hour later than expected when we set off. Still, after being awake for 25 hours, I could finally get some sleep.

Saturday 6th September

Well, that was the plan, but I soon discovered that, between slightly too uncomfortable seats and frequent stops for petrol, it is almost impossible to do more than doze on a Greyhound bus. The highways of Texas and Arkansas are difficult to appreciate in the dark and it was gone six in the morning before anything interesting started to happen (and that was simply a glimpse of Little Rock.)

The only real amusement was passing a little town called Beulah, and returning to Forrest City, Arkansas. It's not changed much, though a new motel has opened (to catch the tourist trade?!) and the bus stop-cum-liquor store is now selling six-packs of Hooch for less than three quid. Though not to people three weeks short of their 21st.

Thanks to the shenanigans back in Dallas, it was almost 9:30 when we pulled into a Memphis and I literally walked off the bus and straight into a taxi to the Channel 5 studios, where a large crowd had already gathered for the first ever USWA TV tapings. Among them was Uptown Bruno, who remembered me from February and was busy moaning about the end of the live broadcasts.

As the taping was set for almost two hours, we were all sent to the toilet where another bloke and I had to wait ages for the cubicle to become free. My new companion passed the time with the "You're from England/Princess Diana/Did you know her?" routine, before asking me to explain UB40's name and enquiring whether I'd ever heard of Flock of Seagulls. Well, only when Stevie Richards wore their shirt...

On a trivia note, it turned out that the man with the urological problem was ring announcer Tony Friedman.

Unfortunately I didn't get a chance to make any notes and, now the USWA's gone down the pan, I've been totally unable to find any record of the matches. Among the highlights I can remember were that PG-13 had a couple of great bouts, Brian Christopher overcame old WCW loser Hardbody Harrison before the 'banned' Billy Travis ran in from the car park only to be hauled off by the cops, and Steven Dunn hit a victory roll on Doomsday to capture the USWA title. Yes, the monster Kane went down to a Well Dunn member.

Outside the ring, Jerry Lawler promised to give us all a WWF figure until a little kid called him "Dairy Queen", while I gladly marked out to a taped interview with that evil heel Tommy Dreamer. The main theme of the taping, though, was utter confusion. After the first hour had been recorded, we were treated to a parade of workers coming to the ring and then, for no reason, walking off again. Officials made everyone change seats in a frankly ludicrous attempt to make it look like the two shows had different crowds. And then Bruno Lauer (who'd kicked things off with an arena brawl against Tony Friedman) came out in a Steve Austin shirt and worked the crowd for 20 minutes.

(2005 note: Looking back, I see the shows also featured the Memphis debut of a young hopeful named Steve Corino.)

Come high noon, with one lad still standing at ringside demanding an Austin shirt, and doing the most believable Veruca Salt impression I've seen in many a year, the producers decided to call it a day.

There are many things to do at noon when the sun is blazing, the air is rare, the humidity is high and you are carrying a week's worth of clothing. A three mile walk is not one of them. You may remember that in February Matt Brannigan and I made the journey from the Channel 5 studios to the Memphis Greyhound station in an hour and a quarter, arriving just as the bus was about to leave. Thanks to the show overrunning, I was left with just 45 minutes to perform the same journey in far worse walking conditions.

Naturally, after seemingly being impossibly behind schedule, I made a babyface comeback and literally collapsed onto my seat as the bus pulled out for the trip to Nashville. The four hour bus journey was fairly uneventful, with the only wrestling connection coming in the 1950s town of Brownsville when I bought a Welch's fruit drink. Welch... Roy Welch... Robert Fuller... Tennessee... well, it seemed funny at the time.

Arriving at Nashville at a little after five (making it 41 hours awake) I needed a quick wash-up and shave as I was starting to look a little shabby. Unfortunately a slight cock-up on the razor/dry skin/no foam front later and I was ready to tackle downtown Nashville with a lip that wouldn't stop bleeding. Still, at least the muggers assumed I'd already been done over.

Inside the Nashville Arena I opted for the top price $21 tickets for the night's WWF house show, figuring correctly that the cheap seats were virtually in a different state. Then it was back to the artists' entrance to while away an hour with the self-proclaimed "superfans".

With everyone on the show already inside, I entertained myself listening to arguments about who loved the Undertaker (or "Mark" to the true fans) the most, flicking through picture albums of Shawn Michaels from every conceivable angle, and listening to "inside information" being discussed, including the impending return of Kevin Nash to the WWF. Oh yes.

On the downside, Fat Minger (see *Beyond The Extreme*) had returned. On the upside, I met a Japanese guy who, though revealing himself as a WAR fan, took my address and later posted me a copy of *Gong*. Cool.

Back in the arena I selected from the wide range of food (pretzels or pretzels) and flicked through the new WWF merchandise catalogue, featuring Steve Austin middle-finger t-shirts, Steve Austin waistcoats and Steve Austin tattoos!

The crowd was around 3,000, which I would figure might be a little disappointing for a market like Nashville, but isn't too bad for the night before a pay-per-view. (*2005 note: It's sometimes hard to believe there's been an entire boom and bust since I originally wrote this.*) On the stroke of eight, Uptown Bruno strolled out to ref and were were on with the first match.

1) Buzz vs Some Bloke Who Thought He Was Taz

Hmm. And it sounds far worse when I tell you that Buzz used to be Sir Mo. Presumably this was a tryout match, and it wasn't all that awful, even if Mo did threaten to come off the top rope. 'Buzz' took the win at 4:24 with a spinkick.

2) Jesse James vs Rockabilly

'Double J' got a huge pop when he was announced from Nashville, and it would have been nice to think it was for wrestling ability. This was one of the best matches of the night, and proved why this pair deserved the tag titles. The hometown boy went over with a pumphandle suplex at 5:01.

The Sultan's music began playing, but who should come to the ring but that nasty, stinky Bret Hart. He took the microphone and gave a great speech referring to the events of February's *Raw* in the same building when he lost the WWF title to Sid. As somebody who'd been at that show, this seemed a great way of targeting the local audience to me. Bret also made a quick note of his decision to make the main event a non-title match. Pat Patterson set him straight. (*2005 note: Eight years on, I've just re-read that last line. Honest, I didn't mean it.*)

3) Flash Funk vs Sultan

It wasn't match of the year, it wasn't even particularly great, but it did include the Sultan doing the Fargo strut which was, as they say, worth the price of admission alone. The Iron Sheik held on to Funk, Funk escaped, Sultan hit Sheik, roll-up, 1-2-3, 6:43.

4) Ken Shamrock vs Farooq

Last November, Farooq lost at the Birmingham NEC in just 2:31. They said it couldn't be beaten. But this time he jobbed to a belly-to-belly suplex in 1:48.

5) Street Fight: Legion of Doom vs Godwinns

Some critics of ECW claim that the promotion's style allows crazy brawls and foreign objects to disguise some wrestlers' lack of ability. That theory gained some ground here, because this was great. For a few minutes anyway. The LOD took the fall at 4:33 with a nifty hubcap to the head.

Interval. Boring.

6) Goldust vs Vader

Thanks to an angle on the previous night's special edition of *RAW*, the crowd decided to cheer Vader, which didn't do a great deal for the psychology of this one. Plenty of traditional fat bloke/thin bloke business here, with a Brian Pillman run-in distracting Goldust, who fell to a roll-up at 5:30.

7) Patriot vs Brian Pillman

But not to worry, as Goldust got his revenge by appearing at ringside and leaving Pillman prey to the full-nelson slam at 5:41. Patriot was remarkably popular for someone who used to be in Stars & Stripes.

8) Jerry Lawler & Dude Love vs Davey Boy Smith & Owen Hart

Jerry Lawler had magically turned babyface for the show and came to the ring to the theme from *Rocky*. The entire match was fought like a Michinoku comedy bout.

141

The first gag came with Owen and Dude Love criss-crossing the ring until Dude Love stopped. Hart continued going even when the Dudester left the ring, took a seat and folded his arms. Then came the infamous Super Delfin/Gran Naniwa comedy armwringer spot, which was set up so decisively I was almost falling off my seat before the punchline. The end came with the dastardly heels getting their comeuppance when Owen mistakenly hit Smith with the spinkick, putting him down for the pin at 10:54.

(*2005 note: I now realise virtually all the Michinoku comedy spots came from 1970s Tennessee spot shows. How exactly Sasuke saw them, I may never know.*)

9) WWF Champion Bret Hart vs Undertaker

Well, yes, obviously it was a screwjob, but they put on a pretty decent match getting there. The finishing sequence had ref-bumps, sharpshooters, chairshots and false falls galore, and the less cynical fan wouldn't have been too naive expecting the title to change hands at some points. Of course Owen and Davey put in an appearance at 11:50 to save their man from the tombstone.

It's difficult to explain why I enjoyed this show so much. Last time I went to a WWF house show (the November 1996 Birmingham fiasco), the short match times ruined the show. This time the event was done and dusted in two and a quarter hours, presumably because everyone wanted to get straight off to Louisville and get a decent night's kip before the big show.

You may remember that the typical 15-20 minute WWF house show match used to consist mainly of stalling and restholds (as opposed to working a hold). The 1997 match is nothing more complicated than a few minutes of fast-paced trademark spots and then, before the crowd tires, going straight to the finish. This was a good night's entertainment, plain and simple.

Next stop was the hotel from February, where I spent a somewhat pointless hour confirming that everyone had already gone on to Louisville, before meeting a bloke who promoted in some hick town and had just booked the Armstrongs for his next taping.

The fact that I spent the next house walking around downtown Nashville solely to ensure I wasn't at that bus station when the midnight service to Louisville left shows exactly how ridiculous this latest voyage was.

Instead, once I'd finally persuaded the drunk geriatric next to me to stop going on about Diana's funeral (for the thousandth time, I did not know her personally you dumb Yank), I caught the 2am bus and saved another night's hotel bills.

<u>Sunday 7th September</u>

For those of you with kids or younger siblings who constantly shout out "I'm bored", please tell them that unless they've been in Louisville Greyhound station at six in the morning and waited around for a couple of hours, they don't know the meaning of the word. Fortunately, as the sun came up, the next bus came along and Kenny finally caught up with me:

It's always the way, isn't it. You finish your last day at work at 4:30 and then by the time you've said all your goodbyes, your bus is late and you arrive at the bank to cash your pay-cheque 30 seconds after they lock up. You start to panic, but it's OK because your mum bails you out and lends you almost enough money for the trip you're taking to American in less than 12 hours. Phew!

Ah, but things still don't look too great, because the bus you're catching to London at 10pm is due to arrive just three hours before the largest funeral in living memory. Now, no offence to Diana Spencer/Windsor or her family; I'm sure I can't imagine their grief. But I really don't think that she had more than 12 busfulls of close friends in Glasgow who had nothing better to do that day than catch the overnight bus to London so they could stand in the street for four hours.

As the TV cameras scanned the mourners at Buchanan Street station, showing the world the Creatures Of The Night, the audience may just have caught a glimpse of a guy in a Chris Candido T-shirt mouthing along to Mikey Whipwreck's music and chatting to the only other sane people there, three guys in kilts off backpacking around Europe.

So my bus finally leaves Glasgow (half an hour late, natch) and I doze past Hamilton, then wake up in Carlisle. looking out of my window I think "Wrestling sighting number one! That looked like 'Mr T-shirt' Mark Smith!" Then I fall asleep again. When I wake up it's 8:30 and I'm in London Victoria. Oh my god, that was Mark Smith!

"Where are you off to, Mark?"

"The funeral. And you?"

"Terry Funk's house."

"BASTARD!"

After almost missing the bus to Heathrow (having spotted a golf shop with a poster for 'The Taylor Made Man'), I finally reach the airport only to find everywhere closed. Again, no offence to the Spencer family, but when a waitress in the (closed) bar dumps a tray on my table rather than carry it a further three feet to the bar, because the coffin has just entered the church, something is wrong.

The world takes a break for a couple of minutes of 'respectful silence'. Yours truly, of course, doesn't notice because I'm wearing my Walkman and ECW The Album III *is just so damned cool. So while the rest of the world has a tear in its eye and a lump in its throat, I have a fag in my hand, a smile on my face, and Mr Hughes' music in my ears. Heh heh heh.*

Nine hours later, there we are in Dallas. 90 degrees Fahrenheit and 99% humidity. I knew there was a reason I hated America. The charming customs gentleman confiscates my illegal bananas and then spots my stack of PowerSlams *and initiates the first wrestling conversation of my holiday:*

"You know any of those Mexican guys? They come through all the time. That Konnan's a real nice guy, and I've seen Psicosis and that little guy without their masks a bunch of times." *Then he mentioned that Shawn Michaels comes through quite regularly; indeed, I'd only missed him by 24 hours. Naturally I did my bit for US law enforcement and told him about Shawn's alleged fondness for a certain fine white powder from Colombia. You have never seen such a stony face, not even on Steve Austin.*

Finally, I board my connecting plane to Memphis. Once again I put

*on the headphones and play Volume III of those great ECW Albums.
There's something quite uniquely romantic about flying from Dallas to
Memphis, listening to* Freebird.

*Gee, you gotta love those $25 cab fares from the airport to the
Greyhoudn station, particularly when the driver is such a grumpy git.
Not to worry though, because in his friendly warning he managed to tell
me whereabouts in Memphis I could find both drugs* and *hookers.*

*From Memphis it was a mere four hours to Nashville and then a
lengthy wait before a further four hour drive to Louisville where, after
my 34 hour trip, Mr JL picks up the story.*

Having managed to arrive 11 hours early for the Ground Zero pay-per-
view, we elected to spend the morning eating bagels, drinking Gatorade
and walking three miles so Kenny could attend Mass. I believe that to
this day I am still the first person to go to Mass in a Brian Pillman shirt.
I guess it's lucky I wasn't wearing my Raven crucifix pose shirt.

The first wrestling reference of the day came with a car clamping
notice informing unlucky drivers that they could only get their vehicles
back by calling 1-800-REPO-MAN.

Passing a giant discount food store proved a bad mood as, in the
sweltering conditions, buying 24 cans of Pepsi for $5 (£3) seemed a
great idea. Not only were we still drinking the damn things in Texas,
but a couple of Louisville's finest subjected us to lengthy questioning
on just why two youths (who hadn't washed or slept in two days) were
carrying so many cans.

And those of you who read *Beyond The Extreme* will be pleased
to know that, while subjecting a bookshop attendant to a series of
computer searches for "DiBiase, Ted", we came across the book of *Fly
Away Home.*

With all the frivolity out of the way, it was time to tackle the main task
of the day: getting into the legitimately sold-out Louisville Gardens,
Mostly this involved having security guards threaten to phone the police
if we didn't leave the area, but other fun came with Doc Hendrix saying
he couldn't talk because he had to go to a booking meeting, and Vince
McMahon reading our "Hulk Who?" sign and laughing. But not giving
us free tickets.

Having failed in our ploy of going straight to the top, we took the opposite tack and got chatting with our old mates Bruno Lauer and Steve Lombardi, who disbelieved our claims to have made him famous until he read through our copies of *PowerSlam* and *Beyond The Extreme*. Eventually the magic words were uttered: "You haven't got tickets? Hmm, I reckon we could get you in. Meet us round the back at about 6:30."

We whiled away the next couple of hours by watching the Disciples of Apocolypse ride their bikes down the street, and cooling off back the Greyhound station. Unfortunately we also discovered that it's against state law to sell alcohol in Kentucky on a Sunday. And they call this the land of the free...

Back at the Gardens we bumped into Ian Rotten who was handing out flyers for his next show. As we were chatting about the *Lariat* and the NWA vs IWA feud, a WWF official came over to the master of the barbed-wire baseball bat and things turned ugly, with Rotten eventually claiming his foe had just "called me a prostitute". Alas the expected pier-six was rapidly defused.

Catching up with Bruno again, we showed off our rapidly increasing knowledge by helping him look for a branch of sandwich store Subway. (*2005 note: Yes, in 1997 you really did have to explain what Subway was to British readers.*) After passing the USWA's TV director, who explained that the previous morning's problems had been caused by a faulty tape machine hampering attempts to record the show as if live, we asked Bruno why he was so insistent on reaching Subway, which was a mile or so away.

It turned out his role as 'production assistant' roughly translated as 'gofer'. Contrary to popular belief, the Legion of Doom do not "snack on danger and dine on death", but instead prefer chicken salad rolls.

Having achieved our previously unrealised ambition of walking into a shop and ordering lunch for the Road Warriors, we played an unsuccessful round of taxi roulette before persuading a couple of passing fans to take us back to the arena. The two lads were clearly a little bemused at having just given a lift to Harvey Whippleman.

Watching the capacity crowd having to queue (imagine 6,000 people standing in the middle of the street, at least 50 of them with shaved heads and goatee beards), we noticed a sign saying that Tuesday's USWA show had been cancelled. There went the 'seven shows in seven days' challenge for another trip. Still, things picked up when a load of women started walking about in bikinis and stilettos. In fact they looked like a bunch of... Oh, they were.

Round the back of the arena we caught up with Chris Candido, who seemed a little stunned at our having returned to the US after the epic voyage in February (when we said we'd be seeing him in Amarillo I think he was truly bemused). Our chat was briefly interrupted when he had to "go and watch Tammy open the show". All together now: Ahhh!

Another cute moment was when Mick Foley, the world's happiest man, came over to look at my copy of *PowerSlam* with an article on him, and a little boy ran up from the street and spontaneously threw him arms around the former Cactus Jack. After he'd finished chatting, and borrowed some back issues on the promise of returning them in Amarillo, we were treated to the unlikely sight of Mankind trotting off for a walk down Louisville High Street.

By this time we were starting to panic that Bruno and Lombardi had been playing some sort of hilarious rib on the marks, but eventually they appeared, called us past the evil security guards, and told us to wait outside the dressing room door.

A few seconds later that mythical gate opened and we were rushed through a roomful of half-dressed wrestlers and through a curtain into the crowd. I think Bruno told us to "get lost" in the nicest possible way.

They'd obviously picked an opportune moment to get us in as a certain Steve Austin had just taken to the stage for an interview to conclude the Free-For-All pre-game show. To say we were experiencing an energy rush would be an understatement. Seeing five thousand people in the same arena where we were among just 300 watching the USWA back in February was quite bizarre.

When we eventually found some seats (having bumped into the Japanese fellow from Nashville), we found ourselves right at the back of the arena. Now obviously we weren't in a position to be complaining, and it turned out we were in one of the more interesting locations in the building.

We, and a few hundred others, were actually behind the In Your House set used as an entrance, and could see all the sound and lighting technicians at work. We also had the slightly bizarre experience of seeing the Titantron (which was placed in the house set's window) from behind, with the picture in reverse. Unfortunately we were also only a few feet from the fireworks, which Kenny swears to this day singed his arm at the show's explosive start.

1) Indecent Proposal: Goldust vs Brian Pillman

During this reasonably entertaining opener, we noticed that the curtain covering the entrance to the main set was partially transparent with the lights on full power. This meant we could see several wrestlers watching the match and, quite disturbingly, what appeared to be a midget jumping up and down. Imagine seeing a Tango advert live and you'll get the idea.

Pillman took the win (and Baby Doll, I mean Marlena for thirty days) when he stole her loaded purse and walloped Goldust at 11:04. It was also pretty strange watching the 'Loose Cannon' speeding his car down the alleyway where, 15 minutes earlier, an entire crew of wrestlers were recording interviews and generally hanging out. No wonder security were so keen to clear the area.

2) Scott Putski vs Brian Christopher

This one never really got going before Putski suffered a (legitimate) serious knee injury at 4:38 and was stretchered out literally under our feet. While the jumping dwarf continued his antics, and the crowd mysteriously favoured 'Too Sexy', we turned our attention to Chris Candido who came over and started reading *Beyond The Extreme* from cover to cover while giving us the latest Philly gossip.

3) Triple Threat: Savio Vega vs Farooq vs Crush

Was this one A) eleven minutes of foreign objects and hot brawling ending with all twelve gang members fighting their way out back and into the street, or B) a marathon of restholds with every pin attempt broken up by the third man until Crush floored Farooq him a heartpunch but Vega caught him with a spinkick for the pin at 11:39? I'll let you be the judge.

4) Max Mini vs El Torito

The mystery of the leaping midget was finally solved and this was a damn fine display. Naturally it briefly descended into the realms of referee arse biting, but the lucha action actually got over and MIni's 9:19 sunset-flip victory earned a rousing pop.

At this point Sgt Slaughter made his way to the ring and Dude Love forfeited his share of the WWF tag titles. Steve Austin came down, called Jim Ross a "fat ass", threw his belt to the floor and ordered Slaughter to "get down and give me twenty". Without looking up from his reading, Candido informed us that "Something cool happens here." And right on cue, Austin gave Ross the Stone Cold Stunner for the biggest ovation of the night.

5) Fatal Fourway for vacant tag titles: Legion of Doom vs Godwinns vs Headbangers vs Owen Hart & Davey Boy Smith

At times this match was excellent. At other times the LOD and the Godwinns were in the ring.

The LOD were thrown out at 9:56 for using the Godwinns bucket, though at least they had a tasty snack waiting for them back in the locker room. Just as amusingly, Henry Godwinn was pinned by Thrasher at 12:42, guaranteeing a decent team would be leaving with the belts.

From the moment Steve Austin appeared behind the main entrance, Kenny and I put two and two together and began marking out. 'Stone Cold' ran to the ring, stunnered Owen, and three seconds later one of the most underrated teams in the sport was wearing the gold.

Sometimes, following the godforsaken business seems worthwhile.

6) WWF Champion Bret Hart vs the Patriot

Thanks to the preview package on the Titantron, this match marked the first occasion that Mitsuharu Misawa and Kenta Kobashi have appeared in the Louisville Gardens.

As for the real contest, the US vs Canada feud was generating some serious heat, though this was somewhat compromised by events in our seating section. As Kenny put it to a WWF official during the previous bout: "You might want to take a look at that curtain. A few people are starting to wonder why Bret and Patriot are chatting to each other..."

In the ring this was a competent, if not outstanding match, almost in All Japan style. Bret worked over Patriot's knee for most of the bout, before Davey Boy appeared at ringside, leading Vader to complete his face turn by making the save. After some extremely close false finishes, Patriot put on the sharpshooter, only for Bret to reverse it and get the win at 19:18.

A clean submission in a World title match? Blimey. A crowd of WWF fans chanting "Bullshit"? Coo.

7) Shawn Michaels vs Undertaker

And you thought the main event of Ultra Kaos was, erm, chaotic? This had six ref bumps, fireworks, explosions, Michaels taking crazy bump after crazy bump, outrageous interference from Helmsley, Chyna and Rude, a five minute pre-match brawl around the arena, an unannounced no-contest finish at 16:03, a run-in by almost every wrestler in the promotion, and an utterly incredible tope suicida by the Undertaker to end the post-match carnage.

The chaos continued when we unwisely decided to stand by the curtain to the dressing room to try and say a quick word of thanks to Steve and Bruno. A few dozen fans, who had been watching the curtain all night to see wrestlers watch the matches, and to shout abuse at Rocky Maivia, decided they were going in he dressing room, pushing us in first.

Just as Kenny and I were about to make our way out the back door, and I was glancing at a blackboard with a running order for the post-match pagga, I looked up to find an understandably angry Phinneous Godwin two inches in front of me.

I tell you, he doesn't use that kind of language in promos.

Once that situation had been defused, we couldn't refuse a trip round the back of the arena, where the wrestlers were walking out straight into a public multi-storey car park. There's nothing quite like the sight of drunken hicks trying to cut up Ron and Don Harris. There's also nothing to match the look of envy you get from teenage boys when Sunny drives past and says goodbye to you.

By now were were pretty desperate to get to sleep, but the great state laws of Kentucky deemed 20 year olds too immature to rent a hotel room, so it was off on the bus to Cincinnati. Quite impressively the driver followed the now familiar pattern of not giving my pass a second glance, let alone stamping it, which meant I would save $50 down in Texas as my one week pass would now be good for the full ten days of the trip.

Come Cincinnati, after a half-hour battle with bureaucracy to get Kenny's bag back from the luggage compartment, we decided not to bother with a cab.

After all, the Cincinnati Days Inn where we'd reserved a room was in a "convenient downtown location on Central Parkway", and my map showed Central Parkway was only half a mile long.

Ha. After half a mile, Central Parkway turns off at a 90 degree angle and heads north (which isn't very bloody central in my opinion) for... well... for a very long way indeed.

All I know for sure is that at 3am we were sitting by the side of the road in an area that closely resembled Toxteth. I had been awake for 75 straight hours without a proper meal. It was 65 degrees Fahrenheit. We were carrying a week's clothes and 20 cans of Pepsi. Kenny was in the early stages of a diabetic hypoglycaemic attack. The two empty taxis which had passed had made no attempt to stop and pick us up. And then a man went past on a push-bike and shouted "Hey, guys. Get in my taxi. Ha ha."

There are times in your life when hallucinatory drugs would simply be redundant.

Eventually we got a taxi to stop and made it the last couple of miles to the hotel, at *2880* Central Parkway nonetheless. Naturally there was no record of our reservation, but we were too exhausted to argue and there were still rooms spare. I guess they don't get much passing trade...

Monday 8th September

Whilst once again making a hotel regret the "all you can eat" breakfast buffet offer, we began the day by finding out just where the hell we were.

Despite being several miles north of Cincinnati, we were still about eight miles south of the Cincinnati Gardens, which was not exactly handy. The town planners of America could really do with a bit more practice on *Sim City*.

Still, there was nothing else to do but get a taxi to the arena, passing on the way a billboard reading "Saturn - they've spoilt me rotten". I didn't know billboards did WCW updates.

Once there we realised that the Cincinnati Gardens isn't actually near anywhere. Fear not, though, as we found plenty of entertainment round the back of the arena (ahem) with a quick game of security guard baiting, before chatting to some fellow stragglers. As well as a photographer from *New Wave Wrestling*, who proved to be the embodiment of the term 'mark', another middle-aged man told us his life story.

The gist of his general conversation was that any wrestler you cared to name had "started out with me back in Memphis/Portland/ Indianapolis". These even included "Masa Shoo-noo". Unfortunately he also said yes when we called his bluff by asking if he'd started out with "Ross Gordon, that guy who works indies up in the North-East." He said yes, but unless this gentleman really did work holiday camp shows in Scarborough with *Suckerpunch* editor Ross Hutchinson last summer, we can only conclude he was trying to work us.

Hunger soon came calling, so we went for a ramble and found a Burger King which kindly provided a free newspaper. This included an advert for *Amos and Andy* videos including the episodes *Sapphire's Brother Comes to Visit* and *Is Sapphire a Murderer?*" Well, that mixed tag at WrestleMania VI sure was a killer.

Once we'd been through a video store (which still had copies of the 1987 Great American Bash) and turned all the covers with Hulk Hogan on inside out, it was back to the arena where we found a bobble-hat-wearing Iron Sheik telling us how he had trained Olympic gold medal winning amateur wrestler Kurt Angle. (*2005 note: I remind you this was written in late 1997. Today's lesson is to listen carefully to the Iron Sheik.*)

The afternoon passed in a sunny haze with more and more fans turning up; Shawn Michaels changing in the arena's parking garage instead of going inside to the dressing room; Jim Ross, Bruce Prichard and Jerry Brisco having a lengthy chat (sparking off a lengthy debate among the smart marks over the ladder of power in Titan Sports; and Kenny and myself talking to lots of loveable little children who were too busy enjoying wrestling to worry about how the business works.

After four days of heatstroke, we were the only two people to appreciate a torrential downpour an hour before the show started. Being from Britain has its advantages.

Once inside the arena, we found that, with around 6,000 fans in the 10,000 seat arena, one side was completely full. Coincidentally this was the side that the main camera faced. Uncanny.

1) Tiger Ali Singh vs ?

Squash. Yawn.

2) Brian Christopher vs Pantera

This was the first match taped for *Shotgun*, and it was a good one. The highlight came when the Mexican decided, for no apparent reason, to do a reverse Space Flying Tiger Drop.

Christopher took the win when Pantera came off the top, and 'Too Sexy' neatly caught him in the reverse Russian legsweep.

3) Legion of Doom vs Farooq and Kama

You might not like D Lo Brown and Rocky Maivia, but at least their interference brought an end to this one. Shamrock made the save and according to the *Observer*, later wrestled a squash match. If that's the case, it obviously wasn't very memorable.

4) Truth Commission vs ?

The Cincinnati Gardens have very clean toilets.

5) El Torito vs Little Lucky

Minis are cool. The evil bully Torito won.

6) Sultan vs Flash Funk

Pretty much the same deal as in Nashville, but entertaining stuff nonetheless. Unfortunately this one went overtime and virtually on the count of three Dave Hebner was at ringside telling them to get out of there pronto. The reason for this became clear when the ring announcer encouraged everyone in the building to make a lot of noise as McMahon and Lawler did a live promo during the adverts of the programme that preceded *Raw*. Then, a few minutes later, we were all holding up our signs for the show's opening and the pyrotechnics were in full effect. You wouldn't believe how loud those fireworks are live.

The show kicked off with a Sgt Slaughter interview in which he announced that Steve Austin was suspended indefinitely and the Intercontinental title would be vacated. A ridiculously popular 'Stone Cold' came to the ring, told Slaughter that "it looks like the only order you've been giving is for a whole load of cheeseburgers", delivered the Stone Cold Stunner, and threatened to do the same to Vince McMahon.

7) Non Title Streetfight: Bret Hart vs Vader

This was reasonable stuff, with the action spilling outside the ring and up the rampway. It ended in an unsatisfying no-contest when all of the Hart Foundation started a barney, broken up by none other than Steve Austin. Then, as the Headbangers prepared to start their squash match, the Godwinns turned up and destroyed the jobbers.

8) Headbangers vs Godwinns

The problems of being there live became apparent as we lacked any kind of explanation as to why this was happening. Then Tony Anthony turned up dresses as a country yokel and lamped Thrasher with a horseshoe to set-up the Godwinns win. Of course, had we been watching at home, we'd have known it was an unsanctioned and therefore non-title affair, and that Anthony was actually the Godwinns' long-lost Uncle Cletus. We should have guessed.

The first Intercontinental tournament match was scheduled to pin Dude Love against Brian Pillman (who unfortunately received an overwhelming babyface reaction when his hometown was announced), but Pillman spoke on a telephone link-up and presented the first part of Brian Pillman's *XXX Files*. Several young children embarrassed their parents by asking exactly what he was talking about.

During the opening for the second hour (which didn't include the 'Sunny 4:69' sign behind us), we noticed a couple of interesting things about the television production. By looking at the Titantron (which is absolutely *huge*) we noticed that whichever camera was providing the live feed had a red light lit. From this we soon realised that a handheld camera patrolling the floor was not filming at all, but was instead being used to trick fans into making a load of noise during dead spots. Either that or we'll be appearing in a cheesy music video, perhaps *Land of a 1000 Dances: The 1997 Mix.*

9) Max Mini vs Piratita Morgan

Minis still rule, even if none of the commentators can get their names right. This time the beloved technico had his hand raised. For those who don't know, Mini was previously known as Mascarita Sagrada; yes, the one who leapt from atop a steel cage onto Jake Roberts. (*2005 note: Even better, Mini was also Little Lucky, while Morgan was doubling-up as El Torito. That's two people putting on three different matches in two days. A few more scams like this and they'd have saved enough cash to pay Bret Hart's contract....*)

10) Goldust vs Owen Hart

This was also an I-C tournament match, with Goldust eventually disqualified for using the closed fist. All the Harts ran in and Steve Austin cleared the ring with a broom. Some things never change.

11) Hunter Hearst Helmsley vs Patriot vs Davey Boy Smith

Without commentary, this one really had the crowd baffled. First of all, the Titantron gave the impression that it was part of the I-C title tournament, which really didn't make much sense. Then we realised it was a regular triangle match, which made even less sense. Then Helmsley and Michaels sneak-attacked Davey Boy Smith, which made perfect sense to us as we were looking forward to *One Night Only*, but confused everyone else in the building. Then Smith was replaced by Savio Vega and everyone gave up trying to work it out.

While this was no worse than the pay-per-view triangle match, at least we knew why Vegas, Farooq and Crush were torturing us with their ring presence. This was just plain inexplicable. And it went on, and on, and on. After about 15 minutes they were having to cut to adverts to avoid airing the "refund" chants, and the cries of "boring" were all over the TV broadcast.

For no particular reason, Michaels and Chyna turned up at the end and Helmsley pinned Vegas before what later became Degeneration X took over the ring. The Hart Foundation appeared on the rampway and then disappeared the moment the broadcast went off air.

12) Billy Gunn, Jesse James and a couple of Boricuas vs DOA

Erm, it's starting to get a little confusing now. This dark match was taken by most people to be a cue to go home, which was probably a better option than working out where the other two Boricuas were, and why Gunn and James had made up. The moment all the heels remembered they weren't actually mates, they did the job.

13) WWF Champion Bret Hart vs Undertaker

Picture the scene: The majority of the six thousand crowd have begun leaving the building when they hear Bret Hart's entrance. The start rushing back inside as other fans are filing out. The arena is then plunged into darkness for the Undertaker's entrance and large explosions are set off. The WWF could still learn a few lessons in crowd control.

By the time the lights were back on, several hundred extra fans had magically appeared on the arena floor and made their presence known at ringside. This was roughly the same match as in Nashville, but the crowd was dangerously into the action and the garbage was soon flying towards the ring. This produced one neat piece of improvisation when Bret caught a can that had been lobbed at him and used it as a foreign object. And once the DQ finish had been given, the rowdies rushed round the back to find that everyone else in the promotion had left the building during the match.

Of course, the main event of the evening was yet to come: The Cross-Border Connection of McBride and Lister against the taxis of Ohio. The heels took an early advantage with broken payphones and the language barrier, and when they delivered a sneaky "oh, we sent a cab to you, but it looked a bit busy, so he went home" foul, it seemed all was lost. But a last minute babyface comeback, in the form of jumping in a taxi as some local fans were getting in, provided the screwy finish.

The ride gave us some of the best entertainment of the night, with our fellow passengers proving just why wrestling fans are held in such low esteem by the public.

"Razor Ramon got fired from the WWF because he Razor's Edged Vince McMahon though a table backstage."

"Didn't Dynamite Kid attack Davey Boy Smith in the middle of Trafalgar Square."

"Did you use to speak to Princess Diana?"

"England? What state is that in? That must have been a long bus ride."

Unfortunately the driver proved to be a monster heel, driving into Cincinatti itself and then back to our hotel, mysteriously making an $11 fare rise to $17 and insisting we paid the full amount, letting our new mates travel free for the first eight miles of their trip. Still, we left the bastard almost speechless.

"You *walked* from downtown to here, through this area? Oh my god, I don't believe it! You should have been *killed!*"

Tuesday 9th September

Another free breakfast later and we were ready to start making plans. The idea of going to the *RAW* taping in Muncie, Indiana went out the window when we found the only bus had left at 5am, and WCW was up in Wisconsin (virtually Canada). Nobody was answering their phones when we tried to find some independent shows, and so the only thing to do was head out to Amarillo.

For those whose geography isn't too hot, Cincinnati and Amarillo aren't very close. Cincinnati is in Ohio, as in the northern border of the United States. Amarillo is in Texas, as in southern border. We had 1,100 miles to go.

Still, we got off to an interesting start with the taxi into Cincinnati. The driver was, to put it mildly, a raving lunatic. After hearing that we were from Britain, he declared me a "redneck" because I was from the south of the country. "And I don't know why you're laughing, pal," he informed Kenny. "You're a goddamn Yankee."

Unfortunately once he turned the conversation to Princess Diana, things turned a little unpleasant. The laws of seditious libel prevent me printing his exact views, but let's just say he wasn't a monarchist...

The joys of travelling by Greyhound became clear when we discovered we'd be off to Indianapolis to spend the afternoon. Highlights of the journey there included passing through 'IRA STREET', going through yet another Shelbyville (this time in Indiana) where we saw a firm called 'Sandman Brothers', and being far too excited on recognising Terra Haute as the site of Shawn Michaels' first I-C title win.

Indianapolis' station turned out to be literally in the shadow of the Hoosier Dome, site of WrestleMania VIII, as well as being right on the main street full of gigantic shopping malls and a *Planet Hollywood* with handprints of all the stars, including Freddy Krueger (claws and all).

At last a proper city.

After the first real meal of the trip (all the pasta and pudding you could eat for £3), it was time to go shopping. The biggest mall had a computerised 'You are here' that gave you a virtual reality demonstration of how to get to your desired store.

Talking of technology, we passed an hour in a games arcade where we found *Tekken 3* allowed you to perform the Niagara Driver, while another fighting game was set in a street with a billboard for a JWP show, and one of the characters was Hayabusa!

Being that Indianapolis seemed a pretty cool place, we chanced our luck in a liquor store and got ourselves some beers (turning down the chance to buy 'Hardcore Cider'.) The heavens opened, and it has to be said that sitting on Indianapolis' war memorial in a torrential downpour, drinking alcohol while underage is immoral, illegal, extremely stupid, and quite remarkably enjoyable.

Back at the station we discovered the timetable was about as reliable as Tommy Rich, and we were set to wait until 10 at night. Still, between watching a man whose name badge proclaimed him as 'Virgil' scrubbing the floor, and reading the obituaries in the local rag, we easily amused ourselves. A couple of recent stiffs included, quite seriously, Martha Jane Cowherd Moore Hubble Litton and Keegan Drake Willner Looney. You couldn't make it up.

The bus finally arrived and, save for a quick drug bust which saw the man sitting in front of us taken away for questioning (causing a minor panic when the police appeared to be ready to search through our bags, complete with the alcohol that you're not allowed on buses, especially when underage), we were soon ready to hook up with whomever sang *Meet Me In St Louis*. Though I assume they didn't mean meeting at 2am.

Wednesday 10th September

We left St Louis at a little after 3. We left Missouri around noon. Missouri is big. Unfortunately Missouri is also a field. At one point we drove for three hours without seeing a single hill or town. You know how *Home and Away*'s Summer Bay only has four buses a day? There are towns in Missouri with only three a week. One stop was literally a sign in the front window of somebody's house, and an elderly woman getting on explained that she was leaving her town for the first time in a decade.

What really doesn't make sense is that, once you hit Oklahoma, every four hours or so a city will rise up on the horizon, complete with immense skyscrapers and narrow criss-cross streets. Seriously, guys, spread out a bit.

Still, enough geography and back to the cultural references. After a vending machine stole my money as I attempted to buy a packet of 'Ding Dongs', we arrived in Tulsa, Oklahoma and soon found the building where the UWF used to promote. Also in Tulsa, a dubious looking gentleman offered to sell us an eighth of marijuana for $15 which, erm, I'm led to believe is quite cheap. Especially as this 'eighth' was the size of a Pepperami. Remembering the fate of the man in St Louis, though, we graciously turned him down.

Oklahoma wasn't much busier than Missouri, though the sunsets over the plains have to be seen to be believed. I'm not trying to say that the US is empty, but hoardings for the Big Texan restaurant in Amarillo appeared by the side of the road at a point where they had to admit "Just 250 miles to go."

After passing through Vinita, Oklahoma, which boasted a firm called PG Walker (presumably not the then newest member of PG-13), we found the first stop in Texas was called Shamrock. Here I picked up the *Amarillo Daily News* which included a story on film director Barry Blaustein making a documentary about Terry Funk.

We pulled into Amarillo itself at about 9pm and, after eventually getting a taxi to pick us up (do American cabbies not realise that actually responding to calls or, god forbid, waiting outside bus stations might get them some business?), made it to the Days Inn where, naturally, there was no record of our reservation. Land of good service, my arse.

So, a mere 35 hours after leaving our room in Cincinnati, we were back in a hotel room on the other side of the country. All that remained was to take advantage of the local phone book's freephone information services (which had everything from funeral directors to movie listings, though we opted for a bloke reading the headlines out of the *Torch* and *Observer*) and catch an advert for the WrestleFest show on the local ABC station at ten to midnight, and it was time for bed.

Thursday 11th September

"Do you suffer from genital herpes?" Trust American television to give you a pleasant start to the day.

Once we'd recovered enough to face breakfast, and pick up the local paper with two different stories on the show, it was angle time. Kenny had decided the continual 90%-plus humidity was too much for his Tommy Dreamer hairstyle, and it was time to revert to the ever-popular Steve Austin look.

Unfortunately the batteries in his shaver decided to give out just at the point professionally known as "the Missing Link", and we were forced into a nasty situation with a razor blade and some borrowed scissors.

Of course, this is first time a hotel maid has ever walked into a hotel room on the day of a wrestling show and found scissors and blood on the floor.

Once Kenny had persuaded the local garage to sell him cigarettes (for some reason the staff thought he didn't resemble his passport photograph), it was time for a quick stroll to the Amarillo State Fairgrounds. Forget the crappy merry-go-round at your local park, this was the real deal. We had arrived just as work was starting on the annual State Fair, meaning their were plenty of opportunities for wandering about as people assumed we were labourers.

After picking up a couple of general admission tickets (there were no longer two ringside seats together), we scanned through the adverts for the United States Wrestling Federation (a shootfighting group who had Dan Severn booked for October) and went to have a nose round the Sports Arena.

Inside we found the ring being set up by a gang of workers and a man in his mid-fifties with long hair and a grizzled forehead. Terry Funk said hello and hoped he would put on a good show, before returning to his task. We moved on to have a good laugh at the crew from Channel 4 (the local ABC network station, not the lot who show *Brookside*) preparing for an interview with the great man, cocking up every line as they went.

Also wandering around was Barry Blaustein, writer of *The Nutty Professor*, who was making a documentary on Terry Funk with the backing of Hollywood legend Ron Howard. It turned out that Barry was a serious wrestling fan and actually understood why we had come all the way from Britain. And he talked about Mick Foley and not the Princess of Wales... Perhaps inevitably the clapperboards and boom mikes came out and, while all your mates are off watching *SpiceWorld 2* in the summer, you could conceivably see me and Kenny making complete fools of ourselves in *Beyond The Mat*.

(2005 note: As you may know, we do indeed appear in the film. And this is the place to clear up an ugly rumour. Contrary to popular belief, and the subtitles, I do not utter the infamous words "We're from England, in Britain." I, in fact, say "We're from England... erm Britain", having remembered the presence of a Scotsman mid-sentence. That said, this common misapprehension is still less embarrassing than the unused sequence in which Barry asks whether we have girlfriends...)

As the afternoon ticked by, a couple of hundred people turned up for an autograph session, where we caught up with Chris Candido and grabbed a few words with virtually everyone on the show. Between Candido licking the Bushwhackers' heads for a bet, and Sandman walking around in a huff because the show was sponsored by Coors and he'd been banned from drinking Budweiser, it was an entertaining couple of hours.

When one of the fans asked Terry Funk why the match with Bret Hart was non-title, he explained that it had been signed before he beat the Undertaker at SummerSlam. You can't beat wrestling for creative excuses.

Over at the merchandise stands, staffed by Beulah McGillicutty and Terry Funk's daughters (erm, I'll rephrase that), we seriously considered asking for the parcel delivery form on the boxes as a souvenir. It read, in it's entirety: "From: ECW, New York. To: Terry Funk, Fairgrounds, Amarillo."

After peering over Terry Funk's shoulder at the running order for the show and the pay-offs for the airline fares (aside from this, the entire ECW crew apparently worked for free), and scratching our heads when Taka Michinoku strolled by in an Austin 3:16 shirt, we went over to the paltry concession stands for our tea.

Only in the land of capitalism can you stick a slice of cheese on a stick, dip it in some batter, and charge £1.20 for it.

Whilst I was starting to realise just how spectacularly I'd been diddled, a voice behind me said "with that accent, you've got to be John Lister, right." It turned out to be everyone's favourite tape trader George Mayfield, who'd heard I was coming after he spoke to Rob Butcher. Unfortunately this now meant I was playing delivery boy with a pile of tapes.

Then we finally caught up with *PowerSlam* photographer George Tahinos (who didn't take kindly to being referred to as "my snapper"), who informed me that I was also playing delivery boy with a pile of T-shirts for Findlay Martin's latest competition.

It was finally time to take our seats behind a flag-waving lunatic American patriot and next to a gang of Mexicans (boy, do we pick our seats) in what appeared to be a crowd of around 4,000 people. The press was told it was 5,200 while the *Observer* reported it as 3,800. You be the judge. Either way, it was a hell of a crowd for an independent show.

The show kicked off with the announcement that Fritz Von Erich had died, and a moment of silence in tribute.

1) Wing Kanemura vs RoadKill

This was a by-the-book opener and, thankfully for Kanemura, Gedo and Jado didn't run to the ring with a flamethrower. A few exchanges of basic spots, a round of chairshots, and Kanemura landed a top rope senton at 5:58 for the win.

2) ECW TV Champion Taz vs Chris Candido

The ring announcer very kindly introduced Sunny to the crowd, which was all very nice, but would have been more effective had she actually been at the show. Or, indeed, in the state.

What there was of this bout was absolutely fine, and in a way it was like the beginning of the match at Hardcore Heaven. Unfortunately that old devil time constraints caught up and, at 7:22, Candido tapped out to the Tazmission.

3) Shark Tsuchiya vs Cooga

Your friend and mine the ring announcer managed to get these two mixed up. Here's a hint buddy: the one with 'Cooga' tattooed on her leg isn't Shark Tsuchiya.

This wasn't up to much (that's FMW women for you), but the crowd's attitude meant Manami Toyota vs Akira Hokuto probably would have done great business for the toilets. The gist of it was Cooga legging it around the ring until she got tired, when Shark took the opportunity to wallop her with a series of clotheslines for the 6:54 pin.

4) Bushwhackers vs Youngbloods

Upside: The Youngbloods' father Ricky Romero is a hometown hero and, with him in their corner, the crowd went crazy for every move he made, giving the Bushwhackers the rollicking they deserve.

Downside: This was the Youngbloods against the Bushwhackers.

Chris Youngblood dropkicked his brother during a Luke powerslam attempt and the ref's count of three ended the torture at 10:19.

5) Balls Mahoney vs Sandman

ECW TV had been aired in Amarillo for a few weeks prior to the show, and it seems the locals are into cigarettes and alcohol because Sandman's entrance provoked much footstomping.

Unfortunately he was still too injured to work (which didn't stop him downing a couple of cans on the way to the ring), so it was angle time. Buh Buh Ray Dudley ran in and gave him a couple of chairshots to the nads which, naturally enough, led to Balls and Buh Buh having an impromptu pagga.

A personal highlight came when Kenny attempted to break the barrage of apathy up in the bleachers by starting a "Balls/Nuts" chant. The gentleman to my right promptly took out his Sergeant's badge and threatened to arrest Kenny "for upsetting my daughter".

Neither man seemed to expect the finish to come at 5:56, but that didn't stop the ref counting to three on Mahoney's pin attempt and giving Sandman another excuse to sink a pint.

6) ECW World Champion Shane Douglas vs Tommy Dreamer

The first words out of Douglas' mouth as he worked the crowd were "Dreamer, you're a piece of Texas shit". It was incredibly tempting to demand the Sergeant next to us go down and arrest him...

This proved the pleasant surprise of the night, with the pair working the crowd so well that several of the near falls really did make it appear a title change was on the cards. Naturally Francine and Beulah had their catfight, before a belly-to-belly from Douglas and a Dreamer piledriver ended their involvement.

Douglas then hit a lightning quick belly-to-belly on dreamer to retain the title at the 10:05 mark.

7) Dory Funk Jr vs Rob Van Dam

OK, I'll admit it, I was fully expecting this to be the style clash of the decade. As it turned out, it was one of the night's better matches.

As well as getting the crowd to react to the most basic moves (proving once again the fundamental rule of wrestling: it's not what you do that matters, but when you do it), Funk's age worked in this bout's favour. Normally it looks a little ridiculous when Van Dam, for example, throws a chair to his opponent and they hold it in front of their face until it's kicked into them but, with a 55 year old man, it's a little more plausible.

Of course, all the somersaults and spin-kicks in the world are buggerall use when somebody catches you in an Oklahoma side-roll, and that's why Dory got the win at 11:32.

8) Sabu vs Mankind

Or, the biggest disappointment of your life. When the triple jump and a table spot received literally no reaction, this one was going to be difficult to rescue but, when 8:29 of weak brawling and blown spots ended in a Bill Alfonso run-in for the cheap DQ finish, I really did wonder whether this match was part of a nightmare.

9) Hayabusa, Jinsei 'Hakushi' Shinzaki and Masato Tanaka vs the Headhunters and Jake Roberts

Yup, BattleBowl is alive and well, and being used to book in Amarillo. Incidentally, the beloved ring announcer chose to introduce "Hayabuttu" and "Hayabushka". While this had nothing spectacularly poor in its execution, the crowd never really got to grips with the concept of 400lb babyfaces taking on 180lb heels. Still, what with the Headhunters attempts to climb the ropes putting the ring in imminent danger of collapse, this one proved entertaining, even if Hayabusa's 520 splash for the 11:20 pin did leave 95% of the crowd shrugging their shoulders.

10) Non-title: Bret Hart vs Terry Funk

Once the ring introductions were done, the entire ECW contingent, Funk's family and, Stu, Bruce and Ross Hart came out for a pre-match ceremony. Paul Heyman then presented a replica of the ECW title belt (which all the ECW wrestlers had chipped in for) and declared Terry Funk the "Lifetime ECW Champion". Bret Hart took the microphone and dropped the anti-American spiel for a moment to describe Funk as "the best wrestler I've ever known" before shaking his hand.

The referee was a gentleman named Dennis Stamp, which didn't mean much at first. It turned out, though, that back in the early 70s, Bret Hart was staying with the Funk family and accompanying them to shows on the old Amarillo circuit. Once night a wrestler no-showed and the 15 year old Bret stepped in to make his unscheduled debut against... Dennis Stamp.

(*2005 note: And to think **we** were worried about being embarrassed in* Beyond The Mat...)

The match was the expected mat-wrestling bonanza, broken up by spells of heavy brawling. Unfortunately, and I make no apologies for returning to this gripe, the majority of the crowd acted like they were in church. There's silent heat and then there's simply not giving a toss.

Once Funk had tried to start a chair riot (an idea the fans really weren't going for), he attempted to throw Hart through a table, but took the bump himself, blading on the floor.

With everything else about the match firmly rooted in the classic territory days, the crowd should now have been blowing the roof off the arena. Instead, some people were actually filing out of the building. I only hope they made it home in time for whatever was obviously far more important.

Back in the ring, Funk went for a German suplex and they did the old both shoulders down finish at 25:08. By the time Bret was announced as the winner of this fine match, the general reaction was less "Damn, our hometown boy nearly beat the champ; let's give him a good send off," and more "Yeah, whatever,. I reckon we can make it home for *All In The Family*.

It probably sounds like I'm slating this show, and that certainly shouldn't be the case. While I'd perhaps have preferred a couple fewer matches to allow the rest time to develop, and the main event would have benefited from a clean finish (or even a 30 or 45 minute draw), the ring action wasn't too shoddy.

Instead, it was the reaction of the crowd that left me baffled. For once, the much criticised 'smart mark' fans, particularly those in the $60 ringside seats provided the vast majority of the heat, and I mean genuine passion, not the smartarse comments that prevailed at, for example, the World Wrestling Peace Festival.

Maybe the local audience are far more into the regular shootfighting style (the introduction of the USWF's Steve Nelson got a loud enough response), but the apathy at this show ruined it for me. Watching the worst match in the world at the ECW Arena would still be a memorable experience; I don't think the greatest match in history would have got much of a pop that night in Amarillo.

Terry Funk sold out the Amarillo Fairgrounds for decades and is a legend in the business. For the workers at the show, this was a chance to pay tribute; Chris Candido was literally in tears at the end of the evening. I don't think a little bit of interest by the 'loyal fans' was too much to ask for.

Friday 12th September

Once we'd had breakfast, flicked through the forty-odd TV channels (which included a weatherman named Flip Spiceland, and Tony the Tiger being introduced from Battle Creek, Michigan), seen *Clueless* (in which it bafflingly takes Alicia Silverstone two hours to find somebody to sleep with her) and panicked at the news that *Fly Away Home* was on in the afternoon, it was time to visit George Tahinos.

Unfortunately this involved calling a taxi, so it was the best part of an hour later when we finally set off to the Radisson Hotel where George, the wrestlers, and all the fans on the right side of the Atlantic when they phoned to book were staying.

Compared to our cheap and cheerful Days Inn, the Radisson was a palace, with ground floor rooms having patio door windows opening onto an indoor park complete with swimming pool and restaurant. Still, at least we had somewhere nice to mark out for the day.

George very kindly handed over the goods for *PowerSlam*, which consisted of more than 20 T-shirts and all the Barely Legal bumper signs you could wish for. Spot the muppets who had to lug them around for the next couple of days...

Once Kenny had smoked a cigarette with the FMW crew (including Hayabusa, shock, horror, without his mask!), we wandered over to say hello to Chis Candido and Dory Funk Jr and wound up gatecrashing Candido and Douglas' breakfast. While we discussed the UK television market, we reeled in amazement as Sabu came past and spoke in English, before leaving the scene as Taz began explaining the intricacies of the katahajime to everyone's favourite psycho dentist, Dr Mike Lano.

George Mayfield turned up next, so it was over to the Waffle House for lunch as he recalled the previous day's snack with the Headhunters, where Messrs. A & B chomped their way through $70 (£50) worth of food. Bear in mind that $7 will give the average hungry fan far more than they can possibly eat. Rumour has it they also visited the famed Big Texan restaurant and attempted the 72oz steak challenge. Visitors are given the mammoth meat portion, a bread roll, side salad and baked potato and, if they eat it in an hour, it costs nothing. I've no idea how the boys from Dominica got on, but no doubt they could have done a quick switch if one of them was full up.

Back at the hotel, we went up to tape trader Bob Barnett's room to see a compilation of truly bizarre clips, including Bruiser Brody telling a young Paul Heyman that he had "womens lips". Then somebody discovered we were from Britain and spent the next half hour quoting lines from *Fawlty Towers* and *Trainspotting* while we discussed differing swearwords across the Atlantic.

Once we'd seen George Mayfield's collection of Japanese merchandise, and read the full Funk-Hart match report in the local paper (imagine the *Birmingham Evening Mail* having the Michaels-Smith match from One Night Only as its lead story on the back page), we went down to the foyer for a chat with the Headhunters, who decided that their pal George should be an honorary Headhunter: "We'll call him Headhunter B and a half!"

George went on to tell us stories of trips from Japan, including the time when he filmed Giant Baba walking from the All Japan bus door to the dressing room (apparently it was a close run thing as to whether it would be longer than *Schindler's List*), only to be confronted by an irate Mrs Baba.

And then there was the time when he was stopped at customs:

"I told them that the $1,800 worth of merchandise was all pro wrestling merchandise. They asked me to see one of the books that I was carrying. It just happened to be the Manami Toyota 'art' book.

"After several minutes, the agent asked me to see another book. This just happened to be Takako Inoue's *BODY OIL*. She then asked what other type of porn material I was carrying. I tried to convince her that Toyota and Inoue were female wrestlers, but she would not believe me

"At this point, several addition agents came over. They emptied all of my bags and searched everything. They even opened the new wrestling videos that I had bought because they thought they were porn. After finding nothing else that was porn, they estimated the total value at $5000 minus the $400 that I was allowed to bring in. I had to pay customs charges on $4,600 and 10% for a total of $460 just to get out of customs.

"After all of this, they missed the one porn video that I did bring back!"

By now, time was pressing and, entertaining as watching Dory Funk Jr and Beulah go for a swim, and laughing at the Angel of Death wandering about was, we were starting to get a little concerned about our lack of transport to the Double Cross Ranch. We did manage to persuade a woman called Mo, a friend of George's, to give us a ride but, in a surreal episode, she had lent her hire car to the Headhunters so that they could go to a cashpoint and they appeared to have done a bunk.

Eventually they made it back just in time and, once she'd finished working out how much the rental company would charge her for the broken suspension, we were off.

If you're ever in the Amarillo area, getting to Terry Funk's house is simple. Just drive south down Interstate 27 and turn off at Exit 108. You'll see a whole lot of grass (cue Too Cold Scorpio gag) stretching as far as you can see, with a ranch in the middle. This land, all 600 acres of it (about 100 average football pitches by my GSCE maths reckoning), is the Double Cross Ranch. This guy has his own road and his own river. Do not ever take on Terry Funk in one of those old 'loser mows the winner's lawn for a month' matches...

Once we'd driven down to the barbecue site (how often do you go for a drive in your back yard?) we found a whole host of wrestling personalities and about 50 fans tops. We were truly in Hardcore Heaven.

I only have vague memories of what was truly the best night out of my life (which isn't much of a boast when you live in Stevenage), but we kicked things off by grabbing a couple of beers and sitting with Shane Douglas and Francine, who were soon joined by a couple of Terry Funk's old mates, Kay Noble and Marie Laverne. For those of you with the *Wrestling Queen* documentary, these two ladies are Vivian Vachon's opponents in the film.

The ensuing chat was nothing more than a group of people passionately talking about the business we love, from the horrors of road trips, to the tales of being in the business both today and yesteryear, to the moment during the Pitbull 2 halo angle when Douglas first experienced the "white heat" that Paul Heyman had told him about. It was both enthralling and humbling to see two of today's stars showing genuine respect for the people that paved the way for the business today and, whatever I might have thought about Shane Douglas/Troy Martin in the past, the fact that he truly cares for the business was enough to convert me.

As well as discussing the British scene with Marie LaVerne (she toured here with her husband several times(and the shootfighting preferences of the Amarillo audience (she is the mother of the USWF's Steve Nelson), I spoke to Francine and discovered that, before joining the ECW training school, she was an insurance clerk!

So, we'll just recap. It is a sunny summer's evening. I am sitting in Terry Funk's back garden surrounded by wrestlers. I am drinking beer and eating freshly barbecued Texas beef. And I'm talking to an attractive woman about professional wrestling. Oh. My. God.

Elsewhere, Jake Roberts is firmly back off the wagon, Balls Mahoney and Buh Buh Ray Dudley are fishing, and Tommy Dreamer is running around in a panic after swallowing a fly. Cue Sandman:

"You mean to tell me that Brian Lee can chokeslam you off the fucking roof of the ECW Arena through 18 fucking tables and you get up, but if he came at you with a fucking bug, you'd do the job..."

After a long conversation about legit wrestling and the House of Hardcore training school with Taz, Kenny somehow wound up in an argument with Paul Heyman. I know it stemmed from his reading of *Hulk Who? Beyond Extreme* but it went off on so many bizarre tangents that everyone else soon gave up trying to follow it. In fact it closely resembled one of my university essays on ethics and philosophy.

Kenny also got chatting to Roadkill about my ECW The Albums series, as it turned out the youngster (who was the real first graduate of the House of Hardcore) is in charge of choosing the ring music for new ECW wrestlers. This led to what can only be described as a pants-filling moment when Taz came over and threatened me for making money off his hard work. Thankfully it turned out to be one of those hilarious wrestling jokes (ho, ho) and it ended amicable when Bill Alfonso asked for a copy.

Later on, once a drunken Sandman (who'd started to come round to the idea of this Coors muck) had started playing about with a whip, setting off a bizarre discussion about *Angel Pays The Bills*, we wandered over to see Stu Hart holding court. Ross Hart was leading everyone's favourite octogenarian on a storytelling extravaganza. This was an incredible sight: try to imagine *The Fast Show*'s Rowley Birkin QC, but replace the catchphrase "I was terribly, terribly drunk) with the words "so I started shooting on him and he stopped it."

There were tales of Billy Robinson, Tommy O'Toole, Earl Macready, the time the Sheik bladed a fan in Calgary, and the amazing story of Nick Bockwinkel's dad and "the hairiest pussy in Canada". One of the more amusing sights was Rob Van Dam, quite frankly, marking out big time.

"Mr Hart, Mr Hart, did you know the Sheik? He trained me, he did, the Sheik. He trained me 'cause I'm a wrestler. Yeah, yeah, I'm in the business!"

It's probably worth mentioning at this point that Kenny had opted to wear a kilt for the evening. It's not vital to the story, but it certainly added to the surreal atmosphere He briefly considered asking Stu Hart why he'd never replied to his letter. Apparently a young Mr McBride once wrote to him asking to be trained, addressing the letter to "Stu Hart, Canada".

By now, time was pressing so, after saying hi to Dory Funk Jr, we went to say thanks to the man himself. Terry Funk cadged Kenny's last cigarette and gave us a heartfelt speech on why we should keep supporting the ECW guys who work their butts off every night and would die for the business. After seeing the genuine passion displayed by everyone we spoke to on that wonderful evening, he really didn't need to tell us. If there'd been any doubt before, professional wrestling now had two more fans for life.

Back at the Radisson, we watched Francine, Douglas, Heyman and Roadkill go out on the town (the night before a 5am flight), shook our heads in amazement as Balls Mahoney downed whole bottles of tequila, and offered our views on Funk, wrestling and American taxis for George Mayfield's latest video diary.

As it was only two miles back to the Days Inn, we decided to walk. Ho ho ho. Over an hour and a quarter later, we discovered that the sign should have read five miles. Still, I guess even the best of the days has a crappy moment, and this was certainly one of the best days I've known.

Saturday 13th September

Saturday morning in a hotel on a *Hulk Who?* road trip means only one thing: confusing WCW on the box. And an advert for *WCW Main Event* being headlined by High Voltage vs Super Calo & Villano IV was pretty confusing.

With breakfast out the way, we laughed our way through a children's version of *Wheel of Fortune* as one poor kid got absolutely zilch points, before *WCW Pro* began. It was the usual cluster of unintelligible matches and strange interludes, but here's the full report:

1) La Parka beat David Sierra (3:39)
2) PowerPlant advert
3) Brad Armstrong beat Adrian Byrd (4:09)
4) Dallas Page beat Vincent (2:45)
5) Scott Hall appeared with a foot high piece of cheese on his head.
6) Scotty Riggs beat Jeff Bradley (3:55)
7) Promo for the upcoming lucha match, reading "Coming up next: Flip Flop Fly"
8) Juventud Guerrera beat Psicosis (3:59) followed by a La Parka run-in.
9) Steve McMichael beat Johnny Swinger (2:25)

There was no way to follow that, so it was time to check out. As our baggage meant following everyone else to the State Fair was out of the window, we had one more taxi nightmare (a 40 minute wait) before arriving in Amarillo town centre with eleven hours to kill.

Unfortunately Amarillo town centre is as dead as a very dead thing indeed. Apparently all the shops are in a hip and happening mall: eight miles out of town. And the buses don't seem to run much.

Once the novelty of walking down Route 66 (the town's Sixth Street) had worn off, we took refuge at a car boot sale before searching for shops. There appeared to be all of three shops in Amarillo, and one had closed by 3:30 on a Saturday afternoon. Fortunately the other stores were a reasonable record shop and what appeared to be childhood heaven.

We were attracted into this comic and collectables store by the Transformers in the window, and spent the next half hour reminding ourselves just how old we were. The offerings included such cool '70s dolls as Sonny and Cher, a *Star Trek* Barbie and Ken, Starsky and Hutch, and even Laverne and Shirley figures.

And then there was the little matter of the sign for USWA, ECW, Smoky Mountain and New Japan wrestling figures.

It turned out we'd stumbled across the regular haunt of a man who will customise existing figures to any character you care to choose. Naturally we'd managed to choose the one occasion when both he and his portfolio where out of town, but by all accounts he provides an excellent service, with his favourite production being a Hakushi figure, complete with tattoos!

The shop owners (who clearly enjoyed their job more than anyone else I've met) showed us catalogues for a range of official figures, including the Rodman and Hogan double set, and even dug out a genuine *GI Joe* Sgt Slaughter doll, which they'd had to hide away back in 1991 when sales crashed through the floor after his participation in the Gulf War angle.

After whiling away a couple of hours back at the Greyhound station (which appeared to be the only other inhabited place in the town; the streets were literally empty on a Saturday afternoon), we naively assumed we'd find somewhere to eat easily enough. True to form, after two hours of wandering about, we stumbled on our old favourite, a back-street Chinese.

Starter, main meal, full plate of rice, free refills on the drinks, full to bursting, change from a fiver. I knew there was something we liked about America.

There were still a few hours to spend back at the bus station, but a jukebox with Hendrix at Woodstock and a couple of dollar bills came together to entertain us and annoy most of the cafe (especially when we stood to attention for his rendition of the *Star Spangled Banner*.)

And finally we were off.

Sunday 14th September

Another eight hour bus trip, another bleary-eyed morning. Once we'd waited for Dallas to wake up, I took Kenny to see the Sportatorium, which was even more depressing with nobody about. Once we'd had a wander and discovered that Dallas on a Sunday morning resembles Amarillo on a Saturday afternoon, we had one last struggle with the private transport system, (of course, a public transport system would be far too much to ask for) and got a minibus back to the airport, completing the World Class trilogy by passing Reunion Arena and Texas Stadium.

Dallas Airport is like any other, so we killed a little time ditching our remaining dollars on overpriced sweets, reading about Fritz Von Erich's funeral in the papers, and trying to stay calm when the woman in the bookshop told Kenny his reservation for Ted DiBiase's autobiography hadn't come in as planned, but he was welcome to come back and try again in a couple of days.

Kenny and I said our farewells and it was time for the ten hour flight back. Ten hours, free alcohol and a pressurised cabin always guarantees an entertaining time, and I certainly enjoyed the in-flight movie, *The Fifth Element*. A sci-fi extravaganza, it left me without a clue as to what was going on, but it all seemed lively enough. I was a little confused when comedian Lee Evans turned up in the 25th century, but when the emperor of the universe turned out to be the wrestler formerly known as Zeus, I knew it was time to sleep.

What with the time-zones, we landed at breakfast time at Gatwick and, what with customs and cross-London transport, it was pushing midday when I arrived back at my flat in Preston. Two hours later I started my final year at university.

Hulk Who?: Rest In Peace.

The Match (May 1991)

(*In my year nine English exam, when I was fourteen, one question simply asked me to write an essay titled 'The Match'. It being two months after a certain pay-per-view, there was only one option. Looking back, it's not a dazzling piece of writing, and it does suffer from the schoolboy habit of trying to show off a wide vocabulary, but it earned a mark of 29 out of 30. I can only assume this was because the teacher concerned truly believed it was a work of creative fiction. For carrying out such a deception, I can only apologise and acknowledge the assistance of Pat Patterson!*)

It was the twenty-fifth of March, nineteen ninety-one. A group of us had gathered together to watch the first British showing of the greatest wrestling event of the year, 'WrestleMania VII'. We were sitting in the lounge of my friend David Perkins' house, glued to the screen. There was myself, Paul Radcliffe, the slow thinking Oliver Clark and younger brother Nicholas, Richard Rosenberg, James Wylie just back from university, and finally David's dad.

The action had started at eight pm and we had been treated to some tedious matches, including the changing hands of the tag-team belts. The event was originally scheduled to take place in the Los Angeles Coliseum, but due to death threats against one of the wrestler who carried an Iraqi flag, it had been moved to the smaller Sports Arena with a capacity of 20,000. The minor stadium, and the lack of excitement in earlier matches meant that the electrifying 'WrestleMania' atmosphere was not really there. All that was about to change.

As we sat through the statutory four minutes of pre-recorded interviews and mindless chatter, we suddenly realised what was on next: the big retirement match that promised to be the best on the card. The ring cameras zoomed onto the ring announcer Howard Finkel, whose words were drowned out by the tune of 'Pomp and Circumstance'. A long shot went to the ring aisle where the 'Macho Man' Randy Savage began to strut towards the ring.

To describe his clothes as colourful would be an understatement. He had started with a fluoro-green hat, spectrum shaded glasses and an orange t-shirt. Below were a pair of tights in a multicolour design that incorporated spots, stripes, stars and every shape imaginable. This was topped by a glorious cape that seemed to engulf the man. Behind him walked his manageress Sherri Martel, looking witch-like in a skimpy white dress and make-up resembling that of a cat rather than a woman.

As Savage stood on the middle ropes beckoning for fans support, a distant rock anthem could be heard. His opponent, James Helwig, better known as the Ultimate Warrior, was making his entrance. For the first time in his life, he was calmly walking to ringside. He too wore a cape, and a pair of tights with a picture of the championship belt on, and the words "It goes much deeper than this". The crowd were looking towards ringside, but in the corner of the screen we saw what neither commentator did: Randy Savage's former manager Elizabeth.

When the bell rang, the two men circled the ring, they glanced into each other's eyes. These two men hated each other, and a match stipulation said that who ever lost would have to retire from the sport. There seemed to be a mental staredown, and the Warrior cracked and broke into a wild frenzy of fists and forearms.

Throughout the match, Savage constantly broke the rules, using closed fists, illegal manoeuvres and interference from his manager Sherri.

Eventually he knocked the Warrior to the floor and climbed to the top rope. He circled his finger towards the crowd and leapt down with the full force of his elbow crashing into the sternum of the Warrior. He repeated the move four more times, and finally tried for the pinfall. As the referee's hand came down for the third time, the Warrior kicked out.

In a rage he battered Savage to the floor. He picked him up and executed his finishing move. The Warrior lifted Savage high into the air, threw him down to the mat, and jumped down. The fans said the match was over, the commentators said it was over. Randy Savage, however, disagreed. He simply lifted his shoulder and watched as the Warrior froze in disbelief.

Warrior looked into the crowd as if asking why his move had failed. He slowly walked back to the dressing room still in a mental coma. Randy Savage picked him up and threw him into the ring and for just one brief second the two men thought alike: the sport was more important than either individual.

After more intense action the Warrior went for his finishing move once again, and stood next to the fallen Savage, placing one foot on his chest to make the pin. As the Warrior left the arena, Savage stayed on his floor, his career over.

Sherri Martel realised she was out of a job and ran into the ring, screaming abuse and kicking the already injured Savage. Now, the cameras found Elizabeth, watching in horror as her former protege was brutalised. She vaulted over the crowd barrier and dashed to the ring, where she used her entire strength to throw Sherri to the ground and turn to Savage.

He rose, and in his confusion almost hit her. He then realised what had happened and they embraced. Savage hoisted her onto his shoulder and enjoyed his final moments in a wrestling ring, as "Pomp and Circumstance" played one more time...

Unpublished piece (March 1993)

(Life as a teenage wrestling fan in 1993 was tough. The boom was over, and it was no longer the fashionable pasttime of my peers. When Hulk Hogan appeared on British television and laughed in the face of kayfabe, I felt betrayed and helpless. Writing was my only weapon to fight back and defend the business. Admittedly I had no means of publication, but simply putting these words on paper would put that traitor in his place... OK, I'm not kidding anyone. This article is laughably pretentious, arrogant and misguided. But, boy, did it ever make me feel better at the time.)

In the space of 31 hours, Hulk Hogan has put the final nail in the coffin that has been his career since the events of November 1991's 'Gravest Challenge'. In the most pathetic display by a competitor since Davey Boy Smith's condoning of steroid abuse, he has irreparably tarnished his career, and attempted to do the same to the sport of professional wrestling.

Appearing first on Carlton television's *London Tonight* he was given several minutes of valuable airtime, which he managed to waste in presenting his public entertainer routine to promote his latest 'comedy' *Mr Nanny*. Amongst such vitally important topics as 'putting the underwear on [his] head', Hogan omitted to mention the sport that made his fortune.

The following day, the 'Hulkster' arrived at BBC's *Going Live*. Unlike the previous appearances of Randy Savage and Jim Duggan, it was clear he was here to promote one thing: Hulk Hogan.

Viewing an ill-informed profile of the superstar, presenter Sarah Greene noticed that Hogan's real name was Terry. "So your name's Terry Hogan, then?" she asked intuitively. Paying little attention, Hogan nodded sheepishly, not disclosing his legal moniker as being Terrence Bollea. A lack of attention it must had been, for surely the man's ego would not have been so caught up in his persona that he believed it to be true.

Following a question on why females did not "do WWF" (proving once more the inability of the average fan to recognise the existence of wrestling outside the control of WWF supremo Vince McMahon), Hogan was asked whether children should play wrestling in the playground. Disregarding the responsible reply of suggesting potential stars should join an organised amateur club, he told the young boy that it was "OK if you take it real lightly... you gotta realise we're just out there having fun."

Ignoring for one moment the effect this could have on young children (minor paralysis caused by a 'playful' piledriver), it seems clear Hogan is suffering a severe case of amnesia. Was it not he who, in nine months of 1991, used salt, ashes and fireballs to gain victory while "entertaining the people"?

Next came the moment that sealed Hogan's place in the 'Hall of Shame'. Replying to a question about "how God feels about you hitting each other", he claimed that "we're just having fun. We're not really hitting each other."

The reaction of the nation could be imagined instantly. Those who followed the mat sport were shocked that its media figurehead should denounce the legitimacy of wrestling, whilst the critics of grappling were overjoyed that they now had irrefutable proof that it was nothing more than a pre-arranged sham. Irrefutable, that it, until you consider exactly what Hogan said. "We don't really *hit* each other," shows a deep ignorance of the rules that govern wrestling, and is as irrelevant to the sport as, well, it has to be said, a Hulk Hogan foam finger.

For those who though Hogan could show his lack of knowledge no further, he later appeared on Channel 4's *Zoo TV*. When asked to display three wrestling holds, Hulk exhibited a suplex, a side headlock, and *a punch to the head*. This can only prove two things: either Hogan is unable to distinguish between the sport of wrestling and his own particular branch of 'sports entertainment', or his skills are so poor that he is forced to resort to blatant cheating. The likelihood is that it is both.

The egotistical persona that is Hulk Hogan made several claims during his visit to Great Britain. He may call himself an entertainer. He may claim to be a media celebrity. He may even claim to be a good actor. One thing is certain: Hulk Hogan has no right to call himself a professional wrestler.

What if... Sid Vicious had kept the NWA World title at Havoc 90? (*Hulk Who?* June 1994)

(Many of the columns and articles from Hulk Who?*, the fanzine I co-edited for three years, were not suitable for this anthology. Either they rely too much on topicality, or they are simply the product of a fan who had too much still to learn about the business he loved. One feature that does hold up relatively well is the* What If...? *series, in which I imagined how wrestling's history might have been different had a particular moment been altered. Today we'd describe these pieces as fantasy booking, but as I would have struggled to comprehend the concept of booking when I originally wrote them, I suspect a better description would be fan fiction.)*

27th October 1990

"Though the situation is of highly disturbing circumstances, we are unable to take punitive action without evidence that would be admissible in a court of law." With these words, Jim Herd publicly announced the NWA's recognition of the result of the Sid Vicious vs Sting title match. When, following the pay-per-view's disappointing, yet not unpredicted conclusion, NWA officials discovered a bound and gagged Sting in a locker in the rulebreaker dressing room, even Missy Hyatt became suspicious. As the former champion told of the diabolical plot, red-faced officials considered a cover-up. The Horsemen were contacted by telephone the following day and told that the title change would be allowed, on the condition that a rematch took place at Starrcade. Overwhelmed with title glory, Vicious personally accepted, and the press release was issued. "What a crock," wrote Bill Apter.

16th December 1990

Sting held Vicious in preparation for a scorpion deathlock after dominating the main event. Time spent studying Japanese tapes had allowed him to utilise an aerial assault which thoroughly bemused Vicious. As he signalled the finisher to the crowd, Sting noticed a man dressed entirely in black walking to ringside. And another. And another. And another. Vicious' roll-up on the 'Stinger' ended the match proper, but the surrounding 'Black Scorpions' made it clear that escape would be more important for Sting. With all exits blocked, the situation looked bleak, and the ensuing beating was not pretty. The appearance of Tom Zenk, Brian Pillman and the Steiners produced a stand-off, but the "Whoooo!" of the masked man leading the champion back to the locker room made it clear which side had prevailed.. and solved the mystery of the 'Black Scorpion' saga. The absences of Arn Anderson, Barry Windham and Ole Anderson from backstage did not go unnoticed either. "What a rip-off," wrote Stu Saks.

30th January 1991

The average fan found it difficult to understand why Vicious would want to defend his World title against fellow Horseman Ric Flair. Indeed, the Andersons were the only other people who knew of Flair's threat to tell all about Vicious' title win to the press. ("Not blackmail, Sid, just a warning.") Fearing isolation from all sides, the champion heeded the advice. He did not seem to comprehend the overtone of the 'Nature Boy''s words though, and spent much of the Clash XIV match overpowering the six-time former champion. The behemoth simply laughed at Flair's chops, responding with devastating forearm smashes. Mentions of Flair's 1975 plane crash are frequent in Jim Ross' commentary, but this time the threat to his back was serious. Seeking crowd approval whilst holding his opponent in position for the powerbomb, Vicious considered how strange his actions were for a man cast in the rulebreaker mode. His pondering was cut short though, as Windham and both Andersons stormed the ring and began pummelling the champion. The save made by Sting was a brave one, and cemented beliefs of a turn to good by the man who had retained his belt on a disqualification. "What a champion," wrote Dave Rosenbaum.

24th February 1991

Sid Vicious stepped into the War Games arena for the first time. The world champion came third on his team, following Rick Steiner & Sting. The importance of the match was no lost on him: any person obtaining the submission would gain a world title match, whilst Sid's confidence was such that he declared anybody who could make him submit "could take the damn belt". With Anderson, Flair and Horsemen newcomer Larry Zbyszko having taken full advantage of winning the pre-bout coin toss, Vicious had all the work to do. Flooring all three opponents with running clotheslines, he began attending to the tired Steiner, whose ribs were clearly damaged. Barry Windham was met on his entrance to the ring by an enraged Vicious, who hurled him into the second ring and into the only cameraman inside the case. Once Scott Steiner entered the fray, Vicious began a final period of domination.

Noticing the top rope bulldogs by the Steiners on Windham, Vicious picked up the abandoned camera. Arrogantly he began filming the fallen and bloodied Flair. "Who's the man now, Ric?" he enquired. After placing the camera on the top turnbuckle, Vicious hurled the 'Nature Boy' above his shoulders and brought him down with a powerbomb of which the description "devastating" did not do justice. Kneeling across his victim, Vicious cackled with glee as the Steiners showed Windham that a man *could* be Steinerlined into a Frankensteiner. What he had until then failed to notice was the uncanny teamwork of Anderson and Zbyszko. Taking the traditional Anderson course of working on one limb, but modifying their attack to take care of Sting's 1990 knee injury, they had progressed to a frighteningly simple method of attack: Anderson held the limb in a single-leg Boston Crab while Zbyszko would continually jump upon it. Vicious showed an unusual burst of speed as he made his way to the corner where the devastation was taking place. What happened next is best described by the commentators.

Jim Ross: *Sting is refusing to submit. He's too proud. But Vicious is waving the referee in to help his friend. The match has been stopped!*
Dusty Rhodes: *It's submission or surrender baby!*
Ross: *Well, you have to consider he made the right decision. Sting was beyond... just a minute. Ric Flair has just been given the belt. What on earth?*
Rhodes: *No! This can't be... Surely they're not...*

Ross: *They are! They're declaring him the new champion. Hey Patrick, what's going on?*

Nick Patrick: *I'm sorry, but Vicious in his role as captain surrendered the match to save Sting. That surrender was accepted by team captain Flair. And what Sid said about giving away the belt is legally binding, so Flair is champ.*

Ross: *Ladies and gentleman, I am in shock.*

Rhodes: *What a...*

24th July 1991

World Championship Wrestling is saddened to report that after extensive negotiations with 'Nature Boy' Ric Flair, stretching over the course of nearly one year, the parties have been unable to arrive at a mutually satisfactory contractual relationship. As a result, the WCW board has decided that the best course of action for WCW, and its fans, is to declare the championship title vacant and to determine a new champion at the Great American Bash.

After the fiasco of WrestleWar, and the disputed Flair-Fujinami decisions in Japan and America, the champion's defection to the WWF was hardly the best of breaks. Clearly the title had to be decided in something big, ruling out early suggestions of a bout between the top two contenders. Instead an eight man tournament would be held, with the three remaining Horsemen appearing to be the most likely contenders.

In first round action, Lex Luger fought Larry Zbyszko to a 20 minute draw, eliminating both men. Whilst Luger was clearly the better man, Zbyszko's tactics of leaving the ring at any opportunity were enough to end the chances of the US champion, an achievement Zbyszko described as "better than any stinking title". Sid Vicious simply laughed his way through a bout with the technical wizard Arn Anderson, right fists and one-hand-slams countering scientific knowledge, with a somewhat unnecessary powerbomb providing the conclusion. Sting's bout with Barry Windham ended the "We Want Flair!" chants; virtually move for move, it concluded with Sting shifting his weight during a superplex attempt to come down for the pin. In the final bout of the first round, Steve Austin sneaked past Ron Simmons, with Jeannie Clark's particularly form of distraction swinging the bout.

While Vicious rested, Sting fought a 26 minute classic against Austin. This bout was later cited as the one in which Austin proved his worth as the 1991-model Ric Flair. Sting's advances were evaded by grabbing the ropes, whilst Austin made more than liberal use of the "Oh no, I'm so tired, oh please don't come over and hit me" line which used to gain Flair his breathing space. His Flair-like arrogance cost him though; after a pinpoint 'Stun Gun' move, he draped one arm on Sting's chest for the pin, only to be caught in a small package for the final slot.

Sting was clearly not ready to fight Sid Vicious, or indeed anyone else. Vicious' constant attack was relentless without being aggressive; Tony Schiavone called it "the nicest massacre I've ever seen". As Sid considered simply asking the referee to end the contest, his thoughts were halted by a punch to the groin. Sting clambered to his feet and, in what could only be described as physical sarcasm, powerbombed the champion. The move obviously had little physical effect, but Vicious was to surprised to kick out. The new world champion walked back to the dressing room to a mixed reception. The ex-champion appealed to the referee, almost in tears. "What a wuss" said Eddie Ellner.

What If... Bundy hadn't attacked Hogan during a 1986 Saturday Night's Main Event? (*Hulk Who?* July 1994)

February 1986

"Well, Hulk Hogan sure celebrated his win over Don Muraco in style last Saturday night, Jesse. That *Real American* video was just awesome."

"Yeah, right McMahon. What about the challenge after the show finished? Is Hogan as yellow as his ring attire?"

"Well, you're wrong there. The challenge was made and accepted. Randy Savage will fight Hogan title for title at WrestleMania 2!"

"Oh yeah!"

7th April 1986

The crowd at Los Angeles Sport Arena had begun the evening quietly; there's little to be said when Adrian Adonis fights in a dress. However, the main event was turning out to be a classic. Clearly, booking Sylvester Stallone as guest referee ("both a Real American and a Macho Man") had sold tickets, but his role had been minimal. Savage had learnt from the lumberjack match as Madison Square Garden, and had limited his entourage to Elizabeth. What he hadn't counted on was the presence of George "The Animal" Steele in the corner of Hogan.

Once he had found a way to counter Hogan's powerful punches (namely one-finger jabs to the eye) Savage was firmly on the offensive. Inevitably the elbow drop followed. Inevitably the pin would come... but Hogan kicked out. Ignoring the shocked Savage's punches, the champion responded with three of his own. An Irish whip, a boot to the face and the legdrop had Savage pinned for a three count.

Unfortunately for Hogan, he made the count himself. Stallone was looking elsewhere. Elizabeth was seductively showing some leg to Steele from across the ring; the former *Rocky* star had to physically restrain him from climbing through the ropes to reach her. When Stallone turned around, Savage had Hogan rolled up with his shoulders on the mat. That the guest referee had not been informed of the regulations on using an opponent's trunks for leverage would haunt Hogan for the rest of his career.

28th August 1986

After the excitement of the previous bout, the 74,080 in Toronto's Exhibition Stadium were almost at fever pitch for the main event. Intercontinental champion Terry Funk (having won a tournament at Madison Square Garden after Savage vacated the title) had held on to the belt by the narrowest of margins, disqualified against Hulk Hogan for using a branding iron. The noise of the spectators had been near deafening, but still rose for the entrance of World champion Randy Savage.

His challenger, the gargantuan Andre the Giant, had not ever reached the ring when Savage landed his first axehandle, to the arena floor. Acting only out of fear of the fans' rage, the 'Macho Man' broke the referee's count and allowed the French man to enter the ring. Savage's following tactics reminded many of a boxer's 'hit and run' style, with punches replaced by elbowsmashed and chops from the top rope. Commentator Gorilla Monsoon tried to convince the television audience that Andre was relying on 'rope-a-dope'; in fact he was merely dazed.

With the exception of a lengthy bearhug, Andre's offensive was minimal. Once Savage had swept the giant's legs away such that he was prostate on the mat, the champion began his final assault. Standing kneedrops, chokes broken only on the count of four, and a vicious attack on the knee left Andre immobile. For reasons never explained, Savage opted to grab Howard Finkel's microphone as he climbed to the top rope.

The words "Ooh yeah, Macho Madness is running wild, the top of the mountain looking down, down at Andre, Andre mania" merely offended the fans. "Going down like Hulkamania did," however, proved more costly. The still perspiring former champion allegedly broke sprint records with his charge to ringside. Savage was visibly shaken, enough for him to fall from the ropes into the partially recovered Andre's arms. A shoddily executed belly-to-belly suplex was enough to pin the stunned Savage. The WWF's newest superhero celebrated with his forerunner for over fifteen minutes.

29th August 1986

The press conference at Titan Towers lasted slightly less than fifteen minutes. Hogan honorarily presented a new "Giant size" belt to Andre, and the pair exchanged eulogical praise. Vince McMahon openly rubbed his fingers in promotional glee. Gene Okerlund openly stated his relief that the belt was back in the hands of the good. Jesse Ventura openly vomited. Meanwhile, Savage became the first WWF wrestler in a couple of years to give a press conference to independent magazines. He made numerous allegations of favouritism in the WWF, even hinting at "special relationships" between McMahon and top stars. He never paid the resulting $20,000 fine to his former employer. Ric Flair had a new contender.

18th December 1986

"And now to read the nominees for wrestler of the year, as voted by the fans of the WWF, Gorilla Monsoon!"

"Thanks, Vince. The nominees are... What? My flies? Excuse me..."

"Well, Gorilla appears otherwise indisposed there, but here are the nominees: Paul Orndorff, former WWF champion Hulk Hogan, King Harley Race and WWF champion Andre the Giant. Gene."

"Vince, it was a close run thing, but the winner was the man beloved by millions worldwide..."

"Oh yes, the 'Real American' Hulk Hogan!"

"No, Vince, it's Andre the Giant."

11th January 1987

Andre's time as champion had drawn the crowd, that much was sure. However, while merchandise revenues rose to new heights, the wrestling itself deteriorated to levels even below that of 'Hulkamania'. In effect, title defences became simply a matter of time before Andre fell on his opponent for the pin. Now, McMahon had turned to tag wrestling to boost crowds at Madison Square Garden.

Andre and Hogan were taking on the combined forces of Don Muraco and Bob Orton in the main event. Sadly, the expected monstrous epic never materialised. Andre would periodically enter the ring and push his foes to the floor, then tag back a rested Hogan to continue the assault. Finally, the rulebreakers changed their tactics. Both ran across the ring and dropkicked Andre off the apron, causing him to crack his head on the crowd barrier before slipping into unconsciousness. The brutal beating on Hogan earned a swift disqualification. Nevertheless, it took ten officials to defuse the situation: six to tear off Muraco and Orton and four to revive Andre.

7th February 1987

"I'm the champion. No problems. No problems," was Andre's response to Roddy Piper's enquiries. The fans at the *Superstars of Wrestling* taping applauded his put down of the Scotsman. Suddenly, they burst into a standing ovation. Andre acknowledged their support, realising his error when he turned around to see Hulk Hogan grab the microphone. The crowd support disintegrated when they heard his words.

"I am here for one reason. To challenge you to a championship match at WrestleMania..."

What If... The Hart Brothers had won the tag belts at the 1994 Royal Rumble? (*Hulk Who?* August 1994)

22nd January 1994

"Why doesn't he just tag him?" exclaimed Ted DiBiase as Bret Hart applied the Sharpshooter to Quebecer Pierre.. Bret's knee was clearly injured and some would say the finisher attempt was ill-advised. Jacques, though, wasn't taking any chances as he entered the ring and pulled the 'Hitman' off his partner. As referee Tim White escorted the intruder to his corner, Bret attempted to reach his brother for the tag, only to find himself dragged back by the heels by Pierre. Owen, however, was aware of the situation and, clapping his hands, climbed to the top rope. Hearing the 'tag', White turned around to see the 'Rocket' landing a flying body-press for the win.

30th January 1994

"I don't see how Bret Hart can concentrate on this title defence when he's fighting Lex Luger for the WrestleMania title shot next week," Randy Savage exclaimed as the Hart Brothers entered the ring to meet the Quebecers on *Monday Night Raw*. Vince McMahon did not agree; he had already rejected suggestions of a double title defence at WrestleMania when Bret clearly had nobody to feud with. Instead he was hoping for an eventual Steiners-Harts feud while golden boy Luger destroyed the Jap and lead the new generation into the next decade. Perhaps this explained his dissatisfaction at Savage's commentary throughout the bout.

"Ooh yeah, it's Owen Hart with the Sharpshooter. Too early, brother, and is Bret mad... Funky like a monkey, it's a cover by Bret! What does Owen think he's doing McMahon? The referee is all tied up with him, oh yeah... They were soaring high with the eagles, now they're slithering low with the snakes ya know... Yeah brother, that's the Hart Attack finisher. Clothesline by Owen. Ooh, he's elbowed his brother on the way down... Unintentional kind of thing situation yeah... Bret and Owen having some words bro'... Ooh, Bret's outta here, and he's been counted out... Bret, whatcha doing man?"

After the blame he put on Bret Hart, Savage was not requested to commentate on the rest of the broadcast. Despite the 'Macho Man''s claims, the Hart-Luger bout was taped on the same night. Visibly irritated, the 'Hitman' entered the ring second, having refused to allow Luger the honour. He took the match seriously though, and could even be described as dominating the contest. Luger's power manoeuvres were evaded, and any holds the patriot put on were broken with elbows or forearm smashes. Hart made one attempt at the Sharpshooter only to be nearly pinned as he released it. Bret continues the assault with the elbow from the second rope, and ran up for a clothesline.

To the dismay of his supporters, a clash of heads put both men on the floor. Owen appeared at ringside, still dripping from the showers, and began slapping Bret to revive him. Bret rose to his feet and began glaring at his brother. Three seconds later, Luger's roll-up had won him the title shot he 'richly deserved'. Bret began remonstrating with Owen and finally shoved him. Three punches to the jaw and a chair to the knee were the Rocket's response.

February/March 1994

Cynics would have suggested the vacation of the tag belts and the ensuing tournament were merely for promotional purposes. Certainly, on reflection, Vince McMahon was not overly upset that WrestleMania would feature Luger-Yokozuna, Hart-Hart and the finals of the tag tourney. The shallowness of the talent pool in the WWF was demonstrated clearly in the first round though, but at least brought some interest to *WWF Superstars*. Men on a Mission barely triumphed over the Quebecers when Mabel literally fell on the winded Pierre. Despite Jacques' protest to the referee and Johnny Polo's valiant assault on Oscar (which later won him an award for Outstanding Contribution to Wrestling), the pin was allowed to stand. The Smoking Gunns fell short in their challenge of the Headshrinkers. Their 'sidewinder' finisher appeared to have won the match, only for Fatu to rise to his feet and laugh in their faces. Once Billy was thrown from the ring, Bart was easy prey for Samu's top rope splash.

The best bout saw the Heavenly Bodies defeat Marty Jannetty and the 1-2-3 Kid when the Kid's moonsault was evaded as Tom Prichard caught him in a powerbomb. Jannetty broke the pin with a clothesline from the top rope, and the Kid leapt into the air for a dropkick. Unfortunately for the youngster, Del Ray made it through the ropes at the exact second to grab him by the hair and slam him to the ground. The pin, as they say, was a formality. In the final match, Well Dunn almost caused a major upset when they knocked out Scott by whipping him into his own brother. With Scott out and Rick dazed (even more than usual), it took a disqualification for overenthusiastic double-teaming at Harvey Whippleman's urging to save the Michigan boys. When Scott was revived, unbeknownst to television viewers, who had the pleasure of seeing *Live Event News*, it took several referees to prevent him permanently injuring referee Danny Davis. He walked back to the dressing room several paces ahead of Rick, muttering expletives as he went.

20th March 1994

The Steiner Brothers entered the ring at a slow pace, ignoring the MSG crowd's attempts to shake their hands. Vince McMahon and Jerry Lawler put it down to their nervousness. In fact their minds, Scott's in particular, were focused on the purse they had had to reject from Japanese promoters when McMahon forced them to fight on the supercard, threatening breach of contract suits. Their distraction was clear to see throughout the bout; there were several spells when the Heavenly Bodies were almost handed victory by one brother's mistake. Eventually, though, their tag experience took control and they reached the brink of victory by throwing the interfering Jimmy Del Ray into manager Jim Cornette. With Tom Prichard on Scott's shoulders, Rick mounted the top rope and launched into a bulldog on his foe. Exactly why Scott let go of Prichard prematurely was a matter of conjecture in future weeks, but the immediate result was both the 'Doctor of Desire' and the 'Dog-faced Gremlin' landing head-first on the mat, with the unconscious Prichard on top of his similarly dullened opponent. The awakened Del Ray chose the wrong moment to grab hold of referee Bill

Alfonso. When he turned around, Scott had reversed the position of the two grapplers; the Bodies' protest was in vain.

Action in the Headshrinkers-Men on a Mission bout was not as forthcoming, and much of the bout consisted of long weardown holds upon the gargantuan Mabel, with occasional excitement when the Samoans executed their various doubleteam manoeuvres on the smalled Mo. Predictably the bout concluded with all four men brawling in the ring. It was perhaps acceptable that Dave Hebner should have confused Fatu and Samu, but even he couldn't pretend to mistake Mabel for his partner (the hair gave it away). However, he wasn't about to stop the mammoth warrior from running across the ring and bouncing off the ropes with a legdrop upon the prostate Samu. The Headshrinkers, though, weren't about to stand for such a flagrant breach of the rules, and a nifty dropping of the top rope left Mabel stomach first on the arena floor. With Afa taking care of the mighty Oscar, Mo had no chance of avoiding the Wrecking Ball clothesline.

The Headshrinkers were used to knocking off foes in short time, and it was no surprise that their stamina might be questionable. Rick and Scott, no strangers to fighting multiple matches on one night, took control of the match from the start. Continued suplexes, culminating in the full range of double-team finishers might have been expected to finish off any foe. Any foe that is, except the savage-like Headshrinkers, with both men breaking counts to save their brother from defeat. Their dedication paid off when they caught Scott in their corner and wore him down to the point of exhaustion. Suddenly though, he put Samu on the floor and turned to his brother who was requesting the tag. Instead, he whipped his foe across the ring and leapt up for the Frankensteiner. Samu caught the weakened Steiner and powerbombed him for the win and the tag team belts. Rick's screamed question was to play a major part in future WWF promotions.

"Why didn't you tag me. All you had to do was tag me!"

Talking Point: How have British tours developed? (*Hulk Who?* September 1994)

(*Most of the* Talking Point *articles from the fanzine have dated poorly. What was once considered in-depth journalism looks pretty lame by today's standards. I included this piece, though, as it gives a nostalgic look at what really was a different era.*)

In the autumn of 1989, a small advert appeared one morning in a daily tabloid newspaper. By noon that day, the London Arena had been sold out for the first ever American card to take place in the United Kingdom. In the following five years, a total of 80 live dates have taken place, 62 from the WWF's dozen visits and 18 from WCW's four tours. Five WWF cards have been televised, in the London Arena (October '89 and April '91), the Royal Albert Hall (October '91) and Sheffield Arena (April '92 and April '93). Bret Hart and Shawn Michaels top the visiting list, with eight tours each, with the Undertaker and Jim Duggan (seven), Davey Boy Smith, Ric Flair, Tatanka and the Nasty Boys (six) also heading the list. Bizarrely, Papa Shango, the Bushwhackers and Virgil have all visited more times than Hulk Hogan! With two recent tours within a fortnight of each other, it needs to be examined how British tours have changed, and which federation holds the upper hand.

In terms of arena and ticket sales, the WWF is the clear leader. From an initial two date stop, they reached the pinnacle of the 1993 spring tour, which brought 34 stars over for 15 cards. Contrastingly, WCW's biggest effort, the 1993 *Real Event* tour visited only six cities, with just 14 wrestlers. The most important factor, the selling of seats, has been on the side of the WWF. Whereas capacity arenas are the norm, with 60% a disappointing effort, WCW shows have struggled to gain half-full arenas. Why this is so is a question that needs to be looked at closely.

The obvious place to look is the levels of talent and the quality of the matches. The WWF made a less than auspicious start, with men such as Boris Zhukov, Koko B Ware and Steve Lombardi on the '89 tour. After the giant 'Rampage' tours of the early '90s, where virtually every contracted star visited, the return to single dates (rather than having two sets of wrestlers travel around) has seen a massive improvement.

Traditionally, WWF cards have either featured a fairly average card, or a dire undercard (Kato & Skinner vs Bushwhackers, Repo Man vs Virgil) with an excellent main event (Flair vs Savage, Flair vs Hart). In 1994 though, WWF cards have featured better than average undercard bouts and strong main events.

WCW's first tour, it must be admitted, featured some poor excuses for wrestlers. PN News and Bill Kazmaeir are not exactly candidates for a Hall of Fame. However, the main events were reasonable, with Rick Steiner & Sting vs Lex Luger & Rick Rude the highlight (and Luger vs News some kind of joke.) The March 1993 tour is seen critically as the most successful, with Vader-Sting, Windham-Rhodes and Smith-Rude highlighting the London date. Indeed, the worst wrestler on the card was Vinnie Vegas who, though no Flair, has shown a level of competence in recent years. By the autumn of '93, the talent list had reached its peak. Flair, Vader, Sting, Rude, Regal, Austin, Pillman and Steamboat were all involved. However, many fans noted that the matches, though appetising on paper, were often somewhat of a disappointment in practice, perhaps due to a lack on intensity, or even interest on the part of the wrestlers, who had only just recovered from the Hallowe'en Havoc supercard. This year's effort featured most of WCW's top talent, but that is no longer something to be proud of. Regal, Vader, Austin and Sting all put in solid performances, but Jim Duggan and Dallas Page are little more than an insult to paying customers.

The publicity involved in the tours has shown up the differences in management between the two major federations. WWF tours since '91 have been promoted extensively, with regular updates on TV broadcasts, and even on the last occasion, a vague idea of what the card will be. WCW have apparently never heard of advertising, but the facts speak for themselves: their most successful tour, in March '93, was heavily promoted throughout the British media, whilst the initial and most recent tours, which received virtually no publicity in this country, achieved dire crowds with a half-full arena seen as a major success. The call of "Is there anybody here?" by Jimmy Garvin to a handful of fans in the Sheffield Arena in 1991 is a sad comment on WCW promotion as a whole.

To be fair, the antics of Vince McMahon can be blamed for at least some of WCW's misfortune. Tours have suddenly been announced to coincide with three of the WCW visits, with the postponed Autumn/ Winter tour last year appearing a deliberate move to steer fans away from the WCW tour. It has also been noted that McMahon has, on at least two occasions, prevented ticket agents in the UK from dealing with WCW, threatening to withdraw future lucrative WWF business. This has been cited in the manner in which the '91 R*oar Power* tour allegedly caused its promoters, Bravo Productions, to go bust. WCW is guilty of similar wrongdoings though, with the publicity of last autumn's tour as *Hallowe'en Havoc* causing many London fans, who had not heard about other dates, to believe the Royal Albert Hall card would be the pay-per-view itself.

The major two federations dominate the sport, but that is not to say independent federations have made no attempt to break into the British market. Indeed, three independent tours of the UK were scheduled in 1991 and '92, with the National Wrestling Federation (featuring the Sheik, Wendi Richter and Ivan Koloff), National Wrestling Promotions (with the Lightning Kid, Bob Orton, the Soultaker and the Bolsheviks) and Global (Bad News Brown, Bam Bam Bigelow and Demolition Ax) all proposing live dates. However, none of the cards went ahead, due to a lack of interest amongst the 'Hulkamoron' fans only interested in the WWF, and poor levels of publicity. Indeed, such tours might well appear overly ambitious, with the NWF even intending to hold a card in the 10,000 seater Wembley Arena!

The tours which have gone ahead though, have given us many moments to remember. The teaming of Luger and Rude in '91 under Paul E. Dangerously's management, causing many to speculate that the World champion had joined the Dangerous Alliance. The clean, 25 minute victories by Ric Flair over Randy Savage on consecutive nights in September 1992. The shocking WCW world title win by Sting over Vader in March 1993. The infamous brawl between Sid Vicious and Arn Anderson last autumn in Blackburn. The first defences by WWF World champion Bret Hart against his brother last month. The double title switch between the Quebecers and Men on a Mission. The first major confrontation between Bret Hart and Jim Neidhart this month. A British event can be as unpredictable as any US house show.

196

The question of the tours might best be answered to looking at the most recent visits. WCW offered some patchy competition, with Rick Steamboat, Arn Anderson and Dustin Rhodes questionable choices to leave behind in the US. Only the performance of Vader was outstanding, and the Hogan-Flair contest, the seemingly ultimate confrontation of the eighties, was a major disappointment. Jim Duggan vs Dallas Page was obviously a wind-up. Meanwhile, the WWF London card was possibly their best British card to date. Each contest was solid and varied, with the Luger/Ramon vs Diesel/Michaels tag title contest, and the performance of Michaels in particular, outstanding. For the first time, every champion and virtually every top star appeared on the same card, with the result an exceptional show. The WCW card was exceedingly average. Passable... but that is no longer enough if they wish to be seen as a serious force in the United Kingdom.

What If... Randy Savage had won the retirement bout at WrestleMania VII? (*Hulk Who?* September 1994)

24th March 1991

The Ultimate Warrior was, in the words of Gorilla Monsoon "questioning the gods... is that his destiny?" Cynics would suggest the lunatic was talking to his hands. After kicking out of the gorilla-press/slam/splash combination, Randy Savage had better things to do than question his opponent's mental state. He rolled to the arena floor, where manager 'Sensational' Sherri Martel passed him her garter. As he returned to the ring, the glint of light reflected from it gave Monsoon an idea. "It's loaded with metal! he brilliantly deduced. "Well, what did you think?" answered Bobby Heenan. "He's hardly going to attack the guy with a piece of underwear!"

He did. Having slammed the Warrior to the mat, Savage climbed to the top rope, placed the garter around his elbow, adjusted it slightly, and landed one final elbow. One might have thought the laceration of Warrior's forehead from a single elbowdrop would have aroused Dave Hebner's suspicions. However, the antics of Sherri at ringside (edited on the replay to placate the 'family audience') proved more interesting for the referee. When he turned around, the count of three, slow as ever for a rulebreaker's pin attempt, concluded with no response from the man who followed his now concluded career with a sad decline into drug abuse and self-pity. Predictably enough, Monsoon described Savage's victory as "a miscarriage of justice."

27th August 1991

The ring had been cleared of all traces of 'victory powder', following the heroic victory by Davey Boy Smith and Hulk Hogan, the 'Gulf War Allies' over the pathetic troupe of Sgt Slaughter and company. Indeed, the construction of an altar provided a suitable distraction for the commentators while federation officials tried to reason with Smith, who had just been informed of his positive steroid test of the previous week. Vince McMahon, though, was not overly worried. He had a new hero to support Hogan: Randy Savage, who was about to turn in a beautifully orchestrated skit. Savage would prepare to marry Sherri, but turn away at the last moment and depart with Elizabeth, who coincidentally had a front-row ticket. That at least was the plan. McMahon had obviously not stressed the importance of this to the 'Macho Man' though, who chose to say yes to Miss Martel. Elizabeth was greeted with a shocking verbal and physical attack by the newlyweds. Vince began to cry.

19th January 1992

Ric Flair, Hulk Hogan, Randy Savage, Sid Justice and Roddy Piper remained in the Royal Rumble, with the WWF title the prize they all sought after. Whilst Hogan and Justice worked over the evil Ric Flair (whose despicable behaviour had resulted in the title's vacation), Savage attacked Piper, ducking a series of punches and responding with one of his own, to the groin. A simple toss over the ropes eliminated the I-C champion, leaving the 'Macho Man' free to continue his vicious assaults (an earlier pummeling of the beloved Jake Roberts had left the 'Snake' unconscious.) Attacking Hogan and Justice from behind, he grabbed each of them with one hand and threw them feet-first over the top rope.

Fortunately both men held on and made their way back through the ropes. However, Justice kicked Hogan to the floor, eliminating the former champion. Savage found hilarity in the ensuing argument, mocking the two 'fan favourites' as they cursed each other. The humour was soon on the side of the crowd though, as Savage's attention to the situation left him open to attack by Flair, whose elimination of the 'Macho Man' earned him a chorus of cheers from the usually hostile crowd. As Savage rose to his feet, he saw only Hogan pulling Justice from the ring to hand victory to the 'Nature Boy'. Savage's ensuing gestures to all were less than polite.

30th January 1992

No sooner had Sid Justice abandoned his partner Hulk Hogan in the match with Randy Savage and the Undertaker, than Ric Flair began to 'walk that aisle'. Cue Vince:

"Oh no!... Brutus Beefcake is jumping up and down. He knows what Flair is likely to do... What an excuse for the world's champion to triple-team the man! He doesn't have to wait until WrestleMania VIII. Slowly he steps through the ropes to where Randy Savage is beating on Hogan. Wait a minute! He just slugged Randy Savage! Now he chops the Undertaker! I can't believe what I'm seeing. The Undertaker falls through the ropes... Savage follows him... Ric Flair has just saved Hulk Hogan!"

Flair departed. Nobody was going to have any excuse when he defeated the bald egomaniac on 5th April. No injury claims. He was going to beat Hogan cleanly in the middle of the ring and finish destroying this whole damned federation.

McMahon called a halt to the taping. He had a germ of an idea. Hogan-Flair was big enough to save until SummerSlam at least. Justice had betrayed Hogan. Flair attacked Savage. Why have one WrestleMania main event when he could conjure up two?

5th April 1992

As if Savage was not intense enough already at what he saw as betrayal at the hands of Flair, the banning of Sherri Martel from ringside during his World title challenge was simply fuel to the fire. To be fair, her attack on Flair and executive consultant Curt Hennig at the *March to WrestleMania* show had been brutal. While Flair's injuries were not serious (he retained the title with a countout loss to Tito Santana), Hennig fared worse, being deeply cut in the forehead with the sharpened heel of Sherri's show. Flamboyant as always, Hennig had arrived at ringside in the Hoosier Dome sporting a large black bandage with the words "Mr Perfect" picked out in sequins.

To every scientific move by Flair, Savage responded with a vicious blow; to every aerial assault by Savage, Flair came back with a punishing hold. Eventually, though, the actions of Hennig, who removed Savage's leg from the ropes during several illegal pin attempts, and even took it upon himself to confiscate a pair of brass knuckles from the 'Macho Man', were distraction enough for Flair to gain the upper hand. Sherri removed her blonde wig, left her 67th row seat, and began running down the aisle.

Running barefoot, with a vicious looking heel upon one of the shoes she carried in her right hand, her path was blocked by several WWF officials. Rene Goulet, Earl Hebner and JJ Dillon all attempted to restrain her, but the power of the former women's champion proved too much. She stood at ringside, waving the show and cheering on her husband (in the world of the WWF at least).

Flair began his final assault upon his challenger, locking in the figure-four leglock. Sherri climbed to the ring apron, kicking away the attempts of Hennig to pull her down to floor level. Flair, vigilant as ever, saw the potential attack and broke the submission hold. He ran over to Sherri, grabbed the shoe, threw it into the aisle (Goulet awoke from the blow in hospital) and slapped the valet.

Savage, visibly incensed, rose from the mat and began assaulting Flair. However, the force of the figure-four had severely weakened his legs, and two chops were enough to floor the 'Macho Man'. With a "whoooo!" to the crowd, Flair again began to put on the figure-four. However, Savage grabbed his head, and rolled the 'Nature Boy' into a small package with a handful of tights. Despite the protests of Hennig, Dave Hebner made the three count, and Randy Savage won his second world title.

"Yes! Yes! Yes!" screamed Bobby Heenan on colour commentary.

"He had a handful of tights!" yelled Gorilla Monsoon. "What a despicable individual! He hooked the tights"

Irresistible Force (*Hulk Who?* November 1994)

(*Yes, I had a monthly column called* Irresistible Force. *My colleague Matt Brannigan had a counterpart slot titled* Immovable Object. *This was, quite literally, schoolboy humour.*)

Like many people, I keep a diary of my dreams. With the real life nightmare of Hogan and Duggan ruling WCW, and a forthcoming midget clown match at Survivor Series, I'm going to share some of my more bizarre wrestling related dreams with you:

Junkyard Dog and Bad News Brown fought the Rock 'n' Roll Express at WrestleMania VIII... The first Flair-Hogan bout took place in my CDT lesson... Luger appeared on WWF TV with the IWGP belt claiming to be the real world champion... Vince McMahon admitted taking bribes from Jake Roberts, resigned, and died the next day... The USWA released a commercial tape of Jeff Jarrett vs Vader... Marty Jannetty, Owen & Bret Hart, 1-2-3 Kid and Randy Savage lost to Take That when Owen was accidentally knocked off the top rope by his partners... Rick Rude and Curt Hennig came to team in the WWF... WCW held a card at my local leisure centre... Davey Boy Smith, Sting, Stan Hansen, Vader and Steve Williams came on holiday with me... Hogan was sacked as guitarist of The Doors for taking too many drugs... My tape arrived from Nic Higton... Met Dave Hebner, who admitted he was biased... Tickets to a card at Wembley Arena were £60, while Bret Hart jackets cost £50... The Royal Rumble appeared on BBC1 for 40 minutes, causing my mum to destroy the television... Ron Simmons won a Rumble while Bret Hart captured the world title despite being in a wheelchair... Realised I was an atheist, so sold my RE book to Steve Williams... WCW held a card in a hotel lobby... A riot on *Monday Night Raw* appeared on the *Nine O'Clock News*... Steve Regal and Vader headlined a tour visiting Bristol and Hitchin after Bill Dundee asked me how many could be seated in Hitchin Town Hall... Steve Regal pinned Mike Rotunda on *Worldwide* when Johnny B Badd sat on both of them... Heard rumour that Luger would throw his match at WrestleMania X so he could take up a job for a British promotion... A dispute between Steve Keirn, Bret Hart and Greg

Valentine was to be settled by a game of golf; Keirn won by dressing up as the other two... WrestleMania XI scheduled for a pub near Wembley... Owen Hart and Ricky Morton appeared on *Gladiators*... SummerSlam 2005 scheduled for London... Mabel hid in my loft... Flair and Hogan met on BBC in the 'Snooker Challenge'... Curt Hennig shaved his head to become the second Undertaker... Hogan appeared in a Yellow Pages advertisement trying to find a photo of his last clean victory, but it was before cameras had been invented... Hiro Matsuda refereed our school quiz night... SummerSlam bouts included Curt Hennig vs Sabu, Headshrinkers & Love Machine vs Heavenly Bodies & Diesel, Bret Hart vs Steve Williams and a three-way bout with Badd, Hogan & Ramon... Diesel won a fourth Intercontinental title. The *Daily Mail* covered wrestling results while UWF-i was shown live on ITV... Alundra Blayze beat Akira Hokuto by disqualification in my living room when Hokuto began choking Grandpa Simpson... A monument was erected for Flair's Rumble '92 win... Shawn Michaels continually did top rope moves from the second tier of Wembley Stadium... Yokozuna played for Hitchin Town football club.... Snuck away from school trip to see live ECW show... Bob Backlund revealed he desperately needed a title shot as he was dying of liver cancer... Hogan missed a title defence, but Flair was unable to win even by forfeit... The Sheik came into the school common room asking for a fight... Doink was revealed to be a woman... Jim Crockett and Flair appeared on *Raw* to announce a WWF-NWA merger.

What If... Bob Backlund had been fit to wrestle on 24th January 1984? (*Hulk Who?* November 1994)

24th January 1984

As Hulk Hogan left the ring after a tough victory over the Masked Superstar, the commentators turned their attention to the main event. Questions had been asked about Backlund's fitness, especially after the devastating camel clutch that had cost him the title, bus as he entered the ring without former manager Arnold Skaaland, he appeared as ready as always. Indeed, he soon proved his physical state, flipping the champion over his head as the camel clutch was being applied. A whip across the ring, a duck from the ensuing clothesline, and the rolling cradle into the bridge was all it took to defeat the Iron Sheik at the 5:30 mark. Equilibrium had been restored.

18th November 1984

Looking on from a backstage monitor at Madison Square Garden, Vince McMahon found himself supporting a rulebreaker for one of the first time in his reign as WWF chief. After the fiasco of the "Brawl To End It All" where 20,000 had seen Cyndi Lauper manager Wendi Richter to the women's title, yet only 4,500 stayed to watch Backlund overcome Greg Valentine after 28 minutes of scientific mat wrestling, it was clear new blood was needed. That Hogan kid had been a possibility for a sudden push, but he had left for Japan when he was refused immediate main event status. Hopefully this Randy Savage character would fill the position; the large salary offered to entice him from Memphis had been a gamble. However, he at least had some colour about him, and his manager Elizabeth appealed to at least half the crowd.

10th March 1985

Women were clearly going to be the centrepiece of the WWF's publicity plans. Elizabeth had started it all, removing her skirt to distract Backlund, leaving him open to a vicious, title-winning attack from

Savage. Now Cyndi Lauper's verbal barracking at the hands of Roddy Piper had allowed a turn by the 'Macho Man', and this title match. The only drawback had been the lack of television coverage: the networks had shunned the "theatrics" of the WWF, Turner remained loyal to the purist NWA, and more vibrant stations like MTV were not interested without a recognised star, instead running previews of a hilarious action movie, centred around 'identical twins' Sylvester Stallone and Hulk Hogan.

31st March 1985

Starrcade was one thing, but this WrestleMania was going to be the greatest event ever! Andre vs John Studd! Wendi Richter vs Leilani Kai! Roddy Piper vs Randy Savage! So where were the crowds? Where was the nationwide coverage? Vince knew who to blame.

It was all the fault of Savage. First he had refused to team with film star Mr T, giving the lame excuse that "the guy's just a film star, dude." After that, he was scheduled to appear as host on *Saturday Night Live*. That had been a tough one for Vince: the producers were all ready to give the slot to that Hogan character from the crimebuster show on NBC, and it had taken the offer of a beautiful woman, Elizabeth, to persuade the producers to change their plans. Damned Savage had other ideas, though. Training for a title defence was apparently more important than getting his face on nationwide television. Vince could rely only on the words of his father and forerunner: "In the end, all that matters is the action in the ring."

What action it was, though. Piper and Savage fought as if their lives depended on it. Piper brawled relentlessly, causing Savage to take to the air. His axehandles from the top rope were astounding, and he dropped an elbowdrop, literally fully across the ring. After he grabbed a chair from ringside and bloodied his opponent, the Scot came close to victory with a series of punches to the head. Savage escaped only by drawing inspiration from the emotional crowd. Over twenty minutes later the end came as Piper attempted a full nelson; Savage dropped to the floor and a slide between the challenger's legs and a 180 degree flip into a sunset flip retained the title. The 13,000 in attendance had got their money's worth.

6th April 1986

The first attempt at a wrestling pay-per-view had been bold, and the co-operation of the other promoters was an important step. The three site idea of David Crockett had been a good one, and the *Triple Title Threat* was an impressive headliner. NWA champion Ric Flair vs Dusty Rhodes in the Omni, AWA champion Stan Hansen vs Nick Bockwinkel at the St Paul Civic Centre and WWF titleholder Savage against Ricky Steamboat at the Rosemont Horizon couldn't fail. Initial crowd figures were reasonable but unspectacular; about 35,000 was the combined estimate. The PPV figures weren't so good: receipts of of $187,000 from the paying audience were unlikely to cover the huge bonuses offered to the main event stars. The major bouts didn't disappoint: Flair hooked the tights for the pin after an epic 48 minutes of close action; Bockwinkel appeared to have captured the AWA belt, only to be awarded a disqualification victory when Hansen punched President Stanley Blackburn; and Steamboat reversed a flying bodypress to take the WWF title in what was later referred to as the "aerial war of the decade". Wrestling fans who paid loved the show. Indeed, underground tape traders did record business with pirate copies of the event.

29th March 1987

It was somewhat ironic that the greatest match of all time was seen by so few fans. As *Pro Wrestling Illustrated*, the remaining Bill Apter publication, reported, it was an hour of history that would never be repeated. Flair and Steamboat had battled for the World title in a classic bout featuring aerial excellence, scientific skill, power and unmatched speed. In the year end awards, 95% of the 31,000 worldwide readers voted it match of the year, with the remaining votes being cast for the February draw. After draping an arm over the collapsed Steamboat, champion Flair dedicated his victory to "every one of you fans here in the Omni". The 3,200 present felt truly honoured.

The financial failure of the show was a subject of hot debate over the following days. Vice Presidents of the World Wrestling Association McMahon and Blackburn claimed the decision to hold the card in

Georgia had been wrong. President Crockett disagreed; he pointed to the falling crowds in the North and the cancellation of the regular MSG show.

Every fan had their own reason for missing the match. Richard Evans of Gulfport, Missouri had not been allowed to stay up to 2AM to watch the delayed broadcast on TBS. Dave Szymanak of New York was forced to take his younger siblings to Central Park, where "Arnie and Hulk" of *Predator* fame were making a public appearance. Rita M Buda of Chicago, Illinois had intended to listen to commentary on pirate radio, but her husband drowned it out with his tape of the Rolling Stones. They'd drawn over 90,000 in the Silverdome, you know.

14th August 1994

"John, Dean Ayass here. Just got a new tape in. There's an awesome ladder match between Michaels and Ramon. Want a copy?"
"How much?"
"Twenty, I'm afraid."
"Twenty quid? Bit pricey isn't it?"
"Well, you're welcome to go and get it in the shops."
"Point taken. How's the saving going."
"Not bad, another three hundred and I should have enough to go to Philly this summer."
"Just imagine it. Actually seeing a live card! You might even get to see Steve Lombardi or someone!"
"I doubt they'll have any of the big stars like Steve. Still, any wrestling's got to be better than none."
"Try telling that to a TV company. How's the fan convention going, anyway?"
"Pretty good, come to speak of it. Should get about thirty there if we're lucky. There's even a rumour somebody might bring a copy of one of those American magazines..."

What if.... Ric Flair had made Curt Hennig retire in January '93? (*Hulk Who?* December 1994)

18th January 1993

The combatants had been fighting furiously for over 25 minutes when the ending came. Curt Hennig was whipped across the ring but, as he bounced off the ropes, he noticed Flair with his head down. Three seconds later, the perfect-plex had gained victory and Hennig had won the *Monday Night Raw* loser-leave-town match.

Bobby Heenan was not happy. "He had his shoulder up! Oi, Hebner, look at this. Show him, McMahon."

"Well, Brain, I don't think instant replay is acceptable here in the WWF."

"Oh yeah it is. What do you say Dave, me old buddy?"

"Erm... Continue!"

Curt Hennig was on the second turnbuckle, displaying his glee for all to witness. When he turned around, a rested Ric Flair awaited him. A series of chops, a delayed vertical suplex and the figure-four later, and 'Mr Perfect' was slipping into unconsciousness, into the pin and out of the WWF...

4th April 1993

Hennig had felt his departure to be unjust, and the frustration was clear in his brutal elimination of Flair the the Rumble; Howard Finkel had come close to suing for injuries sustained when the 'Nature Boy' was slammed upon him. It was Flair, though, who had the last laugh, defeating Bret Hart for the WWF title on 22nd March at a *Raw* taping; as usual, six months had been long enough for him to regain the championship from his initial conqueror.

It was somewhat ironic then that Hennig should make his official return to the WWF as Hart's manager at the year's biggest event. Though Bret Hart hardly needed advice as to how to wrestle his opponent, 'Narcissist' Lex Luger, Hennig did influence the outcome. Not only did he attract the referee's attention when Luger's backslide pin was invalidated by

Hart's feet being placed upon the ropes, but 'Mr Perfect' pulled the 'Hitman' from the ring when he was knocked unconscious by Luger's mysteriously powerful running forearm. As the referee leant over Hart and began counting him out, Hennig entered the ring and floored Luger with a pair of brass knuckles taken from his diamond studded suit. As female fans and Pat Patterson commented on the now-explained bulge in Hennig's trousers, Hart rolled back into the ring at the count of eight. The pin, as they say, was a formality.

13th June 1993

After such a display, it could be imagined that Hart would be perceived as a rulebreaker. This was far from the case though, as endless promotion, scientific skills and appeal to the female species had placed him atop *Pro Wrestling Illustrated*'s 'Most Popular' rankings. Flair though, was not so clear-cut. Certainly he had been the crowd favourite at WrestleMania, but against the 'Nefarious Nippon' Yokozuna, even Benedict Arnold would have been cheered for his patriotic roots. Indeed, such was the rapturous applause for Flair's submission victory, Hulk Hogan abandoned his plans to make a dramatic challenge; the possibility of being seen without his usual overwhelming support weighed heavily on his mind. At least he could rely on support back in Hollywood.

However, Flair had reverted to his more familiar facade for the King of the Ring title defence against the 'true American' Tatanka. With his lengthy 'unbeaten' stretch, the Indian challenger was a credible opponent, and he took the advantage throughout several parts of the bout. Chops to the chest, suplexes and mis-timed aerial attacks are traditionally part of Flair's gameplan, but here they were used against him to great effect. As the match passed the 15 minute mark, Tatanka caught Flair off the ropes and lifted him up for the modified Samoan drop nicknamed by Bobby Heenan as the "papoose to go". Fate though, was on the side of Flair; his opponent slipped on a patch of oil left on the match in an earlier Bret Hart matwork spell, and fell forward, breaking his nose on impact with the ground. Only Flair made it to his feet by the count of ten.

The aforementioned matwork had been a vital part of Hart's gameplan against his larger first-round opponent Razor Ramon, though it was a shift of bodyweight in Ramon's back suplex that gave him the pin. The 'Hitman' continued his run in the semi-final bout, taking on his own brother Owen, conqueror of Doink the Clown and Mr Hughes in previous rounds. The bout was a scientific classic, with the pair's parents, situated at ringside, the only onlookers disappointed with the way the bracket had worked out.

It was after Bret took the advantage on the mat that Owen changed the tempo of the bout. Taking to the air, he began to come close to victory with bodypresses, clotheslines and even a splash from the top rope. Finally he went to the top for the finish: but Hennig was to decide the outcome. He had consulted with Bret prior to the bout and, based on his own previous bouts with 'Blue Blazer' Owen and close study of the 'Rocket''s Japanese bouts of the eighties, Henning had prepared his charge for such an eventuality. Bret caught his brother in mid-dropkick and placed him in the sharpshooter for the finish. Owen clearly bore no grudge, taking a place by parents Stu and Helen for the final between Bret and Bam Bam Bigelow. It was Stu, though, who played the most part; he physically restrained Luna Vachon from her interference attempts when the action spilled outside the ring, while Hennig rolled Bret back inside, where a victory roll gave him the win and the SummerSlam title shot.

30th August 1993

A storyline was hardly necessary to promote a Ric Flair-Bret Hart world championship match, but it had been handed to Vince McMahon on a plate. At the press conference to announce the bout, Hart had been accompanied by most of his immediate family. Unfortunately the champion had chosen to make a few too many comments about Helen Hart's seniority and a predictable wild brawl had ensued. The traditional crew of Rene Goulet, Tony Garea, Earl Hebner *et al* had been insufficient and only the intervention of Hennig had prevented serious injury.

With none of the timing difficulties of certain other federations, there was ample time for an extended preview of the bout (allowing the entire Hart clan to be relocated to the first three rows, much to the displeasure of the displaced Dean Ayass, who had purchased front row seats in a special telephone offer.) Clips of the pair's two title change bouts were aired, along with the press conference incident in its entirety, and a barrage of interviews with both men, and Owen & Bruce Hart. Stu and Helen appeared on camera too upset to speak, and finally there was a somewhat dubious skit featuring an AT&T official investigating abusive calls to the Hart household, traced to a North Carolina address.

Unlike so many hyped bouts, this lived up to the publicity. Hart took the match to Flair early on, landing vicious blows to the jaw, and it was not long before the champion was bleeding profusely from the forehead. Hart landed several two counts in a row from a series of small packages and looked to have the match sewn up. He had not counted on the versatility of the 'Nature Boy' though, and Flair instantly changed the course of the match with a punch to the groin and a swinging neckbreaker. At the ringside barrier, Hart's 'dream team' management squad of Owen & Stu Hart and Curt Hennig conferred. As Flair landed a barrage of knees, Hennig returned to his corner position and began shouting instructions to the 'Hitman'. Hart took his advice and waited until Flair draped the challenger's left leg over the ropes and leapt up to crash down on the knee. At the last moment, Bret snatched his leg away, leaving Flair to land painfully on what Johnny B. Badd would refer to as his "booty". Hart took it to the champion with his standard series of moves (a Russian legsweep, backbreaker and second-rope elbow), almost as if he were fighting a preliminary bout for *Superstars*. Bret began to put on the Sharpshooter, turning around to answer Hennig's cry.

Flair snatched Hart's legs away from him and, with incredible speed, locked in the figure-four. No sooner had referee Dave Hebner turned his back to check for the submission than Hennig had grabbed Flair's arms, holding them for extra leverage until well past the moment when the challenger gave in. Stu Hart was openly weeping at ringside, not at the betrayal or the defeat, but at a Hart submitting.

Meanwhile, in a Minnesota apartment, a man watched the pay-per-view broadcast with a beaming smile. "That's my boy. You did it like I said, Curt," exclaimed Larry 'The Ax' Hennig.

What If... Terry Funk had made Ric Flair submit at Clash IX? (Hulk Who? January 1995)

15th November 1989

With 18 minutes of the "I Quit" contest between NWA World Champion Ric Flair and Terry Funk elapsed, Flair had locked in the figure-four and was demanding submission. The very nature of live television meant responses had to be considered; the Texan was not renowned for his politeness though and, questioning Flair's parentage, turned him over with what could only be a final effort. The scorpion deathlock was hardly a picnic at the best of times, but with Funk actually attempting to insert the house microphone where it had surely never been before, Flair's submission was inevitable. The appearance of the Great Muta at ringside, repeatedly moonsaulting the now retired 'Nature Boy' only prompted a typically wild brawl to end the Clash; Sting dashed to the ring to show exactly how his finisher was best used, while Lex Luger demonstrated that a chair to the knee was the best counter. Flair departed on a stretcher as Sting received the crowd's applause.

16th December 1989

The retirement of Flair has champion inevitably led to the vacation of the belt, and the announcement that the winner of the Starrcade Iron Man tournament would take the title was little surprise. The only unexpected moves were the replacement of Flair by Steve Williams, and the J-Tex representative being Funk and not Muta. This 'corporate decision' had something more to do with the fears of Jim Herd that a champion Muta might well disappear back to the Orient, title in hand.

The opening match saw something of an upset, as Funk pinned Steve Williams. After initial flurries of brawling by both men, Williams having taken everything Funk could dish out, 'Dr Death' began using his natural wrestling skills with devastating effect. The conclusion was only natural; the cagey veteran was planted on the mat with an Oklahoma Stampede powerslam and the referee counted to three. However, this did not constitute a pin, as Funk had reached under the bottom rope.

More specifically he had reached his trusty branding iron and, as Williams protested to the official, caught him painfully in the groin, unseen by Nick Patrick. Meanwhile, Sting took a similar advantage in the tournament, successfully facing Lex Luger. With both Andersons in his corner, the 'Stinger' used a brilliantly executed mix of aerial and power moves, before dodging a Luger clothesline and catching him with a backslide for the pin. He departed with his mentors, each raising four fingers in the air.

Funk cemented his position at the top of the table (both he and Sting having received 20 points for their pinfall victories) with a countout victory of Lex Luger. Luger, used to facing a string of scientific-based wrestlers, such as Rick Steamboat or Brian Pillman, seemed genuinely flustered by Funk's unorthodox attack. Expecting regular power moves to carry the day, he found shots to the groin and chokeholds a more than adequate defence on the Texan's part. However, Luger finally gained the upper hand, with facerakes a not inconsiderable part of his success, and steamed across the ring for a finishing clothesline. Funk, though, ducked the move and was fortunate not to be disqualified for tossing his opponent over the top rope; even more fortunate to see Luger land on his knee and make no attempt to beat the count. Sting was unable to keep up the pressure, dropping his second match to Williams. The bout remained relatively clean, with Sting evading much of Williams' attack by using his speed. However, the earlier match with Luger had taken its toll on the young star, and eventually his gameplan backfired. Taking too long climbing for a top rope bodypress, he was caught on his descent in the 'Oklahoma Stampede', unlike Funk, being clean in the centre of the ring.

With both fan favourites on 20 points, and Funk ahead with 35, Luger was out of the reckoning. However, his match with Williams, despite the Chicago native's obvious panic as 'Dr Death' more than matched his power attacks, went to the 15-minute time limit, giving both men five points, and putting Williams out of the running. Whatever Jim Ross' analyses showed about his mathematical failings, even Sting's fourth-grader core of support could see a pin was the only thing that could prevent the belt hanging over the doorway of the Double Cross ranch.

Such a result appeared a distinct likelihood in the early going; despite

Funk's experience, Sting clearly had the greater conditioning necessary to compete for a third time in the evening. Indeed, he almost scored the winner with a series of Stinger-splashes, culminating with a top rope splash owing much to Jimmy Snuka. However, Funk's guile caused the turning point of the match, as Sting whipped him across the ring and bent over prematurely for a back-bodydrop. Piledrivers have a tendency to halt an offensive spell.

The legendary brawler lived up to his reputation, continually flooring Sting with blatant punches and eyegouges; Ole Anderson, even aware of the situation, informed the referee of the consequences of calling for a disqualification, the 10 points for such a victory being of little use to the 'Stinger'. Finally, as the match clock reached its final minutes, Funk applied a series of spinning toeholds, content that Sting would not consider it worth holding out until the time limit expired. At this moment, with distinct overtones of Magnum TA at the 1987 Crockett Cup final, Ric Flair made his way to ringside, hardly limited in mobility by his crutches. As Funk dropped his guard he found the conclusion of the Clash match coming back to haunt him; Sting reversed the hold and placed Flair in the scorpion deathlock. Not hearing the announcer's call of "fifteen seconds", besieged instead by Flair's barrage of oral abuse, Funk gave up his challenge to the belt. For the first time, a popularly-supported Four Horsemen had custody of the world title.

6th February 1990

Four minutes and eight seconds was all it took for Sting to reject the challenge of Buzz Sawyer at Clash X. In fact, the highpoint of Sawyer's offense was when Gary Michael Capetta missed his cue and announced the 'Mad Dog' as the defending champion. Indeed, Sawyer's sole reward for his efforts was the renewal of his 1983 feud with Tommy Rich, though with somewhat less ferocity. The talking point of the evening came after the bout, though, as Terry Funk made the final assault for J-Tex; assault in its most literal sense. It required both Andersons to save Sting from the madman's attack, and Flair's grasp of office politics to ensure his ejection from the promotion.

214

25th February 1990

Sting was presented with something more of a challenge at WrestleWar, in the form of US champion Luger. The contest was a legitimate match of the year candidate, lasting for over a half hour, with a good two-dozen discernible changes in momentum. No sooner had Luger's power given him control than Sting had used an aerial counter to regain the upper hand. Luger, though, was the most likely to take victory as the 33 minute mark passed, placing his foe in an seemingly unbreakable 'Torture Rack'. Flair realised the extent of the danger, and climbed to the apron in order to pull Sting free from the hold. As referee Randy Anderson's complaints were disputed by his namesakes, Flair and Luger began brawling at ringside for more than the ten seconds allowed by the official's count, Luger chasing his former Horseman leader to the dressing room. A winner in name only, Sting was aided from the ring by both Anderson brothers.

19th May 1990

Following Flair's triumphant return to the ring, showing no signs of his back injuries in a comprehensive defeat of Sid Vicious, and the Andersons' victory over Tom Zenk and Brian Pillman for the US tag belts, it was left to Sting to complete a victorious night for the Horsemen. Meeting Luger's challenge of a clash in the Thunderdome cage, he thrilled the Washington DC crowd with a classic comeback to take the match with a flying bodypress from the cage wall. Luger departed, Arn Anderson and Ric Flair scrambled under the cage just before it was lowered again. (Ole Anderson was later found to be responsible for the security officer concerned being knocked unconscious.) 'Double A' soon made it clear what the point of discussion would be:

"Sting, boy, Mr Flair here is back. I think you'd better do the polite thing and offer him a title shot."

"Sorry, Arn, that's not down to me. Anyway, whatever happened to 'One for All and All for One'?" queried the champion.

"I think you misunderstand me, boy. I said you'd *better* give Ric a title shot..."

Irresistible Force (*Hulk Who?* March 1995)

You may remember last month's *Immovable Object* in which Matt pointed to the uncanny similarities between professional wrestling and soccer. Since then, numerous examples have occurred to me. Most prevalent is the way Tottenham Hotspur, originally banned from the FA Cup, are now looking likely to win the tournament. What is this, if not a copy of Lex Luger and the 1994 Royal Rumble? Meanwhile, Joe Kinnear's touchline band has been inspired by Jack Tunney's annual Rumble rulings, while England's 1966 World Cup win in Wembley Stadium was a clear pre-emptive reproduction of Davey Boy Smith and SummerSlam '92. The 1990 World Cup saw Gazza cry as his second yellow card saw him banned from playing in the final. However, this also occurred at my leisure centre, when Mal 'Mouth of the South' Sanders broke down after his second public warning led to him losing his place in the evening's battle royale. Similarly, the 1988-89 English league season saw the two teams capable of victory meeting in the final game, a blatant rip-off of the 1993 AJW Tag League the Best event, while Michael Thomas' league-winning goal came seven minutes into injury time, strangely reminiscent of Pretty Wonderful's 20:57 victory over the Sullivans at Wembley Arena last year in a 20 minute time limit match.

Other sports are guilty of this transgression though. Sumo contests are all reproductions of the Big Daddy-Giant Haystacks Wembley Arena clash of 1981. Ben Johnson of athletics shares training methods with Hulk Hogan. Andre Agassi's throwing of his shirt to the crowd is taken from the identical actions of Hiroshi Hase. The recent Eubank-Collins match, between two champions from the same federation, but at different weights, was copied from last year's Shinya Hashimoto vs Jushin Liger contest. Eubank's ring entrances are inspired by the Undertaker, Great Muta and the Road Warriors. Cricket's ball tampering is no different to removing the ringpost padding. The aim of cricket, to get the most runs, was surely originated by David Von Erich. Indeed, the famed darts cry of "One Hundred and Eighty" was first said in relation to the Mongolian Stomper.

Talking of darts, the show *Bullseye* adapted its catchphrase from Hulk

Hogan's financial policies in WCW: "Keep out of the black and in the red; there's nowt in this game for hair on your head." *It's A Knockout* is nothing more than a toned down version of FMW shows. *Catchphrase* was inspired by the endless clichés of Gorilla Monsoon. The numbers round of *Countdown* greatly resembles the accounting needed to show a WCW profit. *Play Your Cards Right* often sounds like Hulk Hogan negotiating his match fees: "Higher! Higher!" Finally, the most blatant rip-off of all must be *BlockBusters*. Everybody knows it should feature Eric Bischoff as the host: "What 'C' am I?"

<u>*Wrestling Insight*, April 1995</u>

(*Aside from my own fanzine,* Wrestling Insight *was my longest running writing gig. I used it as a chance to try out different types of column, trying to create something different to the rest of the newsletter.*)

This month, after a spell of writer's block, I decided to let my computer play with a couple of hundred wrestlers' names and spellcheck them for alternatives. It soon became apparent where our ticket money goes.

Apparently Tamon Honda is a tampon hound, whilst Stan Hansen has claimed his tobacco chewing caused a stained harness. Keiji Muto went to a restaurant to order Kiev Mutton. Mashahiro Chono was unpaid though, as he is a chin masher. Unfortunately their ally Hiroshi Hase disappeared in a Hiroshima haze.

Antonio Inoki cannot be contacted, as he has an inky antenna; beware though, as Riki Choshu would be a rich choice. Chris Benoit bought time on public access televangelism, arguing there is a bent Christ, whilst Jushin Liger has spent the cash repairing his broken leg, so he will no longer be known as Justin linger. Tony Halme is entering theatre, taking on the role of tonne Hamlet.

Over in the car factories, Atsushi Onita has been conferring with astute auntie, whilst Tarzan Goto has retired to breed tartan goats. Tiger Jeet Singh is writing a book, claiming that his tiger jeep sings. Meanwhile Toshiyo Yamada has opened an electrical goods store named Toshibo Yamaha.

Akira Maeda is still recovering from the shock of finding his maid afire, and Los Payasos were found in the grocer's buying loose peas. Hogan is hogging the glory, whilst 'The Natural' unfortunately spent his paycheck on a Rhodesian dustbin. Jeff Jarrett's new business involves religious persecution; he believes in the jew garrotte.

The unpaid Lex Luger can now only lug lager, whilst Bundy has been exposed as a King Conga Bunny. Jerry Lawler, after narrowly escaping jail last year, has replaced his jerky lawyer, though his low pay policy means stars such as Doug Gilbert can still only afford a diet of dog giblets.

Vince has bought vice and Hakushi is looking for hookers. Sabu has invested his money in a new Saab, whilst the Rock 'n' Roll Express were not paid as they were revealed as a rich moron and a robber gibbon. Whatever money paid will be wasted on the Great Sasuke though; he is suffering from great seasick.

Wrestling Insight(May 1995)

You know you're a wrestling fan when...

...under 'Referee' on your CV you write 'Dave Hebner'.

...you can't stand to watch *Cat on a Hot Tin Roof* because of the character Big Daddy.

...you only buy AAA size batteries.

...you go into KFC and can't resist ordering chicken-wings.

...you refer to incidents in soap operas as great angles.

...you know more about steroids than your friends.

...people think you're always talking about the film *The Elephant Boy*.

...you love the section in record stores headed 'Funk'.

...you always think of Steve Lombardi during 'Bob-a-job' week.

...you take A level English just in case you have to read the part of Charles in *As You Like It*.

...you but the *Midnight Express* soundtrack for only one track.

...you've lost money to Nic Higton.

...weekdays are only the irritating bits between all the wrestling shows on TV.

...the first thing you do with the TV listings is put a cross next to *Worldwide*.

...you spend school assemblies trying to remember every world champion since Frank Gotch.

...your parents go away for two weeks and, instead of trashing the house, you watch WrestleManias I to X without a break.

...you spend ten minutes of every exam trying to work in a wrestling reference, such as "after intense deliberation", "the muscle of the Allied Powers" or even "the Franchise covering blacks."

...you know that Eric Cantona's dropkick had nothing to do with kung-fu.

...you can't stifle a cheer when the headteacher mentions the Four Horsemen of the Apocalypse in assembly.

...your tape collection has more languages than Linguaphone.

...you watch *Wrestling Challenge* and *Action Zone* on the same day.

...non-fans think you must like rap, as you always talk about NWA and Public Enemy.

...you can't stand the comedian Richard Morton.

...you nearly cry when, on a TV show, somebody calls in the Bomb Squad.

...your favourite parts of the bible are Genesis 30:8 and Genesis 33:24.

...you stay up until 4am on a weeknight to see a match involving characters called Dink, Wink, Pink, Sleazy, Queasy and Cheesy.

What If... Tony Anthony had retained the SMW title at Bluegrass Brawl '93? (*Hulk Who?* May 1995)

3rd April 1993

It had been little secret in the wrestling community that the storyline with 'Dirty White Boy' Tony Anthony had gone too far. Every insider newsletter and premium rate line had given news of the Ku Klux Klan's involvement and their threats to help Tracey Smothers in the Bluegrass Brawl chain match. As Jim Cornette had said, "By God, they believe!"

As a certain television prankster would say, though, "Ron Wright wasn't in on the joke." A fraction of a second before Smothers touched the fourth turnbuckle, the former Tennessee legend threw a handful of talcum powder into his eyes. Anthony fell on to the turnbuckle and was declared the winner, to more than a little dismay from the fans. To steal a second line in the same paragraph, it was time for a sharp exit.

Without going into lurid details, Anthony did not have a safe journey home, and would probably have breached a 30-week rule for defending the title, let alone the traditional limit. However, Jim Cornette, the human set square himself, could always find the right angle. It was announced by Bob Caudle the following week on television that Anthony was refusing to defend his title "in front of those redneck jerks" and that the title was vacant.

The ensuing sixteen man tournament was somewhat ambitious for the regional promotion, but with two first-round bouts a week, the television show suffered little from the experience. Dutch Mantell's victory over Killer Kyle, when both members of the Stud Stable interfered, upset many fans, but was compensated for when Brian Lee took a page out of opponent Nightstalker's playbook, taking the win with a top rope clothesline. The following week saw the continuation of the Heavenly Bodies-Rock 'n' Roll Express feud, with Stan Lane's win against Ricky Morton (Tom Prichard holding the leg during the pin) prompting Morton to appear at ringside for the Prichard-Gibson match a simple yet illegal reversal of a small package gave victory to the Rock 'n' Roller. Newcomer Tazmaniac proved overzealous in his choking of Tracey Smothers, earning himself a disqualification. Tim Horner vs

Robert Fuller proved the tightest match of the first round, with both men eliminated via a 15 minute draw. The only disappointment came with the last week of the proceedings, with the Mongolian Stomper and Kevin Sullivan gaining wins with such ease that their respective opponents, Jimmy Golden and Rob Morgan both joined Tony Anthony in the state hospital.

9th May 1993

Jim Cornette had hardly planned that his second Volunteer Slam show would again see eight men chasing the Smoky Mountain title, but then the Klan had not been part of his long-term strategy. However, the show was considered a success, boding well for the future. In the opening bout, Brian Lee's simple victory was highlighted, for obvious reasons, by the appearance of Tammy Fytch at ringside, departing as 'Prime Time' took the win with a superkick. The Lane-Gibson contest unsurprisingly turned into an impromptu tag affair, with referee Mark Curtis having no option other than to call for a double disqualification. Kevin Sullivan's victory took only six minutes, but still saw four fans knocked to the floor as he and Stomper brawled through the crowd. Tracey Smothers, taking a bye, spent the first half-hour of the show meeting with fans. "Let us know if you want any more damn Yankees sorted out," was amongst the stranger requests he received.

The frightening success of his promotion as the 'Wild Eyed Southern Boy' obviously weighted on his mind as Smothers took on Sullivan in the semi-final; the rulebreaker took the win with a neat spike attack behind the referee's back. The commercial video of the bout saw a split screen, with backstage footage of Fytch entering Lee's dressing room and later leaving with a wry grin. Lee came to the final alone, and dominated much of the bout with his extra stamina from the semi-final bye. However, it was Fytch who proved the deciding factor. Kevin Sullivan's loss of concentration at her cheerleader's outfit not only cost him the title, but required a hasty explanation to the lovely Woman that evening.

14th August 1993

The second Fire on the Mountain show was significant for events other than the continuing Cornette-Armstrong saga and the Rage in the Cage main event. After the Jimmy Del Ray vs Steve Armstrong status match, Kevin Sullivan destroyed Tim Horner, literally carving up his face, and attacking him after the match with a series of brutal kicks to the groin. ("That one was for you, Nancy," he disclosed in a post-match interview.) 'Crybaby' Chris Candido fell in defeat to recent WCW departee Ron Simmons, who dedicated the bout to "every one of his fans, wherever and whomever they are."

In the semi-final contest, Lee defended his belt against Tracey Smothers in a much-hyped contest between the two fan favourites, a "contrast to the brutality of the main event." Admittedly the first fifteen minutes of the bout were an exciting and clean series of scientific manoeuvres, with Smothers' speed pitted against Lee's size. However, it only took Fytch to pass a blatantly loaded black glove to Lee for him, to snatch an easy win. Disregarding the outraged fans in the background, Fytch dedicated the contest to the women's rights movement.

25th December 1993

The return of Tony Anthony and his unanticipated sneak attack on Bob Armstrong had angered the crowd, and it was fortunate that their aggression could be let off vocally in the main event. The first match of the 'Triple Threat' main event was a vicious affair with Lee and Smothers tearing into each other on their first meeting since Lee's "betrayal of a friendship". After ten minutes of action, Smothers was bloodied. After twenty minutes, Lee too was losing plasma. After thirty minutes, the bell to signal the time limit was something of an anti-climax.

Lee's strategy in his second defence, against Ron Simmons, was to bring the 'All American' down to his level, in terms of physical condition at least. The method by which he achieved this was simple; every so often Tammy Fytch would begin talking to referee Mark Curtis, while Lee wore down his foe with brass-knuckles shots. By the time Curtis noticed him passing them back to Fytch and banished the manageresses to the dressing room, the damage was almost complete. All Lee had to do was climb to the top and leap at Simmons with a clothesline... which he avoided, catching Lee and slamming him spinebuster-style into the mat. Presented with the belt to rapturous applause, Ron held one fist aloft in victory.

13th February 1994

The feud was simple to promote. Ron Simmons, the boy from the backstreets of Georgia, friend of the common man and a credit to his people, against Tony Anthony, the Yankee turncoat, the man who denounced the champion's roots and vowed to make Simmons the first "black ex-champion in Smoky Mountain". The Knoxville Coliseum was filled to capacity, and Jim Cornette's share of the proceeds would be a great return on his investment in the weekly look at Simmons' background which had highlighted the television show.

With Anthony's unique balance of brawling and scientific skills (unique for the apparent absence of the latter), Simmons took advantage of his limited, but useful technical knowledge. Experts compared his performance to that at Hallowe'en Havoc '91 where he so nearly dethroned the then-awesome Lex Luger. The challenger's only breaks came when he took the action outside the ring and began a battle of fists. The last occasion on which this happened saw the pair tumble over the ring barrier and begin brawling on the floor amongst the crowd. As both men returned to the ring, Simmons was clearly worse for wear, bleeding heavily from the forehead, with bruises beginning to develop on his ribs. Three punches to the head clinched the title change cheered only by one small group of fans.

"Go get him, DIRTY WHITE BOY" proclaimed the white sheet they held aloft.

What If... Bret Hart beat Davey Boy Smith at SummerSlam '92? (*Hulk Who?* June 1995)

29th August 1992

It had been an ironic evening for Bret Hart. Despite fighting his own brother-in-law for over twenty minutes in a classic scientific bout, with the 'Hitman' giving a superb performance, the crowd had largely booed him, preferring instead to support their countrymen. The fans had not been best pleased when Hart kicked out of both a powerslam and a crucifix and, as he went for a sunset flip, the crowd held its breath. The 80,355 in attendance felt sure Smith could lever himself into a pinning position, but after a seemingly endless struggle of balance, he fell into the pin.

Hart must have lost an element of reasoning in his jubilation to then expect the crowd to applaud his victory. So hostile was the atmosphere in the near silent stadium, he simply snatched the belt and walked back down the aisle. In the ring, the despondent Smith raised an arm in appreciation of the fans, who first began clapping, then burst into raptures of applause. The crowd soon changed their response when Bret Hart returned to the ring, floored his opponent with the belt, and departed.

27th October 1992

The entrance of Jeff Jarrett was not shown on the *Saturday Night's Main Event* broadcast. Instead viewers were treated to a special announcement of the Ultimate Warrior's withdrawal from the Survivor Series main event. Randy Savage then appeared backstage to announce his new partner, "The Most Macho man around... after me, that is. The master of machismo himself, Razor Ramon!"

While Bobby Heenan began choking at the way his charge Ric Flair has now partnerless, commentary colleague Vince McMahon led the boos for Bret Hart. The Memphis fans, hatred for Hart notwithstanding, gave an overwhelming response to his "unknown" challenger. Their support clearly lifted the amiable young Tennessean, who baffled Bret Hart with his escapes from every move the 'Hitman' had to offer. Jarrett made mistakes, certainly, and was near to defeat on many occasions as Hart went through his traditional offence. However, after thirteen minutes of action, Jarrett found the long searched for counter to the Sharpshooter. Simply pulling his opponent's leg away as he attempted to lock the hold on, Jarrett adjusted his legs and captured the Intercontinental title after four minutes of a devastating figure-four.

Bobby Heenan began to hyperventilate.

25th November 1992

The series of skits in which Jeff Jarrett had taught children how to spell had earned him acclaim from several education experts. His popularity had grown immensely, and this explained the tremendous reaction to his victory over Bret Hart in the opening bout of Survivor Series, retaining the Intercontinental belt in the process. It was astounding how he feigned injury, then leapt into the air as Bret Hart came off the second rope with an elbow drop *and caught the 'Hitman' in a frankensteiner!*

Jarrett returned from the shower to personally introduce the "majestical Memphis legend, Jerry 'the King' Lawler". Cynical comparisons with Jim Duggan were not without grounds both men were unexplainedly popular as monarchs despite an apparent lack of orthodox grappling skills. This was to prove irrelevant in his WWF debut tough, as his opponent, the Berserker, was no Kenta Kobashi himself. Lawler took the pin after just five minutes of intense brawling action.

The true brawl, however, came after the bell. As Lawler shook hands with fans in the aisle, one turned on him with a vicious slap to the face. By the time the floor manager placed the spotlight on the battling pair, blood had already been shed. Commentator Bobby Heenan fell unconscious when he checked his monitor not once, but twice. It was beyond the improvisational skills of Vince McMahon to explain why Randy Savage had just attacked 'the King'.

Upon Savage's return, for the final contest of the evening, he was greeted with generally mixed applause; an unfortunate tribute to the promotional skills of the WWF television staff covering Lawler's impending arrival. Indeed, after locking up with both Flair and his last-minute partner Curt Hennig, Savage went to tag his partner. Ramon misread his intentions and remained on the outside for a brief moment. As the 'Macho Man' gave his partner the lightest of taps on the shoulder, the crowd finally erupted into verbal abuse. Savage looked around, hesitated, then hiptossed his partner into the ring before storming down the aisle.

The legendary gift horse's new denture work went unseen as Flair and Hennig, 'Naturally Perfect', began beating on the fallen 'Bad Guy'. Only his new-found support inspired Ramon to escape the repeated pin attempts, while the rulebreakers faced a dilemma in finding exactly how many liberties could be taken with double-teaming before referee Dave Hebner lost his patience. However, the partners in crime decided the moment was rife to land their well-rehearsed finisher, even easier with no opponent to break it up. Hennig simply caught and held Ramon in the Perfect-plex, at which point Flair locked in the figure-four. A truly 'perfect' conclusion it would have been, had not Jerry Lawler appeared on the scene. Leaping from the top rope, he brought both feet into the groin of Hennig. Hebner, unsighted for the interference as he had been checking for a potential submission, counted Ramon's pin before he even saw Lawler.

23rd January 1993

It was somewhat unfortunate that, just as the unlikely combination of Jerry Lawler and Jeff Jarrett had reached the heights of WWF popularity, they met their downfall. Jarrett lose his Intercontinental title to the first three-time champion, his former victim Bret Hart. Once again, Jarrett appeared to be controlling the third of their classic series. With fifteen minutes gone, he had Hart stunned from a DDT, and played to the crowd with the 'Nature Boy' strut of his hero Buddy Rogers. How ironic it was then that WWF champion Ric Flair decided that was the moment to intervene. While Curt Hennig awoke the 'Hitman', protesting to referee Joey Marella as he shook Hart's head, Flair dived into the ring and clipped Jarrett's knee. It was not until later that Bobby Heenan made the connection and informed the viewing audience that, naturally, Flair knew exactly the way to damage the joint before Hart locked in the figure-four. Lawler's defeat came in the tag team headline contest pitting himself and Ramon against the evil duo. As Hennig put it, "this time we know what we're taking on." Lawler was clearly outmatched by his AWA title victim, with the years taking their toll more visibly on the 'King', while Flair's technical skills were hardly challenged by the man who once boasted a blonde perm and fluffy moustache. Indeed, Flair and Hennig, along with new ally Hart, faced more of a challenge in the actual Royal Rumble. With the Last two men left in the ring, the three terrors waited until Yokozuna criss-crossed the ring and then pulled down all three ropes simultaneously, causing such a thunderous landing for the 'sumo star' that he suffered serious bone chips in his spine. However, despite his physical inferiority, Lawler retained his sense of cunning; as Savage leapt from the ring and departed with his new-found friends, Lawler pointed out an anomaly in the rules to both WWF officials and Yokozuna, still prone on his back, *his feet still waving in the air.*

15th February 1993

Few fans in the Mid-South Coliseum were surprised to find Yokozuna's compounded spinal injuries had caused him to pull out of the special challenge match of the MemphisMania card pitting the "greatest Horsemen ever" against the King and his Knights. The crowd favourites were at a clear disadvantage in this elimination series, in which the loser of each match would be replaced by a teammate until none remained. Razor Ramon displayed a clear lack of confidence and was easy prey for Savage's top rope elbow. The over-energetic Savage, however, underestimated the stamina required to continue competing in the tense Memphis atmosphere and fell to Jarrett's figure-four. Flair fared little better and, his desire to win overriding his reasoning, he earned a disqualification for using a piledriver. Jarrett was only removed with the sacrifice of Hennig, with both men counted out during a brutal brawl in the aisle. Bret Hart then claimed victory for his side; as the referee warned Lawler not to complete his piledriver attempt, Hart flicked upwards into a mule-kick that earned the pin. It was at this point that the 'Hitman' learned the true meaning of the words "hometown advantage" as Lawler grabbed the microphone and, with the permission of the referee, introduced a replacement fourth member of his team: independent star Davey Boy Smith...

Spotlight (*Hulk Who?* July 1995)

(Among the hardcore wrestling community in Britain, one man was infamous: Nic Higton. He defrauded many people by failing to deliver fanzines, videotapes or play-by-mail games. Bashing him became a regular feature, but I particularly enjoyed writing this piece in which we took our monthly wrestler profile section and applied it to an unorthodox subject. Those of you who remember these days will understand why it had to be included in the book.)

REAL NAME: Nic Higton **HEIGHT**: 5'11"ish **WEIGHT**: Slightly over **DOB**: 2/4/76

DEBUT: 1993 **HOMETOWN**: NCC-1701, 20 Bute Gardens, Wallington, Surrey, SM6 8SS (0181-669-7232)

AKA: Jean Pierre LaFitte, Dick Turpin, Robert Maxwell, Buster Edwards

CAREER: 'Education' ('81-'92); Play By Mail and merchandise business ('92-4); "Not available" ('94); Back on the scene ('95)

MANAGERS: Phil Jones (Wrestling Insight '94-4)

RING PHILOSOPHY: Face (-'93); began defaulting on contracts; Heel ('93-)

REGIONAL/FOREIGN TITLES: Words PBM service ('93, '94); Dodgiest tape trader ('93, '94)

WWF/NWA/AWA TITLES: Offers many, such as WrestleMania or Starrcade, but rarely delivers

RINGATTIRE: Interesting coloured jackets; XL T-shirts

BESTMOVE: Left home for brother's home where customers could not contact him

RINGSTYLE: Slow. I once waited for twenty but he didn't answer.

SPEED: 1 tape, two months.

STRENGTH: Powerful forces of persuasion.

STAMINA: Kept up charade for many months.

MATWORK: Apparently manages to clear it of complaint letters every day.

AERIAL ABILITY: Many tapes sent out by air mail, one would presume.

SUMMARY: Like Sid Eudy, only not so professional.

INJURIES: Nothing serious, one would hope.

GREATEST VICTORY: Persuaded British Telecom to allow him use of a premium rate information services line.

GREATEST ACHIEVEMENT: Rumoured to have updated the aforementioned line.

TRIVIA: Once had to send a letter of apology to more than 900 customers. Attended the last two WCW tours where he picked up several pointers on ripping people off. Longstanding record was recently broken with reports of a £60 rip-off in one transaction.

SHORT-TERM PROSPECTS: Offer of refund/supply of goods in return for £10 'registration fee' should be profitable.

LONG-TERM PROSPECTS: About six years unless he gets a good lawyer and doesn't try to rip him off.

***Wrestling Insight*, March 1996**

(Although the writing style in this column is effective, my goodness does the content ever look naive with hindsight.)

Professional wrestlers are still using anabolic steroids.

This is 1996, the dangers of stunted growth, hair loss, bone decay and serious organ damage are widely known, fans appreciate the skills of the smaller athlete, and yet professional wrestlers are still using steroids.

The WWF has what appears to be a widespread reliable testing programme. WCW had some form of drug testing, though steroids are conspicuously absent from the list of substances tested for. Wrestlers are still using steroids.

They are using them in Mexico. They are using them in America. They are even using them here in Britain. Wrestlers are sill using steroids.

This is the era of the junior-heavyweights. High-flying action is the order of the day. One of the world's most entertaining athletes, Rey Misterio Jr, weighs just ten stone. The most exciting match I've ever witnessed, the Michinoku match at Croydon last month, featured six athletes all smaller than myself. Yet wrestlers are still using steroids.

Young wrestler, barely adults, are breaking into the sport. They may be performing for crowds that struggle to break into three figures. They do not have years of drug-based habit behind them. Drug abuse is no longer an integral part of the wrestling culture. Yet wrestlers are still using steroids.

George Zahorian served time in prison for supplying steroids. The WWF almost lost its existence through standing back while drugs were abused. Proposed government legislation will make it illegal to simply possess steroids in Britain. Yet wrestlers are still using steroids.

The Ultimate Warrior cost the WWF thousands of dollars in payment for hotel rooms he destroyed when steroids put him into an uncontrollable rage.

Billy Graham can barely walk, his liver destroyed, his hip literally crumbled away.

Eddie Gilbert died of a heart attack at the age of 33.

And professional wrestlers are still using anabolic steroids.

<u>Wrestling Insight</u>, October 1996

Critics of professional wrestling often derogatively compare it with a soap opera. I'm sure we've all tried to deny this, but the weekly ongoing storylines are not the only similarities.

Australian soap actors often jump to different promotions; remember Henry/Grant and Mike/David leaving *Neighbours* for *Home And Away*? Neither man's past was referred to.

Characters often make unexpected turns: who can forget Don Fisher's days as a killer heel?

Storylines are revealed ahead of broadcast by press reports, though some fans feel this spoils the surprise.

When an actor or actress is ill or on holiday, their character is given an excuse to disappear, while when they leave the show, a reason has to be found for their departure. Oddly Albert Square is yet to have its first 'loser leaves Walford' bout. If a character is particularly important, the actor will sometimes be replaced without reason; at least in wrestling this only happens with masked stars.

When a character is removed from the opening titles, attentive fans know he or she has had their marching orders.

Neighbours has recently introduced a music videos at the beginning of the show, recapping all the major incidents of recent episodes. How long then, until *Coronation Street* ends in a *Misirlou* montage, with soundbites from all those involved in the Platt family feud.

Home And Away's Sergeant Chris Hale has recently become corrupt and is well on the way to being the most hated official in Australia. All he needs now is a whistle to blow. "I'm Chris Hale, and you're not, and you can take that to the bank."

Alf Stewart: Bob Armstrong. Enough said.

Certain soaps, such as *Prisoner: Cell Block H, Blue Heelers* and *Shortland Street*, focus on a particular situation, be it prison, the police or a hospital. This is no different to the variety of wrestling styles, such as AAA's lucha, UWF-i's shoot style or FMW's bombs.

Coronation Street and *EastEnders* have begun a bitter Monday night war, with both sides expanding their output. Critics feel the need to fill extra TV times will mean the product is diluted and lowers in quality.

Sounds familiar?

When a soap star's time is up, they inevitably end up performing in the seaside towns of Britain. Say hello to Cannonball Grizzly.

Coronation Street filmed a special episode available only for those paying £13.99, ten years after wrestling hit pay-per-view.

Finally, as well as their TV commitments, soap stars have to travel around the country performing live shows at the theatre every night, performing even when seriously injured. No, hang on, that's just wrestling...

Wrestling Insight, **November 1996**

There's been so much fantasy talk about ECW and the WWF joining forces that this issue I'm going to create my own co-promotion hypothesis: What If... Brian Pillman wasn't really injured?

Imagine the conclusion of Starrcade: Hogan has just pinned Roddy Piper and the nWo are celebrating. Hogan gets on the mike and announced the newest member of the nWo, Brian Pillman. The 'cripple' wheels himself down the aisle, only to leap to his feet and run around like a madman, screaming '"I fooled you all!"

A few weeks later, on the post-Rumble live Raw, Shawn Michaels beats 'Razor Ramon' by disqualification, when 'Diesel' interferes. The two frauds work Michaels over, only for Kevin Nash and Scott Hall to make the save. The crowd react with confusion, followed by anger when the pair turn the beating on to their former Clique partner, sending him home on a stretcher.

The following Monday, both shows break for a simultaneous announcement. The nWo challenges "the rest of professional wrestling" to a best of five non-title series. If the nWo lose, they will disband; if they are victorious, the group will gain control of WCW and the WWF. A week later, Eric Bischoff and Vince McMahon agree to the proposal and reluctantly shake hands.

SuperBrawl and In Your House XII are both cancelled to allow for a special $30 pay-per-view, 'This Means War'. The opening match is an inter-promotional battle royale where the last two men will represent WWF/WCW against Hall and Nash. The 40 man affair is filled with long awaited clashes, including Jesse James against Jeff Jarrett and Vader's revenge on Paul Orndorff, but Sting and Bret Hart are the two survivors.

In the first challenge match, Chris Benoit falls in 15 minutes to Syxx. 1-0 nWo. Steve Austin pins Pillman to even the score, claiming "the more organisations I go through, the better." The Giant upsets the Undertaker with a chokeslam through a casket, but Hart and Sting save the series after Hall mistakenly floors Nash. In the final match, Hulk Hogan (with Ted DiBiase) takes on Shawn Michaels. Hogan dominates the match, with Michaels taking unheard of bumps, but as the WCW champion goes for the legdrop, Michaels catches the limb and locks in a perfect figure-four. Cornerman Ric Flair, proud that his coaching has worked, shoves the microphone into Hogan's face in time for the world to hear him give up.

The event draws a 2.5 buyrate, the promotions pocket millions, WrestleMania with Hart vs Michaels is a sell-out, Bischoff begins hyping the Gall vs Nash feud, and everybody lives happily ever after. Well, it's no more unlikely than Shane Douglas working with the WWF...

Wrestling Insight, December 1996

Where are they now?

Erich Bischoff, regularly abused by nWo members last summer, including an infamous jackknife through a table. *Now: A leading member of the nWo.*

'Dirty White Boy' Tony Anthony, long-time Tennessee top draw, recently respected for tough guy role in non-nonsense Smoky Mountain Wrestling. *Now: Working as a plumber at the NEC whilst young children throw taunts of "You've got diarrhoea!"*

Giant Haystacks, former veteran star of the seventies and eighties. *Now: Still working regularly in Britain.*

Kip Allen Frey, pulled from WCW shortly before replacement Bill Watts condemned modern wrestling as "a macabre cartoon". *Now: A leading executive in Ted Turner's Cartoon Network.*

Brian Pillman, strongly rumoured to be of unsound mind early this year. *Now: Enjoying a $400,000 a year contract with no impending signs of actually working for it.*

Jake Roberts, made a special one-time only return at last year's Royal Rumble. *Now: Preparing to enter this year's Rumble, his sixth consecutive full-price PPV.*

Hanzo Nakajima, visited Britain as part of a flying world tour this past February. *Now: Still here, with no escape in sight.*

Mark Henry, signed to a reported $10 million contract this summer. *Now: Erm... any ideas?*

Big Dick Dudley, a character whose gimmick involved having spent extensive time in prison. *Now: In prison.*

Marty Jannetty, seems to leave/be fired from the WWF every January. *Now: Rumoured to be leaving the WWF in coming weeks.*

Lance Wright, 'hip' dressed ECW announcer known for making gags at the WWF's expense. *Now: Wearing a formal looking suit while announcing for the WWF.*

Hiroshi Hase, amicable nature taken advantage of by New Japan for many years with unjustifiable losses a regular occurrence. *Now: About to debut for rival All Japan.*

Atsushi Onita, retired May 1995, definitely not coming back, no, not ever. *Now: Celebrating a successful return to the ring.*

Scott Steiner, among the most visually obvious abusers of the anabolic steroids which led to Billy Graham's hip decaying. *Now: Facing forced retirement after hip surgery.*

Nic Higton: *No, really, where is he now?*

Wrestling Insight, June 1997

Picture the scene. 100+ ECW conventioneers are having trouble understanding our eloquent English diction. Perry Saturn's presence makes Ken Shamrock look as threatening as Mikey Whipwreck. Later, New Jack is slashing a paper cup to ribbons. Both are tearing into the wrestling press.

I'm keeping quiet.

In the more restrained media of *Wrestling Insight,* though, I have to take issue with the points that they raised. As one often hears, certain wrestlers claim the views expressed by wrestling journalists are invalid as they aren't, to coin a phrase, "in the business". The theory goes that people who haven't worked in the physical side of the wrestling industry cannot understand the intricate details of how the business works.

Consider for a moment the journalists that work in 'the real world'. How many football writers have played professionally? How many music journalists have released chart-topping albums? Indeed, when did Trevor McDonald ever chair a cabinet meeting?

A 'sheet' writer may not have the experience of how difficult it is to put a wrestling match together, but it is ludicrous to say that they cannot tell the difference between a good performance and a bad one.

A further criticism put forward is that so much of the contents of wrestling newsletters is unrelated to the in-ring action; New Jack makes comparisons to the *National Enquirer.* Yet take a look at the 'legitimate' press. We see reports of soap stars' personal lives. We read details of sports players' business dealings. We see these things because people pay to read them. Surely a wrestler would be the first to acknowledge that making money is the ultimate goal of any endeavour.

The idea that wrestling journalists know little or nothing about the wrestling business is an ill-conceived fallacy. Many (though certainly not all) writers, and the true 'hardcore' fans in general, dedicate the bulk of their spare time to studying the history of the wrestling business, viewing tapes spanning time and geography and, most of all, actually thinking about wrestling.

During the aforementioned Q&A session, Chris Candido admitted that the daily grind of the WWF wrestler made it impossible to keep informed of happenings elsewhere in the business. While some wrestlers have legendary videotape collections, many others lack the time, or simply wish to detach themselves from wrestling in their leisure time. ECW itself seems a particularly odd body to be condemning the so-called sheets. Not only has much (if not most) of its following been derived from such coverage, the fact fans have become more informed about how wrestling operates is surely in ECW's favour. Without breaking kayfabe, one could logically conclude that the Ultimate Warrior is the world's greatest wrestler because he never loses, or that Shane Douglas is a reject who couldn't make it in the 'big leagues'.

Generalising about wrestling journalists, on either side of the argument, would be quite ridiculous, in the same way as it is invalid to make sweeping statements about fans who use the Internet. Even with the unique secretive nature of the wrestling business, it is a subject as appropriate for media coverage as any other.

Perry Saturn says that "If I can't fly a plane, I'm not going to tell you that the pilot's shit." If that is the case, why does he feel entitled to criticise journalists?

The No-Show ditties (*Suckerpunch*, December 1997)

(*This list, like so many things at the time, came out of a drunken conversation with Matt after a night in the student bar. What started as an off-hand remark about Buddy Landell's alleged unreliability when it came to making booked shows turned into a parlour game that was libellous, utterly pointless and curiously addictive.*)

1) You never can tell with Buddy Landell.
2) Life's a bitch when you book Tommy Rich.
3) You may pay his bill but you won't see Doug Gilbert.
4) You ain't seen tardy till you've booked Barry Hardy.
5) There are many examples of an AWOL Mike Samples.
6) You must be unstable if you trust King Mabel.
7) It's not fun and games when you book Jesse James.
8) For unreliable brawler see Mongolian Mauler.
9) You've not seen moody till you book Sid Eudy.
10) Trouble always ensues when you book Mr. Hughes.
11) You'll lose out on the deal with Jungle Jim Steele.
12) An experienced booker won't use Jimmy Snuka.
13) The show'll be over before you see Super Nova.
14) Only true fools will trust the Pitbulls.
15) You'll be sitting alone waiting for Carlos Colon.
16) Best rebook the show if you've hired Sir Mo.
17) Life can be hell with Jim Brunzell.
18) Don't Say You'll Be There to B. Brian Blair.
19) It really ain't fun when you wait for Bart Gunn.
20) It's sure to go wrong when you book an Armstrong.
21) You'll soon be forgotten if you trust Ian Rotten.
22) It's gonna be hell when you book Rick Martel.
23) You'll need a good lawyer with Wing Kanemura.
24) A real act of folly is booking Bob Holly.
25) Only a gambler would pay cash for NAMBLA.
26) There's usually no sign of Greg Valentine.
27) For professional worker forget the Berserker.
28) The locker room's bare with Koko B. Ware.

29) In a month of Sundays you'll never see Bundy.
30) Advances? Don't bank `em if you're waiting for Yankem.
31) There's absolutely no way you'll see Jimmy Del Ray.
32) I want to let every guy know not to trust Tommy Cairo.
33) It's really bad form to book Devon Storm.
34) You'll be refunding fans if you've hired Otto Wanz.
35) You'll soon kill your town if you trust Bad News Brown.
36) You'll be back to shelf-stacker if you book Pat Tanaka.
37) Only a schmuck would trust Bunkhouse Buck.
38) Trouble always ensues when you book Curtis Hughes.
39) Unreliable Latino? David Sammartino.
40) Forget word of mouth when it comes to George South.
41) You're acting madly when you pay for Boo Bradley.
42) A blind man can see not to trust JYD.
43) I'm too long in the tooth to book Flaming Youth.
44) For well-known slackers try the Bushwhackers.
45) If you hate no-shows forget the Romeros.
46) Even Houdini can't produce the Blue Meanie.
47) There's little appeal in booking George Steele.
48) When he's late and he's greedy you know it's Bill Eadie.
49) You'll be looking forlorn when you wait for Matt Borne.
50) Best call the show off if you've booked Ivan Koloff.
51) You will never be sorrier than when you book Vampire Warrior.
52) You'll be waiting a while if you've booked Killer Kyle.
53) It really ain't that nice being let down by Rod Price.
54) You'll need damn good specs to find Moondog Rex.
54) He's taken a hike? Yep, that's Moondog Spike.
55) You lose everything when you book Moondog King.
56) Want them there on the dot? Forget Moondog Spot.
57) There's no one that's later than PWA's Hater.
58) King of the liars is surely Hack Myers.
59) You'll have to search far to find Jesse Barr.
60) We were turning the corner till we trusted Tim Horner.
61) My first major fumble was to book Tony Rumble.
62) I was playing a blinder till I booker the Spellbinder.
63) It all ends in tears with Colonel DeBeers.

64) It works out much dearer with Primo Carnera.
65) Only a moron would swallow an excuse from Ray Apollo.
66) Week after week there's no Iron Sheik.
67) It could take a stalker to find Bobby Walker.
68) Only the insane would trust Sweet Stan Lane.

What makes a great worker? (*Suckerpunch*, September 1998)

As all wrestling fans know, this business (or in-DUS-try as Jim Ross puts it) is like no other. You'll have encountered this enigma when trying to answer that question... just why do you like wrestling?

As wrestling isn't a pure sport, we can't dig out statistics to prove just who is a good performer. A great sprinter is someone who runs quickly, a good centre forward is someone who scores lots of goals, but the matter of a good wrestler is far more difficult to define.

It would be simple enough to take the practical view and look at who draws the most money, but unless you want to read *nothing but* buyrates and TV ratings, we'll have to take a more subjective view at the reasons for a worker's artistic success.

Naturally there are many important aspects that come into a wrestler's ability, like natural charisma, and even turning up to shows on time, but we're looking at the specific job of putting together a great wrestling match, of the type Matt Brannigan described last issue.

We just referred to a wrestler as an artist, and it's worth following through this comparison. Think of a novelist, whose task is to tell a story, similar to that of a grappler. The writer has to both select the right words to use, *and* the correct order to use them in. Think of wrestling moves as verbs, highspots as adjectives and basic holds and transitions as all the other bits (*'conjunctions'* - *Mrs. Barker*).

The adjectives brighten up a piece and give it flourish, but a whole sentence of them would be utterly meaningless. Similarly, a wrestler has to know *when* to perform a move as well as possess the ability to pull that move off.

Of course, wrestling differs from writing because it is a live medium, with a need for improvisation. While Pat Patterson worked some creative miracles with the Ultimate Warrior in the late '80s (for a piss-poor worker, his battles with Rude and Savage were pretty darn gripping), the carefully scripted 25 minuter isn't much use when you're out on the road every night, or performing within the constraints of live television.

The live performance can then perhaps be compared with that of a stand-up comedian (no, not Doink.) While the performer will go out with a basic routine, he needs to adapt to the crowd, improvise where necessary, and interact with hecklers. One example is Lee Hurst, whose live show features a set routine, followed by a session of improvisation on topics selected by the audience.

Naturally he tends to relate these subjects back to his planned repertoire (whatever the subject, the gag about accidentally calling his gran a c*** always comes into it), but the performance's tempo needs to be judged for the audience.

Within the squared circle, the same holds true. If five hundred Arkansas hicks are calling Jerry Lawler a "Burger Queen", it's a lot more effective for him to respond to them, rather than worry about setting up the planned armbar into side-headlock. Yet if Buh Buh Ray Dudley has destroyed Tommy Dreamer, insulted the fans, and the crowd are about to hop the rail, it's a good idea for Dreamer to make a brief comeback to cool things down.

Meanwhile, our comedian is performing in a Newcastle working man's club. A few gags about Freddie Shepherd and Douglas Hall would seem in order. But the next night he's in Islington, so some political satire is on the menu. It's all about the audience - if you tell a joke in a forest, and there's nobody about to laugh, it isn't funny.

And while Steve Regal and Robbie Brookside can wrestle for an hour at the Power Plant, besides impressing Dallas Page, there isn't much point. Back in *Hulk Who?*, we once related how Eddy Guerrero could perform a frog splash in the ECW Arena and it was seen as a tribute to his deceased partner. Yet if Marty Jones tried it at Croydon, the crowd would think he'd lost his marbles.

There's also the strong likelihood that Jones would completely cock up the move, as with our hypothetical comic starting a long complex joke, only to stop halfway through and realise the first line was wrong. Working within your capabilities is a vital part of any performance industry.

Take the highspots of everyone's favourite love him or hate him grappler, Rob Van Dam. The first time you cock up a treble reverse somersault through a flaming chair is unfortunate. The third time you screw it up is being unprofessional: not in screwing up the move, but in attempting it again. A comic telling a joke three times to get it right benefits nobody, and neither does Sabu's determination to go through a particular table, even when it patently isn't about to break.

With all this in mind, it's worth taking a few examples and looking at what makes them so good. Steve Austin, Shawn Michaels, Chris Benoit, Jerry Lawler and Jake Roberts are all, for various reasons, what I consider a good worker.

Austin can easily be accused of living solely on a few catchphrases and sign language, but this underestimates what he does in the ring. Austin is a master of what I consider 'working smart' - with the need to protect his injured neck, he knows exactly when to perform a move to best effect, the 'ring generalship' we all remember from Ric Flair. Try and remember the last time you saw Austin climb the ropes.

Michaels is never going to win any awards from a personnel officer but, amid all the backstage bullshit, he remains employed for one reason - very few people possess his ability to work with any opponent. Remember, this is the guy who had a decent match with King Kong Bundy. As well as adapting to the crowd, a good worker needs to mesh with his opponent and bring out the best in him.

Benoit is probably the only man who is an annual nominee for awards in brawling, matwork and aerial ability. Like Owen Hart, this is the result of a solid grounding, and a willingness to learn from around the world - the U.S., Mexico, Canada, Europe and Japan. It's all about having enough respect for your profession to learn more about it.

Lawler and Roberts would probably be the most controversial on this list. But think carefully about why Mark Henry had his debut against 'the King'. This is the same man I saw in Forrest City, Arkansas in a 20 minute bout with Mike Samples that featured a grand total of one recognisable wrestling hold. Yet with every possible variation on cheating behind the referee's back, it was also one of the most heated bouts I've seen.

Admittedly much of Roberts' abilities lie outside in-ring working, and he'll always be remembered for his interviews. But think back, if appropriate, to the matches you saw Roberts in during your early years as a fan. Would they score highly on the ***** rating scale? Of course not. Were they utterly compelling? Hell, yeah.

What makes a great worker is always going to be a subjective affair.

In any case, the wrestling performance needs to be a variety act, which is how Jim Helwig and Eddy Guerrero can work for the same company. But there could be more to this working than we'd like to admit.

Mark Mero once related a tale of how, after his 30 minuter with Brian Pillman at Fall Brawl '95, he lay exhausted in the dressing room, having his battered ankles attended to. Hulk Hogan walked into the room, took a look at the injured limb, and informed Mero that "if you knew how to work, you wouldn't have to do that stuff."

He might just have had a point.

Unpublished journal (September 1999)

(*In September 1999, I made another wrestling-centred trip across the United States. As I was now in full-time employment, another extensive journal was not on the cards. However, I did send the following account to some friends by e-mail, and I'm particularly pleased to have this opportunity to immortalise Mac the cab driver through the printed word.*)

I flew via Amsterdam to Memphis on Friday 24 September, and found that transportation hasn't got any better. Eventually I picked up a taxi and pissed away some money. And Memphis Greyhound stations aren't any better. And they still genuinely cannot understand an English voice.

Fortunately I got the hell out of there on a bus to Nashville, and then arriving in a surprisingly big Knoxville at 5am, where various Jehovah's Witnesses bothered me. Let's just say that the Smoky Mountain region is a little religious.

Anyway, onwards I went to North Carolina where I found out that the Smoky Mountains... are. A quick stop in Asheville and FINALLY I arrived in Charlotte for Saturday lunchtime. Charlotte is actually a decent city for America: clean, accessible, friendly... quite a surprise for a Manchester resident.

The hotel not being ready yet, I sauntered along to the Grady Cole Centre, which looked remarkably like a school gym, for the NWA fan expo convention thingy. This was perversely entertaining; imagine an entire room of people adamant that they are 'in the business' because they once cleaned Tony Rumble's car.

To be fair, you did get the opportunity to support the retirement funds of the likes of Abdullah the Smiling Butcher, Stan 'the old man' Lane, Lou Thesz (who I don't believe will ever die), and Rick Steamboat. Believe me, there are few things more worthy to do on a Saturday afternoon than to chat to Rick Steamboat about matches he had with Flair. In case you are wondering, the little dragon is now approaching adolescence while winning the North Carolina amateur wrestling title, while Steamboat himself is busy curing cancer. And he posed for the attached pic for free!

Anyway, the novelty of seeing some old guy's collection of AWA Southern Tag belts wore off, so I checked into the Travelodge, hit Burger King and settled down in front of the TV... where I found wrestling in eight seconds. After WWF Jakked, I caught up with Saturday Night where it appears the Armstrongs are in a long term feud with Brian Knobs, Hugh Morrus and Jerry Flynn. Ahem.

Back at the arena, the joys of crowd exaggeration came into full effect. Officially, it was a disappointing 700. Wink wink. Try 200 tops, including all the comps from each promotion's lackeys, and you might be closer. Apparently this was because of the WWF show the next day. Because obviously having wrestling fans in town is bad for business. I ask you.

First up was a six team tag tourney, with the winners to meet NWA tag champs Knuckles Nelson and Dukes Dalton. The opener was a bit of a shocker, a real decent match between the local team Triple XXX (Drake Dawson and Curtis Thompson who, now I come to think of it, used to be Firebreaker Chip) against Gene Austin & Tommy Star, the, er, pride of Michigan. Well-worked stuff, with the highlight being Triple XXX's valet Strawberry Fields, who will be big in the business one day. Though she's pretty, er, big, already.

Moving swiftly on, we had Team Extreme (Khris Germany & Kit Carson) of Sportatorium 'fame' against New Jersey's Misfits, who have clearly seen a few 'hardcore' tapes. Pagga ensued, Team Extreme won. And finally we had Samu and a fat bloke against the legendary (?) Crusher Carlson and Michelle Starr, a big Adrian Street fan. It ended with Team Extreme running in for a big fat punch-up, and the fat bloke & Starr going through a table, causing a very convenient double DQ.

Britain's own Sebastian P. Sterling then had a good old style clash with Canadian E.Z. Ryder for the Queen's Cup, which he lost on a fluke. The tag tourney continued with Team Extreme cheating their way past Triple XXX, which was a shame because their valet was wearing less clothes than before, and the final would have been more interesting with her.

And then Hammerlock's Gary Steele took on Brian Anthony and Naoya Ogawa. Cue local 'smart' fan shouting out that "this oughta be good cos those Chinese guys know some real cool moves." Ahem. Major clusterfuck, with Steele & Ogawa's matwork clashing with Anthony's comedy. Ogawa choked out Anthony, but Steele immediately caught him in a roll-up to crown a British heavyweight champion of the world, who will no doubt be recognised in that list of British world champs in the BBC Sports Personality of the Year. And even though he jobbed it back a week later, I can now tick off another of Bill Apter's '37 things you must do to be a real fan' because I have (loosely) 'followed' Steele's career from his debut on the Hammerlock 'Climbing the ladder' show to the world title... so there.

Then came NWA Mississippi champion Big Don Brody vs Abdullah. Cue massacre, cue fork to head, cue large security guard shitting himself, cue very old brown haired Ron Garvin run-in. An Abdullah match is something every wrestling fan should see once in their life.

During half-time I checked out Ms Fields' talents a bit more, then scammed a drink from Andre Baker and Mike White who, considering I've never been in the ring and therefore know shit, were surprisingly friendly. After a bit of British bonding through slagging off the local drinks and humidity, I returned for the second half, where we were all invited to show our appreciation for Nelson Royal. As you do.

There was then a junior-heavyweight Rumble, with our highlight being Hammerlock's Johnny Storm. Alas, he was eliminated and the dubiously named Twiggy Ramirez was the last survivor, only to then fail in his challenge to NWA champ Logan Caine. All pretty much what you would expect from indy juniors.

By now it was getting real late, but most people stayed on for the legends match, featuring Ron Garvin against a visibly aging Stan Lane, still the master of the microphone. All went well as it was enjoyable rather than *****-laden and, as soon as it got to the point where some spots were called for, Garvin twatted Lane very hard and took the pin. It now being past 11, the crowd was well below three figures for the final bout, Team Extreme vs tag champions Nelson & Dalton. They decided to help clear up early by destroying several chairs in a brawl through the crowd, and something or other that was interesting enough to make me say 'oooh', but not interesting enough to remember two months later, led to the title change, and hometime.

Except, of course, Nelson and Dawg had actually dropped the belts in New England to Curtis Slamdawg & Jay Kobain three days earlier, so there were two sets of champions, and no unification match, and nobody was happy. Which pretty much sums up the NWA.

Anyway, come Sunday and I was spending the afternoon watching the Carolina Panthers playing the Bengals. I couldn't get tickets for the stadium, so I sat watching in the middle of Charlotte High Street on a big screen, downing beer and burgers and developing sun burn. USA, USA, etc. Despite my Pillman shirt, the Panthers finally won a game, to the absolute apathy of the Yanks, who have no passion at all for sports, with the game a backdrop to the adverts.

With the Unforgiven PPV a good eight miles out of town, it was taxi time. Ho ho ho. I called one: no luck. The hotel manager called one: no luck. The hotel manager called Gold Cabs: no luck. Then 'Mac the Driver' turned up. Without being called.

I can only conclude that he had been listening in on Gold Cab's radio and intercepted the call. Because one thing this Mac was not, was a taxi driver. In fact, he happily admitted that he was looking forward to the day his probation ended and he could get his driving licence back. Red lights, lanes, speed limits: none of these meant anything to Mac. And he smoked a big fat joint the whole way. At the arena, I asked what he wanted for the fare and he replied 'just give me some money, that'll cover it".

The show itself you probably all saw. Only notes are that the heat was actually way way up on what came across on TV, so the sound guys must have had an off night. The Kennel from Hell match was quite literally unwatchable through the two cages. The weird atmosphere during Jericho-X-Pac was because a fan held-up a sign saying 'Y-2-Jackoff' which was confiscated (boos). He then held up a bizarre 'Eat More Beaver' sign (cheers) which the guards went after (boos) but he passed backwards and it kept appearing throughout the crowd (cheers) until it was confiscated (boos) and then the crowd began a spontaneous 'Eat More Beaver' chant. Oh, and the false finish with Rock over HHH fooled absolutely EVERYONE in the building.

Post-show, I realised there was no hope of getting home, except, that is, to call Mac on his mobile. He arrived with several people on board and told me to climb in the back. As in through the back window. Or where it would have been if there had been one. It soon turned out that Mac's style of taxi driving involved anyone who wanted climbing in or out, going wherever the cab went, and then giving him any cash they had. Two passenger wanted to be driven to their car, though they couldn't remember where their car was. One got in solely so he could hang out the back to lean in old ladies' car windows and call them faggots. Another two gave their destination as 'anywhere with pussy', leading to a tour of every strip joint and table dancing venue in the city, complete with Mac's expert commentary. Every time a police car went past, we had to lean out the window and cover up the license plate in case the cops ran a check on our licenceless driver. Then Mac suddenly realised he had been carrying a deaf and dumb Puerto Rican in the front passenger seat for three hours, forgotten to take him to the airport, and that was the reason for all the flustered hand gestures from the mute immigrant.

Monday took me to Greensboro, which is a horrible, horrible town, reminiscent of the worst parts of Preston. And it rained so hard that even I decided not to walk to the hotel. On the way to the arena, however, I did steal a Jimmy Valiant indy show poster. The show was the *RAW* with the infamous 'This is Rock's life' segment which was a blast live and, to my surprise, wasn't a big channel switcher. Unfortunately it was the night of the referee's restored powers angle, which meant DQs aplenty.

Back in the hotel, I was unexpectedly joined in my room by a large homeless man who had just walked out on his junkie wife, and was intent on committing suicide in my bathroom. Budget motels, eh?

Tuesday was a five hour trip, with me nearly left behind for a 24 hour wait in Dansville, Virginia. Phew. The evening's entertainment was the Smackdown taping in Richmond though, to be honest, food and sleep deprivation left me almost unable to appreciate anything. There was, however, a decent Midian match (vs Al Snow) which has to be a rarity. Trivia note saw Fatu debut as Sammy Sumo, but the entrance bombed so regally that he came back out to be repackaged as Rikishi Fatu. And I saw Hardys vs Edge/Christian, which was nice. After the main event, we were all kept hanging about for 20 minutes on the promise of seeing some more action, which turned out to be Steve Austin's sole appearance of the night, doing the beer cans angle with HHH, all without the tiresome business of having a wrestling match first.

So, another trip over, and I suspect this may truly be the last. At the grand old age of 23, I really felt the trials and tribulations of life on the road. There's only so many Kurt Angle squashes you can take in a lifetime. Then again, I never did get to that museum in Iowa...

Jobber (unpublished, 2000)

(Everyone writer has plans to author the great novel. This was mine. As you can see, it didn't get very far. I only wish I could remember what was meant to happen next...)

There's only three sets of people who work on New Year's Eve 1999: hookers, hawkers and pro wrestlers.

Of course, if you're going to be realistic for a moment, there's nothing special about the last night of the millennium. Forget the pedants' argument about 2000 vs 2001, it's just another night that we happen to have got all excited about for entirely artificial reasons.

Kinda like how you think a hooker is going to be a woman making love to you. And not just someone you pay to do something you can manage fine on your own.

Kinda like how you think a paper hat is worth ten bucks because it's got '1999-2000' written on it, so it'll be a souvenir. And not just another contribution to some guy's next Caribbean vacation.

And it's kinda like how, if you really try, you can believe the ad in the local newspaper that says a WWF superstar is going to wrestle in Tacoma, Washington on the last show of the century.

And when you get there, it's just me. A WWF jobber.

And now, thanks to putting a local kid over in seven minutes, I'm technically a Pacific Wrestling Federation jobber. All 87 people who showed up tonight think that makes the kid a star. As the booker come owner said, I gave him the celebrity rub.

Now for my reward. This and the $50 I got, most of which was for gas. It's half an hour before midnight and, unless there's some outlaw show in Hawaii nobody knows about, I get to work the battle royale, the last wrestling match of the millennium. There's no extra cash for my efforts, but that's the wrasslin' business for you.

<u>20th Century Fakes (*Wrestling Wrap-up*, January 2000)</u>

Professional wrestling is a business, not a sport. Any further confusion can be resolved by Dave Meltzer's two golden rules of pro grappling: 1) Everything you see is a work designed to draw money. 2) If you ever suspect something may be real, refer to rule 1.

This concept is the entire essence of professional wrestling. Once this rule is breached, whatever is being presented ceases to be pro wrestling. But giving such an illusion has been the basis of countless cons, what we will term here as the worked shoot.

Ironically, for a phrase that garners so much discussion, the pure meaning of a shoot (a professional wrestling match without a predetermined outcome) was virtually non-existent for most of the 20th century.

Naturally there isn't a single date when wrestling 'became a fix', merely a gradual process across the first couple of decades of the century. The first elements of working came with late 19th century Greco-Roman wrestler William Muldoon, the first 'World Heavyweight Champion', who would regularly lose suspicious decisions to competitors in other styles of grappling, before winning a rematch under Greco-Roman rules.

What is probably the first bout we can record with any degree of certainty as a work saw American champion Frank Gotch lose his title in a major upset to Fred Beel (the originator of the hip-toss style throw bearing his name) on December 1st 1906. Despite protests to the contrary by Gotch's historical supporters, the result looks suspiciously like it was prearranged to promote a rematch 16 days later, in which Gotch regained his crown. Whether through luck or planning, the 'fluke' loss paved the way for at least half a dozen profitable rematches.

Gotch's two other famous bouts, his world title victory over George Hackenschmidt in 1908 and a rematch win three years later are both the subject of historical mystery. The 1908 match was undoubtedly on the level and, although some accounts portray Gotch using repeated foul holds, there is little evidence of these stories surfacing until Hackenschmidt was defending his reputation back in Europe.

The 1911 match was a little more suspicious. The action in the ring saw an easy Gotch victory, but Hackenschmidt later claimed to be suffering a knee injury; in many accounts this was from a deliberate attack by a paid Gotch ally, but these accounts do not stand up to any serious investigation. Another story has it that promoters didn't dare risk cancelling the show, which drew a record $87,000 gate (worth $1.5 million today, more than WrestleMania 2000) and told Hackenschmidt he would be allowed one fall on his way to an inevitable loss. Whatever the truth, Gotch was most certainly fighting to win. Wrestling may still have been, at heart, a legitimate sport, albeit one run by some unscrupulous characters.

'Fixing' matches at this time was generally in the traditional sense, to defraud gamblers of their money. A popular con involved a fall guy throwing matches to unsuspecting challengers from the audience, who would then be invited to take on a second grappler at a later date. Of course, the challenger's friends and family would back him with the bookie/promoter, who was the third leg of the triangular con. Local stepped in the ring, second wrestler destroyed him, and all three jumped town with the takings. The accompanying code of secrecy took its name from a pig Latin corruption of fake: kayfabe.

Probably the first time a worked wrestling show took place in the form we'd recognise today came with a New York tournament in 1915, highlighted by 'the Masked Marvel' issuing challenges from the audience and holding the legitimate shooter Ed 'Strangler' Lewis to a draw. When the Marvel unmasked a month later as low-ranking grappler Mort Henderson, more than one onlooker was suspicious. A police investigation saw numerous participants admit under oath that the tournament was a sham; though naturally this was a one-off deviance. Wink wink.

The credit for inventing the business we now know as professional wrestling, belongs to Joe 'Toots' Mondt, a highly talented legitimate wrestler who hooked up with Lewis, and his manager Billy Sandow, known collectively as the Gold Dust Trio. Mondt came up with the idea of taking the con process to the next level. Instead of wrestlers travelling around the country on their own ('barnstorming'), Mondt decided all concerned would benefit from a central promoter organising a company of workers, who would trade wins amongst each other for the benefit of promoting rematches. To put things into context, a legitimate July 4th 1916 bout between Lewis and Joe Stecher had gone to a draw when the referee called a halt after five deathly dull hours in Omaha, Nebraska. Such results could only help Mondt and company do record business with pro wrestling as a show, where drawing heat to sell tickets replaced legitimate grappling as a wrestler's job.

Working was thus pretty much the rule after Gotch retired - while he was involved in predetermined finishes, his era was the last in which any real level of 'shooting' existed. Certainly when Gotch's former training partner Martin 'Farmer' Burns followed Mondt into promoting and introduced submissions as a finish in the early 20s, most claims of shooting were pure kayfabe.

But while the development of wrestling as a form of entertainment inherently exposed the business, with anyone who knew what legitimate grappling involved being able to spot the difference, and athletic commissions such as Washington (1940s) and California (1950s) refusing to sanction wrestling as anything other than an exhibition, the backlash against the fake product inherently created a demand for reality, or at least a passable illusion.

Possessing legitimate wrestling ability was now far less important than giving the impression that you had such ability. This could involve good P.R., booking politics, or simply double-crossing a weaker opponent mid-match; a widespread practice between the wars, leading to the need for many years to put title belts on those with legitimate grappling skills, such as Lou Thesz.

And at the heart of the whole business of promoting a particular wrestler or match as 'real' was the implicit acknowledgement that everything else was fake. As early as May 6th 1921, Strangler Lewis used this policy to limit the loss of face from a worked title loss to Stanislaus Zbyszko, claiming in the press that he had (in his exact words) been "jobbed out". The implication being that, while matches were sometimes thrown, he did not usually follow such practice. When the supply of shooting appeared so limited (and was realistically non-existent), the laws of economics drove up the price people would pay to see it.

Ironically, it was the defenders of genuine sport, the New York State Athletic Commission, who helped legitimise worked matches in the public eye. They ruled in the mid '30s that all wrestling bouts must be promoted as 'exhibitions', with only title defences against serious contenders billed as a 'match'. The fact that such contests, for example the June 26th 1934 title win of Jim Londos over Jim Browning, were as legitimate as a three pound note didn't diminish the popularity of these 'shooting matches.' (Londos and Browning were part of a recently formed promotional cartel dominating the business at the time)

That's correct: the term that today's smart fans use like it's going out of fashion was a popular promotional tool several decades before most of us were born. The most successful example was when Londos finally accepted Lewis' title challenge on September 20th 1934, after years of refusing to fight him. (He had previously assumed, quite probably correctly, that Lewis would have taken the belt whatever the planned finish).

With so many 'knowledgeable' fans sure that Lewis would never lay down for Londos, the scene was set for what was openly promoted as "the last shooting match in history". 35,256 fans paid a record $96,000 to fill Chicago's Wrigley Field and see... Lewis pinned by his rival. Of course, Lewis had joined the cartel, and the whole affair was business as usual.

Between the emergence of Gorgeous George (who didn't end real wrestling as his contemporaries would have you believe, but merely popularised showmanship rather than wrestling holds as the basis of his worked performances) and Antonino Rocca (the first television wrestling star with no tangible wrestling ability, perhaps the Hogan of his day), the worked shoot lost its appeal in the U.S. after the Second World War.

People have always only been prepared to believe a wrestling bout is really, truly, for real when it appears neither man would throw the match. For the next development in fake reality, we need to follow the wrestling business across the Pacific where, after a few false starts going back as far as 1887, the Japanese wrestling business made its real beginnings in July 1953.

Among the first promoters was the legendary Mitsuhiro Momota, better known as Rikidozan, whose Japanese Wrestling Alliance was the first successful promotion. On December 22nd 1954, Rikidozan became the first Japanese Heavyweight Champion by beating then world judo champion Masahiko Kimura in what was naturally promoted as a shoot with neither man prepared to lay down. (Kimura was just coming off a win over Brazilian jiu-jitsu expert Helio Gracie, the last defeat for the Gracie clan for over 40 years.) As it turned out, Rikidozan double-crossed Kimura, making his reputation for life.

After this incident, the Japanese business returned to the usual affairs, with Japanese babyfaces taking on the heel American tourists in traditional worked bouts, a policy that continued on past Rikidozan's 1963 death, to Antonio Inoki starting New Japan Pro Wrestling in 1972. On October 5th the following year Inoki began a career of introducing new concepts to the wrestling business, many of them variants of the worked shoot.

On that day, Inoki was happily walking down Tokyo High Street when an unknown Indian gentleman beat the crap out of him. Naturally the media went into a frenzy and, when the assailant turned out to be a wrestler by the name of Tiger Jeet Singh, the pair's eventual match had to be for real. Needless to say, Inoki had just innovated the shoot angle and, to cap it off, won the June 26th 1974 grudge match by apparently breaking Singh's arm with an armbar, a move that has been considered a believable submission in Japan ever since.

Earlier in 1974, on March 19th, Inoki participated in the first apparent inter-promotional match. Shozo 'Strong' Kobayashi, champion of the country's number three promotion, the IWE (All Japan being #2), jumped to New Japan. Surely, the logic went, a champion wouldn't job for somebody from a rival group? Despite the IWE stripping him of the title beforehand, Kobayashi's worked loss to Inoki drew a then record 16,500 fans.

Inoki took the concept a stage further by defeating a star from another sport, Olympic judo champion Wilhelm Ruska, on February 6th 1976. The match was designed to set up the ultimate worked shoot on June 25th of the same year: World Champion wrestler Inoki against World Champion boxer Mohammed Ali. Budokan Hall sold out to the tune of $2.5 million, a bigger gate than any in the U.S., even to this day.

All was set for Ali to do the job for a $6 million payoff; although this sum would wipe out any profits, the prestige Inoki gained would be worth far more. The finish would see a bloodied Inoki take advantage of Ali's momentary lapse of attention (played up outside Japan as a gesture of sportsmanship) and land the enzuigiri for the win that would set him and New Japan up for life. Unfortunately, Ali backed out at the last minute and, with no suitable finish agreed on in time, the worked shoot became a real shoot, a dull 15 round draw, with Inoki flat on his back the whole time, and both men too petrified of defeat to aim for victory. It was Lewis vs Stecher all over again.

The fiasco could easily have killed Inoki's career, but fortunately TV-Asahi, the broadcast network who held stock in New Japan and recorded a massive 54.0 rating for the match, kept the company afloat. The subsequent damage repair exercise saw Inoki defeat stars from a variety of martial arts, from World Karate Champion Eddy 'Monster Man' Everett to Olympic judo medallist Allan Coage, later billed as Bad News Brown.

Highlights of these, and the Ali bout can be seen on a martial arts documentary Kings of the Square Ring (keep an eye out on market stalls). As per usual, the popular belief was that a real competitor wouldn't throw a match to Inoki, and he wouldn't even lay down for the greatest boxer in the world, so the matches had to be shoots. In three words, it was business as usual.

Come the early '80s, Inoki returned to the inter-promotional concept. 1981 saw Rusher Kimura and Animal Hamaguchi jump from the dying IWE for a rerun of the Kobayashi feud. But the idea hit its real height on October 8th 1982 during a six man tag match, when Riki Choshu turned on partner Tatsumi Fujinami, telling him after the match that "I'm not a dog that lets you bite me."

Better translated, Choshu was apparently expressing his dissatisfaction with his lack of a push, something the smart fans knew about. Therefore the angle 'had' to be real. Indeed, other workers in a similar position, such as Hamaguchi, Killer Khan and Kuniaki Kobayashi, joined Choshu as the Ishin Gundan (Restruction Force) faction, feuding with the established stars.

While the feud set record business over the next year, with the company achieving a 90% sell-out rate at house shows, behind the scenes disputes raged. When the sell-outs continued after Inoki missed three months with injury, Choshu and company's shoot-style angle became too real; their concerns over office politics were still genuine. The repercussions were to completely change the course of worked shoots.

First, in August 1983, several wrestlers attempted to seize control of the company, with the coup's failure seeing Satoru 'Tiger Mask' Sayama thrown out of New Japan. He responded by exposing the business in his infamous book 'Kayfabe'. Meanwhile, the remaining New Japan stars uncovered massive financial misbehaviour; the massive profits that should have been reflected in their payoffs had been diverted to support Inoki's failing businesses elsewhere.

Inoki being Inoki, he shifted the heat onto business partner Hishashi Shinma, who was unceremoniously given the boot. The angered Shinma decided revenge would best be served by starting his own company, the Universal Wrestling Federation, and basing his group around the young former karate star Akira Maeda. With Maeda on tour in the WWF at the time, Inoki got on the blower to Vince McMahon Sr, and Maeda found himself staring at the lights for such credible grapplers as George Steele.

On returning to Japan, joined in the UWF by New Japan's Yoshiaki Fujiwara and Nobuhiko Takada, an embittered Maeda decided he wanted to work a new style of wrestling: realistic, submission based, with no room for showmanship. In other words, the worked shoot. Shimna's traditionalist views earned him a spell on the dole, and Sayama was persuaded to return to the ring. With the UWF's stars condemning traditional pro wrestling as fake, the Tokyo hardcores bought the style hook, line and sinker.

(Back in New Japan, leading house show promoter Naoki Otsuja, angered with Inoki's business practices, got talking to Giant Baba, and on September 21st 1984 Choshu's brigade left to form their own promotion, Japan Pro Wrestling. Of course, it was part of a worked promotional feud, and the Ishin Gundan stars were soon in All Japan.)

The UWF failed to draw outside of Tokyo, mainly through a lack of television exposure, and Sayama moved into traditional martial arts, while the rest of the crew returned to New Japan in February 1986.

The natural dream match was soon signed, and Sumo Hall sold out in a matter of hours for Inoki vs Maeda. The Tokyo hardcores knew this one had to be for real as neither man would put the other over.

Unfortunately this was the exact truth of the matter. A finish couldn't be negotiated, and the bout was switched to a ten-man tag. The shooters vs wrestlers feud continued to draw well at the houses, with the former UWF workers most popular in Korakuen Hall among the hardcore fans, but the casual audience was less interested in the realistic style, and the television ratings dropped until New Japan's prime time slot was axed, banishing them to the early hours.

Between Inoki's refusal to step aside in favour of the more popular Maeda atop the promotion, and the return of Choshu in October 1987, Maeda soon grew disgruntled with his position. Much like the Bret Hart-Shawn Michaels situation, the office failed to keep matters under control, and matters came to a head with the infamous shoot-kick. On November 27th, Maeda threw a legitimate kick at Choshu during a six-man Korakuen Hall main event, shattering his orbital bone and removing him from the annual tag tournament.

Rather than publicly acknowledge Maeda's offence (which would effectively admit that New Japan's product was a work), management offered him two alternatives: go and work 'unrealistic' lucha in Mexico and then put Choshu over clean, or pack his bags. Maeda chose to reopen the UWF, taking Takada and others with him, and with television exposure having educated the mass audience to the new style, the promotion was a huge success.

The first UWF show, at Korakuen Hall on May 12th 1988, sold out in 15 minutes, with only one show in the next two years failing to sell out. The group peaked on November 29th 1989 for the U*Cosmos show at the Tokyo Dome, the first to sell out the Dome, including a record 40,000 tickets sold on the first day. The image that the UWF was the real deal was taken to a new level with an undercard bout pitting Yoji Anjoh against the historical footnote that was Campuir Davey. If the story that this was a token legitimate contest is true, it was the first in 35 years, with a 1954 June Byers vs Mildred Burke bout the last known pro-wrestling match without a predetermined finish.

Many of the UWF's biggest matches pitted Maeda against stars of other martial arts, such as Gerard Gordeau and Chris Dolman, in a rerun of Inoki's '70s bouts. Inoki himself opted to revitalise New Japan by bringing in Soviet amateur wrestlers for a series of bouts, including the first Tokyo Dome show on April 29th 1989. Once again, the worked shoot was successful, with fans falsely assuming that the Russian wrestlers would not be open to the concept of predetermined finishes.

The UWF's success led to the seemingly inevitable financial mismanagement, and the group fell apart in late 1990, leaving the workers to split off into their own groups. While Maeda formed the martial arts influenced RINGS, and Yoshiaki Fujiwara started PWF-G, it was Nobuhiko Takada's UWF International that had the quickest success.

With Takada regularly denouncing New Japan as fake, and scoring a much publicised victory over former boxing champion Trevor Berbick (which was actually a double-cross in the ring), the UWF-i product probably had the largest gullible audience in the history of worked shoots. Everyone from *Combat* magazine to my old landlord thought it was the real deal, while even Lou Thesz was temporarily persuaded that he was watching a competitive sport.

The façade took a serious knock in 1994 when the group's Yoji Anjoh hopped on a plane and turned up in Brazil at the training camp of Rickson Gracie, generally acknowledged as the world's leading legit fighter, and the older brother of Royce (who was by then a three time champion in the flourishing Ultimate Fighting Championships). The idea was simple: Anjoh would humiliate Gracie and cement UWF-i's (fraudulent) reputation. The problem was that Anjoh, to use a technical ju-jitsu term, got his ass handed to him on a plate. When Takada understandably failed to respond to his fans' pleas to avenge the beating, the emperor's new clothes were looking threadbare.

As per usual though, it was the accountants that eventually screwed things up, and a financially perilous UWF-i found itself taken over by New Japan, leading to the most successful worked shoot in history: Nobuhiko Takada vs Keiji Muto. 67,000 set a new gate record of $6 million for the first bout, and Takada became the biggest short term draw in history, selling out the Tokyo Dome three times in six months.

The most important development in worked shooting, though, rose from the ashes of the floundering PWF-G in 1993, when headliners Masakatsu Funaki and Minoru Suzuki, along with businessman (and former Weekly Pro writer) Masami Ozaki set up the Pancrase promotion, a product that rewrote the concept of pro wrestling.

Since its stunning September 21st 1993 debut, which saw six matches last a combined 13 minutes, Pancrase has taken an entirely different perspective on working and shooting. Instead of a worked product with a shooting influence, Pancrase is basically a legitimate sport, albeit with the tampering that is common with most sports.

Along with RINGS, where the work/shoot divide is often blurred, the element of working between competitors in Pancrase is most commonly in the form of an agreement to fight in a particular style or avoid working on an injured bodypart.

Like boxing, a proportion of matches are fixed for the benefit of the promoters (such as Ken Shamrock being asked to drop the group's title to Minoru Suzuki before risking the promotion's credibility in his Ultimate Fighting Championship bout with Dan Severn), but the essence of the sport is genuine competition.

Unfortunately true fighting does not make for a lengthy career, and this is why both Shamrock and Severn turned to full time professional wrestling with the WWF. Ironically their legitimate skills meant bookers felt neither man should take part in the promotion's failed foray into the world of shooting in 1998.

It's often said that Vince Russo fails to grasp the basics of the business of professional wrestling. No surprise then that he was later credited with the idea of the Brawl For All, an elimination tournament consisting of legitimate matches based on a mix of wrestling and boxing.

Although the matches did boost television ratings, the attempts to create new stars failed miserably. Five of the 16 competitors suffered injuries serious enough to end their WWF careers, and another six were dropped from the roster by the year's end.

Between the Brawl For All, and the use of legitimate fighters in Severn and Shamrock, the WWF never really served any useful purpose. There are, after all, three possible benefits to a worked shoot. The first, that the aura of reality will draw extra money from the fans and the press did not apply in the WWF: even the legitimate fighting of Brawl For All failed to appeal to crowds awaiting the latest in the McMahon-Austin soap opera. The other two benefits (that results can be manipulated to draw more money, and that matches can be worked to avoid serious injury) went out the window with Brawl For All.

(Despite the obligations on journalists to give fair and even-handed coverage, I think the less said about Tank Abbot and WCW the better.)

Had the worked shoot taken off in the WWF, it seems most likely that Shamrock vs Severn would have been the big climax, with an attempt to capture the normally dismissive mixed martial arts audience. Ironically both men would play bit parts in the course of Japan's next major angle.

When Shamrock signed for the WWF in 1997, it came as something of a shock to New Japan staff who had been under the impression he would make his professional wrestling return in their rings. Such a strong impression, in fact, that they had already booked a second Tokyo Dome date of the year and announced him as the opponent for IWGP champion Shinya Hashimoto.

To solve the problem, booker Riki Choshu took a look through the sports pages and asked directory enquiries for the number of Olympic judo silver medallist and national sports hero Naoya Ogawa. A non-title victory for the Ogawa at the Dome and a victorious rematch for Hashimoto in Osaka later and Choshu was depositing the best part of $10 million in New Japan's savings account.

Meanwhile, our old friend Takada was finding fewer and fewer opportunities to scam the public, and in October of 1997 he took the only logical step: a legitimate fight against Rickson Gracie on the first show of new shootfighting group PRIDE. 37,000 of the Takada faithful saw their hero destroyed in under five minutes.

A rematch a year later saw Gracie turn down a virtual blank cheque to 'do business' and another huge crowd saw Takada's myth exposed again. After that match, Takada appeared five more times for the group, a blend of painful defeats and worked victories. Oddly enough, the shoot matches greatly outdrew the works; either more of the old UWF-I fans lost interest with each defeat, or they simply saw through the scam of his unconvincing wins. Either way, Takada's last hurrah was a convincing defeat by Royce Gracie last January, and after one last kicking in October he hung up his boots.

While PRIDE has been tremendously successful through its pro wrestling style hype and promotion, it has been the intrigue of legitimate fights that has kept the company strong. The moral of the Nobuhiko Takada story is a simple one: false claims of fighting superiority can only draw money until somebody calls your bluff.

But while Takada was relying on hype in a world of reality, the complete opposite held true in New Japan with the century's last great 'shoot angle'. Shortly before the 1999 edition of the annual January Tokyo Dome show, officials announced Shinya Hashimoto would be suspended after the event. His crime? Complaining to reporters that an upcoming tournament would detract from the annual G1 Climax series.

Observers noted this as a little baffling, but put it to the back of their minds as they watched Hashimoto and Ogawa compete at the Dome in their first match since 1997. What followed was an Ogawa buttkicking that looked extremely realistic, and for good reason. Inoki had helped cook up a plan where the two would fight for real until Hashimoto gave the signal that he could take no more. And to add to the fun, as Jeremy Beadle would say, most of the New Japan crew wasn't in on the joke.

With the attention that followed, the American Monday night bookers would probably have followed with a series of replicas and variations of the theme leading up to a fraudulent retirement stipulation. Funnily enough that's just what happened, only with a little more patience on Inoki's part.

The pair were kept well apart with Hashimoto returning to New Japan later in the year and Ogawa concentrating on the worked shoot promotion UFO, owned by one A. Inoki. On the group's first major show in March at the Tokyo Dome, Ogawa won the NWA title from Dan Severn.

Inoki then called in a few favours and persuaded the NWA directors to approve a title change to Hashimoto in the big rematch. However, New Japan decided they didn't really want one of their big stars taking off every time Dennis Coraluzzo could afford a plane ticket and booking fee so, on 11 October, Ogawa again beat Hashimoto in the Tokyo Dome. The finish was again an 'impromptu' stoppage, this time with Inoki running into the ring in a throwback to a legendary legitimate incident between our old friend Akira Maeda and Andre the Giant.

The next clash between the two came in a tag match at the January 2000 Dome show where Hashimoto's partner Takashi Iizuka beat Ogawa's team-mate Kazunari Murakami. The match, which was worked to resemble a legitimate contest, drew a strong television rating, based largely on its lack of resemblance to traditional wrestling.

But that was nothing compared to the sixth and 'final' meeting between the two, again at the Tokyo Dome in April. The bout drew an incredible 34 million viewers on live television, many of whom were shocked when Hashimoto lost and announced his 'retirement'.

The worked shoot requires a paying public with enough sophistication to perceive a difference between the worked shoot and the traditional wrestling product. But that public must lack the intuition to realise the match they desire is just a more realistic drama.

Considering many fans were unconvinced by even a legitimate product like Brawl For All, the worked shoot seems unlikely to be a moneyspinner in the United States.

But in Japan, the old saying that 'promoters push what they know' means that as long as the likes of Inoki and Choshu have their fingers in the promotional pie, the blurry line between work and shoot will help the crystal-clear line between profit and loss.

The death of the sheets (*Moonsault Xtra*, July 2000)

There aren't many areas where a 23 year old could be a grizzled veteran, but the world of wrestling writing is one of them. It's scary to realise, but this final issue of *Moonsault* coincides with the 10th anniversary of the first piece I had published in a wrestling magazine, the long forgotten *Spiked Piledriver*. This was a big affair, 60 A4 pages with the then-controversial selling point of refusing to use ring-names and referring constantly to 'Bossman' Bubba Rogers and 'Undertaker' Mark Callous. Ahem. For what it's worth, we outsold the WWF magazine in our local shops, though our sales outside Stevenage could be counted on one hand of an unfortunate leper.

Something that shows how this business had changed over the years came a few months later in the summer of 1991. Just as our quarterly magazine was going to press, our 'sources' (in other words, Wrestlecall, 39 pence a minute to hear somebody read the front page of the *Observer* but protecting kayfabe) informed us that Ric Flair had quit WCW. I'm proud to say that, just three weeks or so after it happened, we had a stop press sheet in the magazine with the important news that Lex Luger had beaten Barry Windham for the vacant world title.

How times change. Now, not only is the idea that a title change was important somewhat laughable, but you can get Battlarts results live from Japan on a mobile phone (possible the worst use of new technology I've ever made).

I hope this doesn't sound too much like a science fiction novel, but it seems fair to say in this look back at wrestling newsletters that technology has played a big part in the boom and collapse of the British sheet scene. Desktop publishing helped many of us veterans (there I go again!) to produce newsletters with a professional look relatively simply. Anyone who has seen the early editions of Glen Radford's *Piledriver* (which launched in 1988) with its stencilled headlines and typewriter text with Biro amendments will know what a difference computers made.

Back in the early '90s though, the only time 'the web' was mentioned was in Brad 'Arachnaman' Armstrong's squash matches. (Yes, the Road Dogg's brother once had the gimmick of a human spider. No, it didn't work.) Since then, the Internet may not have changed the world forever, but it's sure told a lot of people a few secrets about the world of professional; wrestling. When Rob Butcher launched *Suckerpunch* in 1993, he had to decide whether or not to write the magazine on the premise that pro wrestling was not a legitimate contest. Back then it was actually an issue. Feeling old yet?

The difference, and what I now consider a major reason why the sheets have largely died out, is that discovering the inner workings of the wrestling business was once a voyage of discovery. Fans would uncover the secrets step by step. You certainly didn't go down your local cinema and see Rock and Mankind planning a finish. By learning gradually how the business worked, the 'smart' fans of the 90s grew to appreciate the profession more, rather than coming straight in with the idea that it was all just a show. Why read speculation about the backstage dealings of the industry when the promotions are virtually forcing reality down your throat? What chance does a newsletter stand when you can read all the same 'inside' information in *RAW* magazine... and get some hot pictures of scantily-clad women too?

The nature of the Internet affects the sheets in other ways too. One is the sheer speed of news. The idea that electronic media would kill off newspapers has been proved false, but newspapers are part of our daily culture. When it comes to the relatively closed world of wrestling, timeliness and print just don't go together. Nowadays, a new WCW champion wouldn't just be old news by the next issue of a weekly magazine; he would probably be an ex-champion.

There's also the sheer scale of the web. There is more wrestling information available on-line than anybody could ever hope to read. It's like walking into a newsagent that stretches as far as the eye can see and being told that you never have to pay for anything. Quite frankly most of us old hacks spend so much time trying to keep up to date, we never have a moment to step back and write anything anymore.

And that, perhaps even more than new technology, is the reason the sheets have trickled away. We are at or just past the biggest peak this business has ever seen. It's no coincidence that the heyday of newsletters in Britain was the mid-90s: the last wrestling recession. We are all devoting pretty much the same amount of time to the business as then, but in different ways. Waiting for an ECW tape to come through the post was once an exciting event. Now a fan with a satellite dish can see ECW every week, not to mention WCW on TCM and Channel 5 and the WWF on Sky and Channel 4. In a WWF pay-per-view week, you are looking at something like 16 hours of first-run television a week. Add in on-line radio shows, daily news updates on the web, a couple of hours reading the *Observer* and there's not much time left over for journalism. And can you really show that much interest in Japan, Mexico and the indies when you hardly ever get a chance to watch the tapes?

Still, we shouldn't mourn the sheets too much. After all, we newsletter veterans have got pretty much everything er ever dreamt of. We can hear wrestlers discussing the business in-depth every night of the week. We can get ECW pay-per-views within a few days of the show. We can tune into Sky and see Benoit vs Guerrero on regular TV. We can even get Battlarts results on a mobile phone.

When it comes to the death of the British sheets, I can only quote my dear old Mum: "In my day, we had to make our own entertainment."

Who killed WCW? (*Wrestling's Last Hope*, September 2001)

(For a year or so I was the guest 'letter-answerer' in Wrestling's Last Hope. *I thought this was an interesting example as it is a rare objective look at the finances behind the greatest personality-led whodunnit of our time.)*

Dear WLH

I wonder if Mr Lister could let us know who was really responsible for the WCW collapse. Everyone I argue with has an idea of which angles were worst, but we need some actual figures to settle the argument.

I think Russo did an OK job of salvaging the company, but it was in such a mess by his two runs that nobody could do anything to help it.

Yours
Tim Perry
Boston, Lincs

Dear Tim

It's probably impossible to do any kind of analysis of WCW without the finger pointing, but we'll give it a try.

We need to look at the business overall, so our best bet is to use the figures the *Observer* published each month. Now the WWF business is split pretty much evenly between TV revenue, house shows, merchandise and PPV. With WCW, TV ratings play a slightly larger role as all the advertising revenue went to WCW's owners, while WWF gets part of its TV money as a set fee.

I'll take the following set of three indicators from which to work our business levels:

Monday *Nitro* average ratings. I would prefer ratings for all WCW shows, but that would be too much number crunching for us to handle.

House show average paid crowds. Probably better to use the number of people rather than the money total as this is affected by the ticket prices. In most wrestling cases, the ticket price has far less effect on the number of people going to shows that the general level of interest in the company does. The number of people prepared to pay for house shows probably has a fair relationship with merchandise sales: both represent people prepared to pay for the product rather than just watch on TV.

PPV buyrates. Again, counting actual revenues would be affected by the price changes, but the number of buys tends to be more reflective of the interest in the product.

Next we need to decide timeframes. The company's peak in all areas was 1998, during which Eric Bischoff was in control of the product. We'll take the following eras from that point on and compare each with its predecessor:

1998: Eric Bischoff
January 1999-September 1999: Kevin Nash leads a committee.
October 1999-January 2000: Vince Russo produces the show.
February 2000-March 2000: Kevin Sullivan and company take charge.
April 2000-September 2000: Russo returns (with Bischoff in management).
October 2000-March 2001: A committee takes life support duties.

This is of course a little crude as the changes in control do not perfectly match the beginnings of each month. However, it seems to work out pretty fairly as, for example, Russo gets credit for Hallowe'en Havoc 99 (which he booked on the night but had little involvement in the promotion of the event), but also gets the blame for Souled Out 2000 (which he promoted but left before the show took place.)

The results, showing percentage changes compared to each person's predecessor, are as follows.

In Charge / **H**ouse Shows / **TV** ratings / **PPV** / **O**verall business / Overall business **A**verage per month

Nash (compared with Bischoff)/ **H** -14.6 / **T** -13.8 / **P** -35.8 / **O** -21.4 / **A** -2.3

Russo (compared with Nash)/ **H** -27.8 / **T** -19.7 / **P** -35.5 / **O** -27.6 / **A** -6.9

Sullivan (compared with Russo)/ **H** -41.2 / **T** -11.1 / **P** -63.1 / **O** -38.4 / **A** -19.2

Russo II(compared with Sullivan)/ **H** -7.7 / **T** +0.9 / **P** +35.6 / **O** +9.4 / **A** +1.56

Committee (compared with Russo II)/ **H** -7.8 / **T** -16.9 / **P** -31.5 / **O** -18.7 / **A** -3.11

From this we can draw several conclusions.

* The rot truly started during Nash's reign. Clearly the abortion of Goldberg's push and the return to the same old characters began to hurt.

* Russo's first reign actually sped up the decline. In particular, his reign hurt house shows very quickly, perhaps the result of hotshotting on TV.

* The brief Sullivan reign took an incredible chunk out of what was left of the business. It is probably fair to say that the loss of Bret Hart (to retirement), Goldberg (to injury) and Benoit & company (to the WWF) had a very dramatic effect in early 2000. Who deserves the blame for these various losses is open to question.

* The second Russo run overall picked up some of the slack from Sullivan and represented the only upswing of any kind after 1998. However, his figures still compared poorly to his own previous performance, so it was simply a case of stemming the flow. With only a slightly smaller TV audience than he had the first time round, Russo's second reign saw much smaller house show crowds and PPV buyrates. Artistically he came back strong with the New Bloods vs Millionaires Club angle which gave the focus to the promotion that was lacking under Sullivan. But the follow-up failed to draw money outside of TV.

One possible conclusion is that the tactics Russo used to drive up TV ratings were not those which were best for turning TV interest into house show and PPV business.

* Finally, under the post-Russo committee, figures slid back to at, or just below, where Sullivan left off. It's probably a safe bet that the audience left at this point was the WCW hardcore contingent, which would not give up on the company under any circumstances. Had the sale to Fusient Media gone through, the only sensible strategy would have been concentrating on getting a greater percentage of this core audience to spend money on house shows and PPVs.

As for who really deservers the blame, there are dozens of candidates, but ultimately Bischoff was the man in charge during the glory years of 1996-1998, and it was under his watch that Nash and pals were able to start the road to ruin in 1999. Bischoff may have got the company to the top of the mountain, but he was also there when it started rolling downhill. Those that followed may have helped or hindered the decline, but the momentum was already there.

I love 1994 (*Wrestling's Last Hope*, December 2001)

You'll be pleased to know this column does not feature Kate Thornton's rentaquote utterings. Neither does it feature Jamie Theakston's memories of a childhood that mysteriously seems to have run for 30 years. But if I were on BBC 2 on a Saturday night, I'd be telling the viewers how I love 1994.

Writing in a snatched moment between work, sleep and general adulthood, I long for the year when I turned 18. The year of lower and upper sixth form, with the euphemistically titled 'study periods', most of which were spent with Matt Brannigan at my house watching wrestling tapes, or catching the train to London to hang about hotel lobbies waiting for Jeff Jarrett to ignore us.

Whatever the state of the product, 1994 was always going to be a glorious year to be a hardcore wrestling fan. It was the year where Rob Butcher's Suckerpunch was, while not the first insider sheet in the UK, was the first to feature widespread reader participation. It was the year that the tape trading scene took off, with Rob and Glen Radford making it into a full-time business.

It was also the year that we launched Hulk Who? fanzine and began our journey into the mysterious concept that pro wrestling might not be on the level, and that there was an even more fascinating story beyond what Bill Apter told us.

It was the year when, for my 18th birthday, I was offered the choice between a shit-hot video recorder or driving lessons. Needless to say I still take the bus. And come the glorious day I entered adulthood, I tried out my new machine's Video Plus feature by taping Eurosport's wrestling show. Expecting to see the usual edition of Challenge with Ted DiBiase providing vague commentary to avoid local references, you can imagine my joy at seeing Jushin Liger in the first episode of New Japan wrestling.

But most of all, 1994 was the year when wrestling rocked. In the WWF, it took just six men to make a year. The various combinations of Bret & Owen Hart, Shawn Michaels, Diesel, Razor Ramon and the 1-2-3 Kid made for excitement on every major show. Chuck in a good year for Jeff Jarrett, the underrated Quebecers and the last decent performances from Marty Jannetty and the dire undercards were easily worth sitting through.

Over in WCW, Ric Flair had the book for the first few months of the year. As the old saying goes, there was something for everyone. Flair, Steamboat and Austin with the science. Regal and Anderson on the mat. The Nasty Boys, Cactus, Maxx Payne & Kevin Sullivan brawling from the heart. Rude & Sting still on top form. Pillman and Johnny B. Badd duelling with highspots and Vader & the Boss duelling with their fists. Hell, Dustin Rhodes didn't suck all the time.

Then Hogan came to town.

ECW became the sight to see. The undercards may have been over-hyped, but with Cactus vs Sabu, the Public Enemy and the Funks, Benoit & Malenko taking on the Tasmaniac, Douglas and Funk making it look oh so real, 911 and Mikey Whipwreck becoming cult heroes and Santa going down to the chokeslam, it was clear the business had an extreme future.

As far away from ECW as you could get, but just as engrossing, was Jim Cornette's Smoky Mountain. Sure the no-shows and failed angles began to bite, but you had the Heavenly Bodies, the Rock 'n' Rolls and the Moondogs. You had cake at TV tapings. You had embarrassing music videos with Storm & Jericho. You had Jake Roberts interviews. You had 'fans' using a camcorder to film themselves getting an autograph from the Thrillseeker just so there would be a logical reason for a camera being present for a Heavenly Bodies sneak attack. You even had Bob Armstrong and Jim Cornette in a feud with such a detailed history that it took 45 minutes to recap.

It was the year that the Ultimate Fighting Championship answered all the questions about what real wrestling would look like. Royce Gracie became the unstoppable star. Dan Severn became the man who almost stopped him, while showing what a real suplex was supposed to look like.

AAA caught fire, becoming one of the biggest draws in the United States before running a pay-per-view that defied WCW management's piss-poor promotion and petty attempts at sabotage. Chris Benoit's bout was the worst of the show. In the last match of his life, Art Barr teamed with Eddy Guerrero to work the definitive example of a perfect match with El Hijo Del Santo and Octagon. Konnan didn't suck as much as usual.

And then there was Japan.

US trader Bob Barnett cottoned on to the idea of the Best of Japan TV tapes. Each month you'd get every match that mattered from the country, with perhaps a couple of US indy spectaculars and some UFC highlights to round it off. And what a year to do it in.

All Japan's Triple Crown main events were state of the art. Hansen vs Kawada in the Championship Carnival final, Kawada's title challenge to Misawa in the first match Rob Butcher ever rated as *****+, Misawa dropping the belt to Williams, Williams defending against Kobashi and Kawada taking the strap from Williams. It's unlikely any company will ever have five major matches in a row of such quality.

New Japan's heavyweights may have been lacking in comparison, but it was the year of the juniors. The Super J Cup swept the board for show of the year. If you haven't seen it, just imagine Sasuke, Liger, Hayabusa, Taka Michinoku, Benoit, Malenko, Guerrero, Ohtani, Delfin and Samurai in one tournament. Then came the Top of the Super Junior tournament with Delfin getting the super-push. And to round the year off you had the Super Junior Tag League with Sasuke & Guerrero vs Benoit and Ohtani so much fun they did it twice.

Elsewhere FMW was violence at its best, WAR vs New Japan made for some classic 8-man junior bouts, and the women managed the minor matter of a 42,000 crowd for a ten hour show with 15 matches at ***1/2 or more.

Yes, I love 1994. In fact the only part of that year that truly blew was Johnny South doing a rip-off of the LOD gimmick in the halls of Great Britain. But some things never change…

Jim Barnett (*Pro Wrestling Press*, April 2002)

Ask many fans to name the most influential men in the history of wrestling and a few names will come up again and again: Frank Gotch and George Hackenschmidt, Strangler Lewis and Toots Mondt, Lou Thesz and Sam Muchnick, Andre the Giant, Ric Flair, Vince McMahon and Hulk Hogan, Rikidozan, Inoki and Baba, Steve Austin. But mention the name 'Jim Barnett' to most fans and you will be met with a bemused stare.

Yet in a 40 year career Jim Barnett played a key role in developments that shaped the wrestling business as we know it, from the growth and death of the territories to the emergence of national companies coining it in from pay-per-view television.

After earning a masters degree in business studies, Barnett started in pro wrestling in the mid-1950s as an assistant to Chicago promoter Fred Kohler (who later promoted the famed Buddy Rogers-Pat O'Connor NWA title match in Comiskey Park). Working with Kohler allowed Barnett to learn from legendary promoters, including Vince McMahon Sr and San Francisco's Roy Shire. Televised wrestling had just started to take off, and Barnett's business skills helped Kohler cash in by securing a $100,000 contract to produce a show for a Chicago station.

Within a couple of years though, television coverage of wrestling had reached the inevitable saturation point, and gates were dropping across the country when fans realised they could watch shows live in the comfort of their homes rather than go to arenas. In 1955 Barnett, then working in Indianapolis, stumbled across the solution by accident. One week the local station was unable to transport the production equipment to the arena. Barnett took the practical approach and set up a ring in the television studio itself. It suddenly dawned on him that not only could he produce a better looking show under these conditions, but he did not need to give away the arena experience for free. From here it was a simple step towards using the TV show as a weekly taster designed specifically to promote live events. Studio wrestling, the heart of the American wrestling business for the next 30 years, was born.

In 1959, Barnett took the business of TV wrestling to the next step when he began promoting in Detroit with Johnny Doyle. Until this point, most promotional work for wrestling simply came through the old "I'm better than you" interview. But in one of Barnett and Doyle's early shows, they ran a match with Angelo Poffo (father of Randy Savage) and Wilbur Snyder. The match saw the referee knocked unconscious, missing a pin by the babyface Snyder. Manager Bronco Lubich jumped in the ring, knocked out Snyder, and revived the referee to count the pin. All run of the mill today, but at the time it was one of the first major televised angles, and it paid off big time. A rematch at Detroit's Olympia Stadium sold 16,226 seats, and the company went on to average 10,000 a show over the next five years.

While Barnett and Doyle found success expanding the territory, and even promoting as far afield as Denver, they didn't make the mistake of waiting until business hit a stale patch. Instead, in October 1964, they moved to Australia, where television was just taking off. Repeating their earlier successes, they made the *Big Time Wrestling* show an institution on TV, and drew large crowds under the 'World Championship Wrestling' promotional banner. They soon gained a reputation for paying good guarantees to American wrestlers coming in for tours. One such visit was by the 'Hardliners' team of mouthy badass heel Dick Murdoch and his quiet but deadly partner Dusty Rhodes. Barnett had other ideas, and suggested Rhodes should be the mouthpiece of the team. It's safe to say the idea caught on…

Doyle returned to the United States in 69, but Barnett hung on until the end of 1973, selling the promotion to wrestlers Larry O'Day (who, for you trivia fans, appeared at Clash of the Champions 20 in the NWA tag tournament) and Ron Miller, who predictably based the group around themselves and just as predictably saw business drop off heavily.

Barnett's next step was Georgia, where the NWA cartel's Paul Jones and Lester Welch (better known as Buddy Fuller, father of WCW's Colonel Rob Parker) had just won a bitter promotional war with Ann Gunkel, whose husband Ray (a wrestler and stockholder in the promotion) had died in 1972. Once the war was won (amid rumours that Barnett had bankrolled booker Tom 'Assassin' Renesto as a mole in the Gunkel promotion) Welch decided to return to promoting in Florida. He sold his stock to Jim Barnett, and Jones did the same in 1978 to leave Barnett in control.

Barnett helped make Georgia into one of the strongest territories in the country, helped greatly by the promotion's success as it's Saturday evening programme became the top rated show on Atlanta's channel 17. This station, owned by a young media mogul named Ted Turner, was beamed across the country by satellite (making Georgia the most watched promotion around), and would eventually become the cable 'superstation' TBS. Barnett's power in the NWA saw him serve as the Alliance's company secretary in the late 70s, playing a key role in the annual conventions. He was also put in charge of booking the NWA champion's appearances, though any title changes had to be approved the Alliance's board of directors.

Perhaps his best known action during this spell came in 1981 when young babyface Tommy Rich somehow upset Harley Race and held the world title for four days. What really happened here is a mystery and the subject of many rumours. The double title switch was barely mentioned outside the area and it is not certain the NWA board had approved it. Among the apparent urban myths that surround this incident are the story that Race was made to drop the title as punishment for undisclosed misconduct, and that the homosexual Barnett arranged the title in return for certain favours by Rich. The most likely explanation is that Race, knowing Ric Flair was soon to become the main attraction in the NWA, wanted to tie Lou Thesz' record of six title reigns. That Barnett chose to put the belt on Rich of all people may have been an attempt to test just how much power he truly had within the organisation.

His control eventually ran out when his booker Ole Anderson persuaded the company's management to oust Barnett from power. It proved to be the spark to a momentous change in the industry. In late 1983, as Anderson was eyeing the opportunity to expand his territory across the country with the backing of the TBS show, first one and then another of his top stars disappeared. The likes of Tito Santana, Paul Orndorff, Brian Blair, Tony Atlas and Masked Superstar each had their own reason to be away, Japanese tours being a popular excuse, but all of a sudden they were showing up on Vince McMahon Jr's WWF television shows. And wouldn't you know, Jim Barnett had somehow wound up working in McMahon's office.

Barnett's experience in television proved extremely helpful as he carried out most of the work that transformed the wrestling industry as the WWF approached local stations across the country (most famously in St Louis) and offered a sweet deal. Instead of selling programming, the WWF was willing to pay to get on air, banking on the increased exposure making back the money through nationwide house shows.

Anderson might have had a shot in a race to go national, but he had forgotten one thing: Barnett still held stock in the company. This, and an offer that couldn't be refused to fellow stockholders Jack and Jerry Brisco, was enough to give the company, and more importantly the television slot, to McMahon. Anderson started his own promotion, persuading Ted Turner to add an early Saturday morning slot on TBS, but in March of 1985 he sold the promotion to Jim Crockett of Mid-Atlantic. The WWF's comparatively poor ratings on TBS caused problems with the station, and a month after buying out Anderson, Crockett paid McMahon a rumoured £1 million for the timeslot.

Once McMahon had firmly established himself as the number one national promoter, Barnett's role became less prominent and, in 1987, he was persuaded to jump to Crockett, now by far the dominant faction of the NWA, having bought up promotions in St Louis, Kansas, Florida and Bill Watt's Mid South/UWF territory. Barnett arrived with news that McMahon was planning to sabotage Crockett's first PPV (Starrcade '87) by running a head to head show (what turned out to be the Survivor Series.) The tip-off allowed Crockett to try to salvage the event by switching it to the afternoon but, as we covered in issue 2, Vince pulled a power-play with the cable companies leaving Starrcade as good as dead.

The loss of these PPV receipts, along with falling advertising revenue when ratings collapsed under Dusty Rhodes' legendary poor booking year in 1988 meant Crockett was unable to pay the huge guaranteed salaries he had offered to stop his stars jumping to the WWF. He faced bankruptcy and Barnett took on yet another history changing role, heading the negotiations to sell the company to Ted Turner.

Barnett worked for what became WCW for the next seven years, primarily in the syndication department, persuading local stations to carry WCW programming, but also having a hand in the various booking committees that sprang up. (With Jim Herd, Jim Crockett and

Jim Ross also on the committees, things may have got confusing). He was eventually released from the company in 1995 when Eric Bischoff began cutting back on expenses and syndication had become a far smaller priority.

Since then Barnett has attended several high-profile independent shows as a guest of honour but has otherwise been largely forgotten as the man whose career shaped much of wrestling as we know it today.

A history of British wrestling (*Pro Wrestling Press*, May 2002)

The idea that wrestling might attract paying crowds first caught on in Britain at the turn of the 20th century thanks to music hall promoters, who put together a variety act with everything from song and dance to what we now know as stand-up comedy. One of the biggest attractions was the bodybuilder strongman, with Eugene Sandow the main star. However, the limited action involved soon meant the gimmick wore thin.

Wrestling first caught on through a Cornish-American ex-miner named Jack Carkeek who would move from theatre to theatre challenging audience members to last 10 minutes with him. His bluff was called one night in London's Alhambra theatre (now Leicester Square Odeon), when the Russian George Hackenschmidt, fresh off a major tournament win in Paris' Folies-Bergere Palace, answered the challenge. Knowing of Hackenschmidt's reputation as Europe's leading Greco-Roman grappler, Carkeek quickly came up with the excuse that his challenge applied to Englishmen only.

On hearing of the incident, promoter and entrepreneur Charles B Cochran took Hackenschmidt under his wing, persuading the Daily Mail newspaper to write a prominent leader article on the Russian titled 'Is Strength Genius?'

After defeating top British wrestler Tom Cannon for the European Greco-Roman title in Liverpool on 4 September 1902 (giving him a credible claim to the world title, cemented in 1905 with a win over Tom Jenkins in the US), Hackenschmidt took a series of bookings in Manchester for a then impressive £150 a week. Noting that his dominant wrestling threatened to kill crowd interest, Cochran persuaded Hackenschmidt to learn showmanship from Cannon and wrestle many of his matches for entertainment rather than sport. One gimmick would see 'Schackmann', a German wrestler using every heel trick in the book, lose a hard-fought match to Hackenschmidt. Another involved Hackenschmidt deliberately allowing his challenger to survive a 10 minute challenge and collect a £25 prize, only to legitimately beat them with ease in a rematch once unsuspecting punters had bet on the challenger.

All that was needed now was a legitimate major challenger, and Ahmed Madrali, one of the few genuine 'Terrible Turks' fitted the bill. Madrali's manager Antonio Pietti upheld the tradition of wrestling promoters by raking in around £100 a week but paid Madrali just £5.

The big day came on 30 January 1904, with a legitimate payoff of £1000 for the winner and £500 to the loser. The stories of the time tell of a jam-packed London Olympia, with traffic held-up throughout the West End. The match itself proved memorable, if hardly the gruelling war that might have been expected. As the opening bell rang, Hackenschmidt charged towards Madrali, picked him up and slammed him straight on his arm, either breaking it or separating the shoulder. The popular story among fans after the event was to claim to have dropped a match at the opening bell, bent over to pick it up, and then sat up to find the match had already finished.

Hackenschmidt soon departed for the United States and was replaced as the main attraction by Stanislaus Zbyszko in 1907, the Pole playing a heel role. One particular promotional scam would see a boisterous Scotsman march into the matinee performance at a rival theatre in the town where a match was scheduled, demanding Zbyszko come out and fight him. The theatre's manager would invariably correct his 'mistake' and unwittingly promote the evening's wrestling show to his entire audience.

The following year saw the beginning of the decline of wrestling in Britain after a match pitting Zbyszko against Ivan Padoubney of Russia ended with Padoubney disqualified at the 20 minute mark for repeated use of elbows and backhands. The crowd, which expected Zbyszko to get his comeuppance, drew the conclusion that the match was fixed. Interest in the sport wasn't helped when the news came through that the much-admired Hackenschmidt had failed in his attempt to defeat Frank Gotch in Chicago. There are also stories of 1910 match at Crystal Palace going to a deathly-dull four and a half hours. In any case, the absence of credible and entertaining big name draws meant the business was already in decline when the outbreak of war in 1914 halted proceedings.

With Greco-Roman still the preferred style, wrestling as a promotional business didn't seem to catch on in the 1920s until word came from the

United States of the success of a combination of gimmickry and using submission holds to liven up matches. Sir Atholl Oakley, a wrestler of the time, writes in his autobiography that he was first inspired to being promoting the new style of wrestling after a colleague, Ben Sherman, beat him in a gentlemanly tussle on the lawn of his mansion one Saturday night, putting him away with a submission hold at the thirty minute mark. Literary licence aside, Oakley did get together with fellow grappler Henry Irslinger and launch what he coined 'All-in' wrestling. On 15 December 1930 Irslinger fought Yugoslav Modrich at Olympia, London, while Oakley took on Bert Assirati at Belle Vue, Manchester the same night.

Needless to say, Oakley would later claim his wrestling was entirely legitimate, with no hint of impropriety in the business until after he retired. Oddly enough, promoter Oakley soon beat Welshman Bill Garnon to become the first British heavyweight champion. If nothing else, the fact that business took off to the extent that many wrestlers were working twice a day shows that wrestling was by that point firmly established as purely business, albeit one where legitimate amateur credentials were part of the job requirement.

Under the British Wrestling Association banner, Oakley's promotion took off with the likes of Tommy Mann, Black Butcher Johnson, Jack Pye, Norman Ansell (Norman the Butcher), College Boy and Jack Sherry on the roster, along with a man named Leonard Abbey, who wrestled as Jack Dale, and would go on to play a key role in the business after the war.

One of the famed 'insider' stories of the time came when Jack Pye met Bert Assirati in what was billed as a supreme grudge match. The pair had agreed to draw the match one fall apiece, but immediately after getting his opening fall, Pye loudly complained the referee was biased and walked out of the match, leaving Assirati the technical winner, but Pye the victor in the crowd's eyes.

Business was going great for a while, with the best part of forty regular venues in London alone, and crowds of up to 14,000. Indeed, if you choose to believe Oakley's recollection, two million people watched a four match show as part of the celebrations when the Graf Zeppelin airship visited Heathrow Airport. It is perhaps worth bearing in mind that Oakley also claimed to have performed what we now know as a headscissor takedown on an opponent that stood over nine feet tall.

Unfortunately the great demand for wrestling meant there weren't enough skilled amateurs to go around, and many promoters switched to a more violent style, with weapons and chairshots part of the proceedings. In the late 1930s, the London County Council banned pro wrestling, leaving the business in rough shape just before the second world war.

Attempts to relaunch the business in 1947 failed to catch on, with a major show at London's Haringey Arena featuring Ireland's Jack Doyle knocking out the Estonian 'Bucth' leaving journalists condemning the gimmickry and as good as calling the show a fake.

The 'shock' of this revelation prompted Admiral Lord Mountevans, a fan of the sport, to get together with Commander Campbell (a member of the popular 'Brains Trust' radio panel show), member of parliament Maurice Webb and Olympic wrestler Norman Morell to create a committee to produce official rules for good clean honest wrestling. They also created seven formal weight divisions: lightweight (154 pound limit), welterweight (165), middleweight (176), heavy middleweight (187), light heavyweight (198), mid-heavyweight (209), and heavyweight, calling for champions to be crowned at each weight.

The various promoters smiled very sweetly and got on with their business, using the committee's existence solely as a counter to any accusations of funny business. Instead, the business was revolutionised by the promoters themselves. Just four years after the formation of the NWA in the United States, a similar idea was adopted in 1952 with the launch of Joint Promotions. Officially this was an alliance of promoters attempting to regulate the sport and uphold the Mountevans committee's honourable ideas. In reality, it was a promotional cartel designed to carve up control of the business between a handful of promoters, and it did so with ruthless efficiency.

The group was represented in London by the Dale Martin promotion, which had incorporated in 1948, and involved Les Martin, and Jackie, Johnny and Billy Abbey, who worked as the Dales. Other promoters included Norman Morell and Ted Beresford in Yorkshire, Billy Best in Liverpool, Arthur Wright in Manchester and George de Relywyskow in

Scotland, with Arthur Green the secretary of the group. By agreeing to rotate talent, and block out rival promoters, Joint was soon running 40 shows a week.

The financial advantages of this arrangement helped the members survive the tough conditions caused by a post-war tax that took 25% of all entertainment revenue. Other promoters were not so successful. The closure of Haringey Arena in 1954 was the last straw for Atholl Oakley, and Joint Promotions were the only major player left to benefit when Chancellor Peter Thorneycroft abolished the entertainment tax in the 1957 budget.

At this point the only independent promoter of any real note was Paul Lincoln, who survived on a shoestring budget, working his own main events as the masked 'Dr Death'. The Joint stranglehold also spelt bad news for Bert Assirati, whose hardman reputation had him marked down as a troublemaker. He held the group's heavyweight title in 1955 but quit without dropping the belt the following year. Such was his confidence, he even showed up in the audience in a December 1957 show at the Royal Albert Hall and issued a grandstand challenge to the visiting Lou Thesz; Dale Martin promoters and security staff made sure Assirati never had the chance to test his reputation.

One of Joint Promotions' first moves was establishing (and controlling) the titles called for by the Mountevans committee. At first this proved a profitable venture, with title matches leading to raised ticket prices. However, perhaps inevitably, attempts to extend this success by bringing in additional titles led to overexposure. While the World and British titles had some credibility (particularly as they were often placed on the more legitimate wrestlers), the addition of European, Empire/ Commonwealth, Scottish, Welsh, and area championships got out of hand, and at one point there were conceivably 70 different titleholders to keep track of within Joint Promotions alone.

But while titles had some success, it was television that took British wrestling to the next level. The first show aired on ABC and ATV (the regional forerunners to ITV) on 9 November 1955, featuring Francis St Clair Gregory (father of Tony St Clair) vs Mike Marino and Cliff Beaumont vs Bert Royal live from West Ham baths. The show was successful, and wrestling became a featured attraction each Saturday afternoon from Autumn to Spring each year. In 1964 it went full-time as part of the new World of Sport show, running from 4pm to 4.45, just before the full time football results. It also had several runs on Wednesday evenings in the 60s and 70s (eventually being replaced by late night football highlights.)

To think of televised wrestling at this time in today's terms is misleading. The shows featured nothing more than two or three matches. There were no storylines. A ten second soundbite before the commercial break was the extent of the wrestlers' vocal contributions, and that only appeared in the 1980s. Commentator Kent Walton's softly spoken style was a gentle backdrop rather than the voice of hype. Indeed, there was barely a hint of promotion for live wrestling shows.

What television did for British wrestling was to make the performers household names. When wrestling started on television, there were just two channels available (the BBC launched its second channel in 1964, and Channel 4 did not arrive until 1982). Indeed, commercial television had only begun two months before the first wrestling show. While the ratings success has been greatly exaggerated through romanticised reminiscence, legitimate figures show audiences were respectable. The peak year of the period came in 1965, when wrestling was among the top 20 shows for 15 weeks of the year, peaking at 7.3 million viewers for a Bolton show featuring Roy Bull Davies vs Billy Howes and Johnny Eagles vs Ken Cadman.

Television was a money-maker itself for Joint Promotions, with rumours of a £15,000 weekly fee going in their pockets, while the wrestlers involved would be lucky to get £200 between them. But the exposure of wrestling on television proved the ultimate boost to the live event business: it became part of mainstream culture. Indeed a 22 May 1963 show at the Royal Albert Hall featured Prince Philip as a guest of honour. By the mid 1960s, Joint had doubled their live event schedule to somewhere in the region of 4,000 to 5,000 shows a year. Every town of note had a show at least once a month, and at some points more than 30 cities had a weekly date. For live events per square mile, Mexico City and perhaps Tokyo are perhaps the only areas to rival this spell of business, and it is doubtful that any territory worldwide has ever seen so many shows putting gate receipts in the pockets of so few promoters.

One effect of television was that, by ensuring weight classifications were based on appearance rather than legitimate weigh-ins, promoters could match similarly sized opponents. This, and the illusion of television, meant that personality could get a wrestler over just as much as size. The two biggest beneficiaries of this were Jackie Pallo and Mick McManus, both welterweight heels. Their feud, pitting the tough cockney McManus against the extravagant Pallo have become the stuff of legend. While their respective claims that they twice outdrew ratings for the football Cup Final on the same day are likely exaggerated (neither show appears in official ratings histories), the feud was so successful that the pair are by far the two best remembered performers of the time. Pallo slipping out of the ring and kissing McManus' wife at ringside was considered major heat at the time.

The style of wrestling at the time was unique, with the system of five minute rounds (three minutes for title matches), best of three falls matches the norm, two public warnings for rulebreaking before a disqualification and no diving moves allowed on a grounded wrestler. Gimmick matches were a rarity; midget wrestling failed to catch on, while women were banned by the Greater London Council until the late 1970s. Tag wrestling proved extremely popular, with Joint putting on a mere eight or so such matches on television each year to keep them special. The Pallo-McManus feud saw Jackie Pallo Jr and Steve Logan added to the mix, while brothers Bert Royal and Vic Faulkner were perhaps the best know permanent team as the Royal Family.

The success of wrestling on television did give a better opportunity for the independent groups. The British Wrestling Federation name was used for a rival title, built around Assirati (who retired through injury in 1960), and later Shirley Crabtree, a young muscleman who had worked working for Paul Lincoln in the 1950s under the names 'Blond Adonis' and 'Mr Universe'. Crabtree quit after a few years, realising he was unlikely to make much money outside of the Joint cartel; he was also plagued by the constant threat of an embittered Assirati exposing his limited legitimate ability.

Another attempt to get round Joint's stranglehold was the Wrestling Federation of Great Britain, a Leicester based alliance of independent promoters such as lightweight legend George Kidd & referee Joe

D'Orazio, 20th Century promotions (consisting of Norman Berry and Max & Brian Crabtree, brothers of Shirley), and Jack Taylor. While such promotions managed to stay profitable well into the 1970s, they would forever be chasing the crumbs of a cake carved up by Joint Promotions.

But, as the old wrestling saying goes, nothing last forever. The men running Joint Promotions were financially well-off from their success, and the day to day hassles of protecting the cartel may not have seemed worthwhile considering their advancing years. When a group of businessmen known as the Hurst Park Syndicate offered to buy out the company but leave the running to the experts, Joint agreed. But by the turn of the 70s, the original promoters had one eye on retirement.

It was at this point that Jarvis Astair (a promoter who had tasted success by pioneering closed circuit coverage of major boxing shows, and as part of the Wembley group would go on to play a key role in bringing the 1992 SummerSlam event to the UK) bought out Dale Martin promotions. He replaced the managing director Johnny Dale with brother Billy, perhaps believing Billy would be more open to change. Astair went on to buy out the remaining promotions involved in Joint, along with Paul Lincoln's independent group.

One might have thought the new finances would be used to spark another boom for Joint Promotions, but it was not to be. With so many of the old guard of wrestling out of the business, Astair was forced to rely on people from outside the industry. Eventually he sold out to the bookmakers William Hill, leaving the wrestling industry run by a public company with little experience of this unique business.

The biggest threat to Joint's dominance almost took off when Jackie Pallo, arguably past his prime in the ring, but carrying name value in negotiations, quit Joint and set up his own promotion with Max Crabtree as booker, and Johnny Dale scheduled to take over the business side. However, Dale died before he could really settle into the role, and Crabtree was headhunted by Joint as the most experienced booker still in the business.

Crabtree had a simple idea to turn business around, one that would spark the next boom... and bust. His brother Shirley, who had been unemployed for the best part of 15 years, was repackaged as 'Big Daddy', the larger-then-life favourite of children and pensioners everywhere. That he was no longer a bodybuilder youth, rather an overweight man in his forties, did not seem to be an obstacle. Every major heel in the country tasted defeat at Daddy's hands, usually in short order thanks to Crabtree's lack of conditioning.

Within a few months of his return, Daddy had even torn off the mask of Kendo Nagasaki, a mysterious heel that had been a top draw since unmasking rival Count Bartelli in 1966. Nagasaki was one of the few men to avoid jobbing to Daddy, instead voluntarily unmasking in a bizarre ceremony in 1977, before retiring the following year.

There is no doubt that, for the Crabtree family at least, the Big Daddy express proved hugely successful. He was by far the best known wrestler in British history, with his own cartoon show on television; Hulkamania without the in-ring ability. His run was extended by carefully positioning him in tag matches, allowing a host of young partners (which included Davey Boy Smith, Dynamite Kid and the future Steven Regal) to carry the match before tagging Daddy in for the finish. His two biggest singles matches, defeating the Canadian 'Mighty' John Quinn in 1979 and perennial rival Giant Haystacks two years later were both inexplicably successful; claims of 18 million viewers may require a healthy dose of scepticism, but both shows sold out the 10,000 seat Wembley Arena.

But, once again, things couldn't last. Within a couple of years, Joint Promotions was down to around 100 shows a month, a notable drop-off. One hero defeating many villains may have made good television, but it left everyone else with limited drawing ability. When Joint were rewarded with a five year extension on their television contract starting in 1982, things looked bleak for the rest of the industry.

Frustration among wrestlers was inevitable, particularly considering how many great workers were around at this point; one could argue that New Japan and Calgary's junior-heavyweight glory days both had their roots in British wrestling of the time. Merseyside promoter Brian Dixon, who had started in the business in his youth, running the Jim Breaks fan club, now had several years experience running his own firm, All Star Promotions, and began capitalising on this disaffection.

Joint had tried their hand at creating a major drawing storyline by crowning Wayne Bridges as the first 'world heavyweight champion' in 1979, with John Quinn taking the title the following year to set up Bridges' chase at revenge. However Quinn jumped to All Star with the title; Joint put the belt back on Bridges, only for him to follow suit in 1983. Within a couple of years, Dixon also had British heavyweight champion Tony St Clair, World mid-heavyweight champion Mark Rocco, British mid-heavyweight champ Chic Cullen and World lightweight champion Johnny Saint on his books. And whatever prestige the titles brought to All Star was more than matched by the superior product, with the fast-paced technical style and show-to-show storylines at regular venues proving more appealing to many than the seemingly never-ending antics of Daddy and company.

But this was hardly the only concern for Joint Promotions. In 1985, regular Big Daddy partner Tony 'Banger' Walsh told all to the Sun about the true nature of wrestling. This was not a first: a 1972 News of the World expose saw a locker room bugged to record two wrestlers discussing a finish. A 1981 court case with wrestler Masambula suing promoters after suffering an injury on a defective ring revealed that he suffered the injury one round before his scheduled defeat. And a frustrated Pallo went into intricate detail in his 1983 expose 'You Grunt, I'll Groan'. But revealing these secrets never truly hurt the business; suspension of disbelief was all too easy for the loyal punters. What really hurt was the suggestion that Big Daddy's warm-hearted child-loving image was in fact a sham.

At the end of 1986, the Crabtrees received another blow when World of Sport was taken off the air. Wrestling instead got its own show, but the timeslot changed from week to week, slowly driving away the regular audience. And far worse for Joint Promotions, with their contract up, they were forced to share the timeslot as part of a rotation system with All Star Promotions and the WWF. While the All Star's product put Joint to shame (a truly atrocious Dale Martin show at the close of 1986 was followed by an All Star extravaganza featuring Fuji Yamada, later known as Jushin Liger, plus the return of Kendo Nagasaki in a bizarre 'disco ladder' match), the shows were limited by harsh restrictions on the part of broadcasting regulators. But it was the exposure of WWF television that many have pinpointed as the death blow for British wrestling. As one British promoter put it, what chance did an ageing

Joint roster stand when young viewers had seen Hulk Hogan and Randy Savage in a wild lumberjack match before 20,000 Madison Square Garden fans.

What appeal Big Daddy still had took yet another blow on 24 August 1987 during a match with Mal 'King Kong' Kirk. After being pinned by a splash from Daddy, Kirk lay still in the ring. He was taken to hospital and never regained consciousness, dying from a heart attack. When Kirk's widow revealed he was earning just £25 a night, the press tore Shirley Crabtree's reputation to shreds; his attempts to portray the incident as a tragic end to a legitimate sporting contest just made matter worse.

The end was nigh, and it arrived in December 1988 when new ITV head of sport Greg Dyke axed the wrestling show as part of an attempt to modernise the station's image, with 'working class' sports such as snooker and darts also falling by the wayside. Having bought the remnants of Joint Promotions from the William Hill firm just two years earlier, Max Crabtree soon suspected he had been sold a lemon. And with rumours that the WWF were asking just £700 a show while Joint Promotions were getting £17,500, hindsight suggests televised demise was already on the cards when Crabtree made his purchase. When newly launched satellite network Sky (which, in its previous form as a single cable channel, had covered the WWF since the early 80s) offered just £500 an hour, the game was up.

For Joint Promotions, there was nothing left to do but tour every town and village to squeeze every last penny out of the remaining Big Daddy followers. But the trick could only work a couple of times at each venue and, despite relaunching as Ring Wrestling Stars and bringing over Davey Boy Smith, just six months after headlining Wembley Stadium, it was a losing battle. When Smith returned to World Championship Wrestling, he took with him the last hope of the Crabtree family.

For All Star Promotions, the end of television was like a shot of venom; it provided a short-term boost as fans went to live shows to get their wrestling fix, and the show-to-show storylines kept them coming back, but by the early to mid 90s, the groups was down to a handful of regular venues. By 1995 promoter Brian Dixon was relying on sold shows on the holiday camp circuit to keep afloat, while turning down a chance to air on cable station L!ve TV because the station offered no fee for the shows.

Since that time, a return to television has been the Holy Grail for countless members of the British wrestling profession. In the early 90s a Jackie Pallo organised taping saw an £80,000 budget, 36 match show sell for just £15,000. Following the resurgence of interest in the American product, former WWF production crew member Dan Berlinka's UWA group persuaded L!ve TV to air their show for free during much of 1999 in return for covering production costs, but the promotion failed to translate the exposure into profitable live events.

A year later the Mondial Sports company's UCW promotion seemed the most serious attempt to get back to the big time, with wrestlers put under full-time salaried contracts, and two shows drawing impressive crowds without imported name talent. But the financial backers seemed to misunderstand the wrestling industry; with one eye on a national television contract they cancelled plans to run regular dates in 1,000 to 2000 seater venues, reasoning that the promotion would look small-time in negotiations. With full-time expenses and no source of income, the result was inevitable.

While the NWA affiliated Hammerlock promotion produced a series of local television shows with the assistance of their Nashville counterparts, the group soon returned to its original plan of running bare bones live shows to complement their successful training school.

And no mention of attempts to put British wrestling back in the big time would be complete without the debacle of WrestleXpress in which a 19 year old somehow sold 2000 tickets and negotiated a pay-per view deal for a launch show featuring everyone from Rob Van Dam to Eric Bischoff. The cynics were proved right when the show collapsed amid stories of champagne dinners and widespread money-mark baiting, leaving goodwill down the toilet and fans waiting up to a year for refunds.

The irony is that, as much as attempts to regain former glories may have fallen short, there have likely never been so many promoters working in British wrestling as there are in the early 21st century. All Star Promotions operates a simple policy of emphasising low costs rather than high revenues, combining a few regular venues with a couple of hundred touring dates each year with a curious mix of former American stars, British veterans, fresh faces and the ubiquitous 'UK Undertaker' and 'Big Red Machine'. Perhaps the most profitable promoters are the likes of Orig Williams (an independent promoter since 1973) and Shane Stevens, whose 'WWF Tribute' shows can draw crowds in the thousands, only bringing closer the inevitable trademark infringement cases. Long-time promoters such as John Freemantle (running Premier Promotions since 1987), Scott Conway (the Wrestling Alliance, 1989) and Ricky Knight (WAW, 1993) continue with steady crowds in the low hundreds and the occasional success such as WAW's crowd of 2000 for its Fightmare show. And there is almost an alphabet soup of 'new school' promotions based around training schools, the most prominent being the Frontier Wrestling Alliance, which provided much of the talent for the nationally televised Revival show.

When considering the future of the wrestling industry, and British wrestling in particular, people often speak of the 'cyclical nature' of the business, with 'inevitable peaks and valleys'. Yet the history of professional wrestling in this country shows that every spell of success began and ended for a reason. The music hall era ended when promoters could no longer provide a product with the finely-tuned balance of legitimate grappling ability and showmanship. The 1930s craze for 'All in' wrestling went by the wayside when quality was sacrificed for quantity. The TV boom trailed off when a generation of wrestling masterminds gave way to a corporate world that didn't realise wrestling was a business like no other. And the fad of Big Daddy went the way of every promotional drive that replaces steady business with an attempt to hotshot to riches.

But for all the lessons wrestling history teaches us, the most important is that each boom was a product of its times. The world of 2002 is a vastly different place of that of 1982, let alone 1962. In this era of multi-channel broadcasting and home entertainment, even national television exposure gives no guarantee of a place in mainstream culture. The wrestling business in the United States no longer exists in Britain merely in the pages of magazines; the WWF is by far the dominant player in this country's wrestling industry. And for a generation of young fans, British wrestling as it was is now neither an idealised reminiscence nor an unshakeable stigma; for today's target audience, British wrestling is starting from nothing.

Whether today's promoters can translate the successes of the past to today's world without falling victim to previous mistakes will decide if the history of British wrestling is a tale ending in tragedy or a story with glories yet to be told.

The age of innovation (*Pro Wrestling Press*, June 2002)

When wrestling promotions try something 'new', the long-time fans will often point out that it is just a rehash of an old idea, perhaps from the 1990s, or even as far back at the 70s or 80s. But for all its stylistic changes, the wrestling business of the 1930s appears very similar to today.

For example, if you thought table spots were something new, this extract may surprise you. It's taken from 'Trouble in Paradise', the autobiography of Irwin Stanton, who wrestled professionally in the 1930s, and went on to be one of the leading technicians behind the launch of network television (and one of the men responsible for the NTSC video system that has befuddled so many tape traders in Britain!)

"Another match was at the Oakland Athletic Club, where Max Baer and other boxers and wrestlers worked out. It also had tables around the ring. It was an exhibition match. We weakened the legs on a table next to the ring and put a Reserved sign next to it. During the match I made a flying tackle at my opponent, went through the ring ropes, and landed on my back on top the table. It collapsed. The audience went wild screaming and hollering."

If you wanted gimmick matches, Dallas was the place for you. During 1937, the famous Sportatorium saw a feud between the Cardiff Giant and Sol Slagel end in a match where, thanks to a pre-match stipulation, Slagel's loss meant he was forced to push the Giant in a wheelchair down Main Street the following day!

Think TL Hopper, Freddie Joy Floyd and Salvatore Sincere had cheesy names? Check out the following, who all appeared at Madison Square Garden in the 1930s: Harry Barry Horse, Farmer Nelson, Wong Buck Choeng, Pat O'Shocker, Chief Little Beaver, Blue Sun Jennings and Professor Pietro Marconi.

As for the likes of Orig Williams and Shane Palmer, their 'tribute shows' are hardly a new creation. After a fellow named Gus Sonnenburg won the world title, rival promoters billed their own performer (a man called Marshall Blackstock) under the same name. The scam on this occasion was to have their 'Sonnenburg' work as an opening match jobber in the hope of the results getting in the newspapers and hurting the drawing power of the genuine article.

The famed 20/20 show just before WrestleMania in 1995 was hardly the first expose of the wrestling business. In 1934, promoter Jack Pfeffer, disgruntled at being double-crossed by the business' leading promotional cartel, went to the New York Times to spill the beans. He would later use his knowledge of promotional tactics to correctly predict finishes of upcoming matches for the columns of Dan Parker, a reporter on the New York Mirror.

And where the business was exposed, the opportunity to make money from the 'smart' fans lay. On 20 September 1934, Jim Londos met Ed Lewis in what was billed as 'the last great shooting match in history'. The fans that closely followed the business knew Lewis had previously been unwilling to job for Londos, a performer with little in the way of legitimate grappling ability. Enough people were willing to accept this as a 'rare legitimate contest' to draw 35,256 fans in Chicago and set a new all-time record at the box office. Of course, it was all business as usual, and Lewis put Londos over.

For all its fame, the Bret Hart-Shawn Michaels incident in 1997 was not the first 'Montreal screwjob'. Back in 1931, Ed Lewis was defending a version of the World title against former Olympian Henri DeGlane, with Lewis scheduled to win. When DeGlane returned to the ring for the third fall, he kept his arm close to his chest. As soon as the bell rang, DeGlane went into a clinch then jumped back screaming that he had been bitten. And, yes, a bitemark was there under his arm. The referee had no choice but to disqualify Lewis and give the belt to DeGlane. The only problem was that, by all accounts, DeGlane had inflicted the wound to himself back in the dressing room. And talking of the dressing room, Lewis returned there to find promoter Paul Bowser and several men carrying baseball bats, just in case he had any ideas of protesting.

This incident later led to one of the most famous lines in wrestling history, which would be used on at least two later occasions. Bowser went on to switch his title from DeGlane to Ed Don George. To 'prove' he held no animosity, Lewis put over Don George in a Los Angeles match. In a rematch, Lewis locked up with Don George and informed him that, contrary to the planned finish, Lewis would be leaving with the title and, "we can do this the easy way or the hard way". Don George chose the former option. These words would be heard again in 1963 when, after several attempts to get out of the match, NWA champion Buddy Rogers finally got in the ring to drop the belt to Lou Thesz, who had no doubt picked up the phrase from his mentor Lewis. Again, Rogers chose the easy way. The incidents became part of wrestling folklore and, in 1998 when Vince McMahon launched his feud with new champion, and anti-authority figure Steve Austin, one big angle saw 'Stone Cold' ordered to conform and given a simple choice... the easy way or the hard way.

And to finish on a more light-hearted note, these rules for '20th century catch-as-catch-can wrestling' printed in a 1938 programme from a show at Manchester's Belle Vue, suggest today's drug scandals are nothing new either!

'Seconds may not give a contestant any noxious drug, nor any stimulant such as cocaine, strychnine or alcohol.'

The truth about smoke-filled halls (*Pro Wrestling Press*, July 2002)

The WWE version of wrestling history is well known and very simple. It was once a low budget regional hick activity that took place in little smoke-filled halls. Vince McMahon stopped pretending it was a sport and made it successful, at one point outdrawing the Pope and the Rolling Stones in a match where Andre the Giant passed the torch to Hulk Hogan. Vince suffered a bit when Ted Turner stole his big stars and the government tried to convict him on shoddy charges, but Vince's creative genius allowed him to win the war and take the business to new heights.

Needless to say, pointing out the flaws in this account could fill an entire issue; indeed, Dave Meltzer has already carried out such a project in his review of the A&E channel's 'history' of wrestling show. Instead this issue we will examine the state of the United States wrestling business in 1983 and see whether it is truly in better shape today.

In 1983, the year that Vince McMahon began his national expansion, the territorial system was still at the heart of American wrestling. Many fans, and particularly independent wrestlers, today have an entirely different idea of what a territory was. Wrestling once a month, or even twice a week, is not the same as working a territory. A territory was a full-time promotion in a particular region, running perhaps five regular shows each week: one town would have a show every Saturday, another every Sunday, and so on. There would also be perhaps one or two 'spot shows' each week in smaller towns, which would each get a live show once a month or so. Add in a weekly morning television taping and it certainly wouldn't be unusual for a wrestler to work up to 8 shows a week. This meant wrestling in a territory was a full-time occupation; the guy you see working five days a week at a pizza parlour today and a couple of matches at the weekend is not 'working a territory'.

In 1983, the **WWF** itself was still a territory, albeit one of the biggest. They had a strict promotional area, stretching from Washington DC up to Boston, with the occasional date in California (where the recent closures of Gene LaBelle's Los Angeles promotion and Roy Shire's San Francisco territory had both left gaps in the market). The structure was slightly different to the rest of the country, with monthly shows in venues such as Landover, Boston, Philadelphia, New Jersey's Meadowlands, Madison Square Garden, Baltimore, and White Plains (New York), with 10,000-20,000 gates the norm. There were many more spot shows than in most territories, with various promoters throughout the Northeast each running shows around their area using the WWF talent.

To put things into perspective, in a usual week now, the WWE runs eight shows, drawing an average of around 6,000 a time, for a total of 48,000 fans a week. In an average week in 1983 you could probably expect to get 20,000 to 25,000 fans from the combined audiences of a couple of the big cities. Throw in ten spot shows drawing 2,500 each and it becomes clear that, while there is a hefty margin of error in both cases, the smoke filled halls of 1983 and the global corporate entity of 2002 both put a similar number of people through the turnstiles.

The main opposition that McMahon faced in his quest to expand was the National Wrestling Alliance: not a promotion in itself, but a body of territorial promoters. At one point in the 1970s, the group had almost 30 members. By 1983, the NWA was arguably at the beginning of a decline, with the unifying force of President Sam Muchnick lost after his retirement, and several territories having closed. However, there were still at least eleven major players:

Jim Crockett's **Mid-Atlantic Promotions** ran in North Carolina, South Carolina and Virginia with weekly shows in towns such as Greensboro, Richmond, Charlotte, Spartanburg and Columbia.

Ole Anderson ran **Georgia Championship Wrestling**, running in its home state, but also making trips into West Virginia, Ohio and Michigan. While down from previous levels (and hitting trouble behind the scenes), business was still good enough to attempt to build a secondary circuit, titled Georgia Championship Wrestling Superstars, running East Tennessee and booked by Bill Dundee. The promotion failed to take off, though some have blamed this on failing to supply the product expected by long-time fans in Knoxville and Chattanooga rather than a lack of demand for live wrestling. The main Georgia circuit had successes with the debut of the Road Warriors, and the TV show on the 'Superstation' (the first national cable station, later known as TBS) drew a record 6.8 rating for a match pitting Pez Whatley and Mr Wrestling II against Zbyszko and Tully Blanchard.

Eddie Graham's **Championship Wrestling from Florida** ran such towns as Tampa, Orlando, St. Petersburg, Miami, Fort Lauderdale, West Palm Beach, and Lakeland. Crowds were healthy, with Miami drawing around 3,000 to 5,000 each week.

Ron Fuller's **Southeastern Championship Wrestling**, based in Alabama and Northwest Florida, had five weekly shows (Dothan, Birmingham, Montgomery, Mobile and Pensacola) plus spot shows, with sell-outs far from a rarity.

Bill Watts' **Mid-South Wrestling** in Louisiana, Oklahoma and Mississippi had a weak year by its own standards, but still attracted two Louisiana Superdome crowds of more than 20,000. An eight-show week was part of the job.

Jerry Jarrett's **Memphis** promotion had its hottest year ever. The weekly circuit of Memphis, Louisville, Evansville, Nashville plus one or two spot shows saw regular 5,000 crowds in Louisville, and Memphis crowds could range from 5,000 to 12,000 depending on the main event.

Fritz Von Erich's **World Class Championship Wrestling** also had a blockbuster year. Business had been sparked off on Christmas night of 1982 with the legendary Freebirds heel turn, and through 1983 it was normal for the Friday night shows at the 4,500 seat Dallas Sportatorium to sell out, as did those on Mondays in the 5,000 seat Will Rogers Coliseum in Fort Worth. A series of major shows saw up to 14,000 in the Tarrant County Convention Center in Fort Worth, and three shows in Reunion Arena, Dallas all sold out at 17,500 fans a time. For the Thanksgiving show pitting Kerry Von Erich against Ric Flair, several thousand ticketless fans stood outside in freezing temperatures peering through the windows at security monitors to see what happened. Spot show business was also strong throughout the year, reaching venues as far away as Amarillo.

Paul Boesch's **Houston** promotion, which shared talent with Mid-South, had a strong year. Taking inflation into account, revenue for 1982 was more than three times greater than Boesch's first year as a promoter in 1967.

Bob Geigel's **Central States** promotion ran 32 shows a month in Kansas, Missouri, Iowa, Illinois, Wisconsin and Nebraska. To put that into perspective, one of the smaller regional promoters was running the same number of live shows as Vince McMahon does today.

In **St Louis** a coalition of local promoters and wrestlers had taken over the one-town territory from Sam Muchnick. His business had never shown any signs of the so-called cyclical nature of wrestling, due largely to the absence of short-term gimmicks and hotshotting. While his departure made a decline almost inevitable, the city's weekly shows was still pulling crowds in the 5,000 range.

And finally Don Owen's **Portland** promotion ran its home city twice a week, with weekly shows in Salem and Eugene (both in Oregon), and occasional dates in Seattle.

There was also a range of other full-time promotions. Verne Gagne's **AWA** was largely left alone by the NWA, and had an established territory across Illinois, Wisconsin and Minnesota, stretching through Utah and Nevada into Northern California. 1983 was the company's biggest year ever, thanks to the growing popularity of Hulk Hogan. There were also at least two 'outlaw' promotions running regular schedules and competing with NWA territories; Joe and Tully Blanchard ran **Southwest Championship Wrestling** in San Antonio, while the Poffo family ran **International Championship Wrestling**, based in Lexington, Kentucky.

And true 'independent' wrestling was still in a healthy state. North Carolina alone had at least six notable promotions, while 400 different men were licensed to wrestle by the Texas athletic commission

So how does the business of 1983 really compare with today's national monopoly?

We have already looked at the live event business of the WWE. In terms of the number of shows, there is still a notable independent scene; in one recent week at least 50 shows took place across the United States. However, crowds are almost insignificant in comparison to the old territories; taking an average of 250 a show would be generous.

Looking solely at live attendance, based on estimates for the promotions we have covered in this article, an average month for US pro wrestling in 1983 (not including the small independents) might have drawn in the region of 850,000 tickets sold. Today, including both the WWE and the independents, that figure is more like 380,000.

Of course, you could argue that you need to take pay-per-view into account. Taking into account both declared figures from annual reports, and estimates for the last WrestleMania, we can add 400,000 a month to this figure, taking us to 780,000 a month.

When you remember that we haven't even included independent shows from 1983, the fact is that, however you interpret the figures, more people paid to see US pro wrestling each month in 1983 than they do today.

Television today sees perhaps 6 million people a week watch pro wrestling (giving the WWE a generous interpretation of how many unique viewers each show gets). Considering Georgia Championship Wrestling alone could get close to a million viewers, and there were more than a dozen major promotions producing TV, it seems unlikely that today's figures exceed those of 1983.

In 1983, there were at least 40 towns and cities where wrestling took place every single week before crowds in the thousands. Today, you are looking at a handful at most running weekly, and a paid crowd of 500 would be considered a major success.

In 1983 at least 250 men made a full-time living as professional wrestlers, and there were at least 15 different employers with whom you could make a living. Today the workforce reaches 100 at a stretch, and if you don't want to work for Vince McMahon, you'd better start praying for the 'next big thing'.

In terms of revenue and profit, wrestling may well be more successful now than in 1983; that is the very nature of a monopoly (both as a supplier to the audience and as an employer). But the facts are that fewer people pay to see pro wrestling, fewer people watch it, fewer people make a living from it, and the business as a weekly live entertainment form has been wiped out.

Vince McMahon's organisation has certainly changed the wrestling business forever, and Vince McMahon's income has been taken to new heights. But for Vince McMahon to claim he took wrestling from a insignificant smoke-filled halls to the big time is arguably a bigger lie than ever pretending a wrestling match was on the level.

The art of booking (*Pro Wrestling Press*, August 2002)

For all the changes that professional wrestling has gone through, the essence of the business has not undergone a major change since the turn of the century. This was when the reasoning behind working matches changed from making money through betting scams to making money by building up interest in future matches. The art of telling ongoing stories through carefully chosen finishes to matches, or 'booking', has been practiced in a variety of ways over the years and around the world.

The first real booker was Toots Mondt, part of the famed 'Gold Dust Trio' of promoters with Ed 'Strangler' Lewis and Billy Sandow, who created the idea of a touring promotion of wrestlers working a circuit of dates. The 1937 expose 'Fall Guys', written by Marcus Griffin (but according to some theories, heavily influenced by Mondt) discussed some of the now-commonplace finishes Mondt came up with to bring fans back for rematches.

"There's the time limit match in which both men wrestle through to the time limit without deciding the victor. Sometimes the match is a two out of three falls contest. Perhaps each man will secure a fall with no deciding third fall. Then, again the contestants will wrestle the time out without a fall.

"In another finish, the men bump their heads together, fall to the mat, are unable to continue and are counted out by the referee and the bout called a draw. The variation of this finish is for one wrestler to recover consciousness in sufficient time to struggle to his feet and be declared the winner. Another variation is for both contestants to knock themselves out by falling through the ropes and onto the floor outside the ring. Still another form is both men through the ropes with one managing to stagger weakly back into the ring before the referee completes his count.

"In another finish, the aggressor is about to rush in to pin his adversary, but in his eagerness misses his opponent, falling through the ring ropes to the floor outside the ring where, apparently unconscious, he is counted out by the referee.

"No prosaic ending of a bout was permitted if [Mondt and company] had their way, and for many years their word was undisputed. The Sandow, Lewis and Mondt wrestling matches had to end with a flash like the old-time vaudeville acts. The Gold Dust Trio believed in pleasing the crowds."

Longtime Houston promoter Paul Boesch, in his autobiography *Hey Boy, Whered'yda Get Them Ears* described Mondt as "a man with real wrestling brains… he had an almost infallible sense of feel for the public's likes and dislikes. [To find the perfect booker] you find a man whose judgement you can trust; who knows wrestlers and has a feel for what fans really want to see. This is an intangible quality that is as difficult to define as it is to find. What the fan says he wants to see is not always what he will pay to see. If the matchmaker has the rare ability to understand fan language and reaction, and translate it into the right matches, then the promoter will reap both money and glory. And the wrestlers will feel they are the stars the publicity men say they are."

For Boesch himself, the principles of booking and promoting were simple. "The solution to end struggling, if you are a promoter, is to recognise talent and to secure that talent to wrestle in your ring. If you do that, and the sport prospers, you are a genius. Fans do not come to arenas to see promoters, even if they think they are geniuses. They come to see wrestlers. They come to see action.

"How do you secure talent? There is a formula. First, you recognise it. Then you apply that recognition to whether the fans to whom you will show the talent will recognise it. A promoter does not make matches to please himself. He makes them to attract fans and please those fans. The matches he makes are not always those the fan would make if he was suddenly given the job of matchmaker.

He went on to defend the growing use of gimmick matches during his spell as a promoter from 1966 to 1987. "Wrestling has always been a sport of loose restrictions, a sport that grew up in carnivals and music halls and theatres and state fairs. With this background, it has never graciously accepted the boundaries set on it by people who have no understanding of what the fans want. And the fans are still the barometer or, to use the cliché of the day, they are the bottom line. If they don't like the idea, or the [gimmick], or the match, they stay at home and any promoter with an ounce of sense would never try it again."

Successful territory promoters in this era were quick to recognise the particular tastes of their fans, and adapted their booking styles appropriately, such that different philosophies prospered across the country. For example, the WWWF (now the WWE) ran major venues only once every three to four weeks, so a wrestler would have fewer major matches during a feud. A 'three strikes and you're out' policy applied to the main events; one of the trio of managers Lou Albano, Fred Blassie and the Grand Wizard would pit their latest monster heel against babyface champion Bruno Sammartino, Pedro Morales or Bob Backlund. The first match would usually see the challenger score a disputed victory, perhaps by countout, disqualification or a stoppage for blood, none of which led to a title change. Depending on the financial success of the first match, the champ would either score a decisive rematch victory, or extend the programme through a screwy finish leading to a third match ending in a conclusive win, perhaps in an appropriate gimmick match.

In a 1982 interview with the Los Angeles Times, North California promoter Roy Shire explained his territory's policy for building to stipulation matches. "The really hard part, the toughest part is figuring the finish. The problem is figuring what can I do that the fans will buy that will get another rematch. Say your heel is the champion, wrestling a babyface. Last fall. Your champion goes into his finishing hold and slams the baby face into the ring post. He blades himself, gets some heat up. Takes the 20-count then comes back to beat the heel, your champion. Thing is, in my territory, the ref is allowed to stop a fight on cuts. He had stopped the fight. Everybody thinks the baby face has won but here comes the ref to announce he stopped the bout because the baby face was cut too badly to continue. Almost have a riot. "The thing to do in this case is to bring them back for the rematch, bill it: 'No stopping for blood.' [Or] fight on the floor to a draw, run out the time limit, then come back without a time limit."

In the same article, Wrestling Observer editor Dave Meltzer explained why these tactics worked in the San Francisco territory. "All of the matches on the card always made sense. If a guy won a match, he'd be moved up on the card; if a guy lost, he wouldn't.

Every match was important, because the guy on the preliminary match, if he won two straight preliminary matches, he'd be moving up to a main event, and then if he won that, he might get a title shot. No one came in and was in the main event the first time. "Every match on the card was important, the title matches were always long, and they always had good endings. He was really sharp at endings, and the rematch always made sense. Promoters now... I'll give you an example... cage matches: of all the gimmick matches, the number-one draw is the cage match. Sometimes they'll just throw in a cage match, to draw. If Shire had a cage match, it was because the two guys were fighting in the stands the week before, and that's why he had the cage match, to keep 'em in the ring. If he had a match where there was no stopping for blood, it was because the guys were bleeding all over the place the card before. His gimmicks always made sense."

Another account of Shire's promotional days has an office underling pointing out that the annual battle royale at the Cow Palace in January was always the biggest date of the year. But when it was suggested that Shire hold a second battle royale each year, he dismissed the idea, arguing that to do so would kill the unique status of the gimmick.

Repetition was not such a problem in Florida, where the weekly circuit could see main events repeated for weeks on end, with referee bumps prolonging the rivalry. (The famed 'Dusty finish', where a KOed referee wakes up and reverses a decisions, was learnt by Rhodes when he worked for Florida booker Eddie Graham.) Yet, because fans in the territory had never encountered another style, it didn't harm business; nobody questioned something that seemed so familiar.

To show the difference in territories, a ref bump was virtually unknown in St Louis, where Sam Muchnick promoted his shows on the back of his credibility with leading figures in legitimate sports. There would be perhaps one match a year with a disputed finish, and it would be corrected in a rematch straight away. Wins and losses were the most important thing, and the basic philosophy was to treat wrestling entirely as any other sporting contest, only with the advantage of working finishes to build future business.

And yet just a couple of hundred miles away, the Memphis style of week to week booking was entirely different. Randy Hales, who booked the territory in the mid-90s, said there were four aspects to successful booking in Memphis: heat ("if baby faces are over, and you do the heat right, you can put heat on the heels every week and never hurt your babyface"), soap-opera style cliffhangers, wild action brawls and personal issues between feuding wrestlers.

"Our entire focus was our weekly towns. On TV we would build something for Louisville, Memphis and Nashville. We would be in these towns ever week so finishes were critical. The secret of it is writing the finish to further the storyline and if you do that, the finish is critical."

But it seems that philosophy, along with every other theory of booking, has been killed by the era of catering to weekly television ahead of the direct money-makers of house shows and pay-per-views. The art of booking by has been replaced by television writing, where characters and skits take priority and the week to week journey seems more important than the intended destination. The emphasis has shifted from winning and losing towards the two overused 'high concepts' of the invasion angle and the heel promoter.

Perhaps, rather than editorialise, we should let the embodiment of this 'evolution' explain it in his own words. Over to you, Vince Russo:

"What we've done now basically is we've basically trained the audience [to short matches]. It's crash TV. It's in and out. What's the finish? Let's get to the next thing.... winning and losing does not mean shit anymore... Basically, the non-finishes and stuff like that you see is just to help us [with] character development and to move storylines forwards.

" I swear to you television is written week to week. There are no more long term plans. I mean, the boys used to come up to me and say, 'Vince, where is this going?' And I used to look at them and say 'I have no idea.'"

Perhaps one day the likes of Vince Russo will learn from history (rather than dismiss it as 'uncool') and realise that the idea, whatever style you choose, is to use your finishes to build your business. It's called booking.

The 25 best angles... ever! (*Pro Wrestling Press*, October 2002)

Believe it or not, the idea of incidents on wrestling shows was not always to draw TV ratings, to amuse bookers or to fool 'smart' fans. The idea of angles was to create something unusual to persuade fans to pay to see a match. As Jim Cornette put it, "The heel pisses on the babyface's leg and then the babyface by golly does something about it". The following are some of the most memorable angles from wrestling history. Some worked at drawing money, some didn't, but all left a lasting impression.

The kneedrop (Ray Stevens and Pepper Gomez, San Francisco, 1962)

There are many ways to get a wrestler over on weekly television. For Pepper Gomez, letting wrestlers punch him in the stomach or run over it with a car and no-selling the move was the trick. The next step was to let wrestlers jump from halfway up a ladder onto his stomach, with similar results. But Ray Stevens wasn't satisfied when his first stomp failed to leave an impression. He asked if Gomez had the guts to let him jump from the top of the ladder. Gomez accepted but, instead of a stomp to the stomach, Stevens crashed down with his 'Bombs Away' kneedrop to Gomez's throat. Gomez was left coughing up blood. When he eventually returned for revenge, the match at San Francisco's Cow Palace drew a record California crowd of 17,000. The figure was perhaps made more impressive by the building's 15,000 capacity.

The teeth (Boris Malenko and Eddie Graham, Florida, 1966)

Boris Malenko was having an easy time with opponent Sammy Steamboat one week on the Championship Wrestling from Florida television show. Malenko bit Steamboat on the ear and began spitting his blood on the floor. Rival Eddie Graham responded by running to the ring, punching Malenko so hard his false teeth flew out, and then stomping the teeth into oblivion. There were consequences...

The streetfight (Tiger Jeet Singh and Antonio Inoki, New Japan, 1973)

Most wrestling angles take place at a television taping or a live show, with a camera on hand. So when Antonio Inoki was walking down Tokyo High Street one night, it caused something of a commotion when a mysterious Indian man began attacking him. Particularly as Inoki was standing outside a high-profile department store at the time. Once the newspapers had reported the story, it came to light that this man was in fact a professional wrestler, Tiger Jeet Singh. In the inevitable grudge match, Inoki 'broke' Singh's arm with a cross-armbreaker, making the move a credible finisher for years to come.

The axe (Jos LeDuc, Memphis, 1978)

Jos LeDuc did a lot of crazy things in Memphis. He'd smash vases over his head. He'd lose arm-wrestling matches that saw his hand forced onto a burning candle. He'd let challengers take a sledgehammer and break a brick over his head. But nothing quite matched the day he vowed to defeat Jerry Lawler and made a 'blood oath' by taking an axe and slicing his arm open to leave a scar as a permanent reminder of his hatred. He sliced his arm open, with no gimmickry, live on television at 11am on a Saturday. Now that's family entertainment.

The concession stand (Jerry Lawler, Bill Dundee, Wayne Ferris and Larry Latham, Tupelo, 1979)

Taped to show clips on television, this Mississippi spot show match saw Lawler and Dundee battle Ferris (Honky Tonk Man) and Latham (a future Moondog) battle to the back of the building and into the kitchen where hot dogs and drinks were sold. They destroyed everything that stood in their path; a hardcore match two decades before the term caught on. The angle was so effective that bookers repeated it two years later with future FMW headliner Atsushi Onita and AJPW's Masa Fuchi fighting Eddie Gilbert and Ricky Morton amid a pool of mustard and broken bottles.

The blinding (Junk Yard Dog & Michael Hayes, Mid-South, 1980)

Kurt Angle wasn't the first wrestler to don a wig and claim his hair had miraculously grown back after a hair vs hair match. In fact, Buddy Roberts did the trick with his magical 'Freebird' hair cream. And partner Michael Hayes took advantage by rubbing the cream in JYD's eyes. The Dog sold it to the extreme of never leaving his house amid rumours of blindness. Fans began sending money to his house to help pay his bills because he was "unable to wrestle". His wife gave birth and fans watching television were told he might never see his baby daughter. When he appeared in the ring to announce his retirement, an attempted angle with Hayes went haywire when a fan jumped over the guardrail and pointed a gun at the heel. Finally the Dog returned, still 'blind' for a dog-collar cage match, begging the fans to help by shouting out instructions. Around 30,000 heeded his call, drawing the second or third biggest gate in the history of the business.

The chairshot (Bruno Sammartino and Larry Zybszko, WWWF, 1980)

The battle of the master and the student is one of the oldest stories in wrestling, but this was the most successful. Zbyszko, after several attempts, persuaded his mentor to let the student test his abilities. Throughout the televised match, Zbyszko gradually became more and more frustrated at his failure to take control. Eventually he snapped and, with two blows from a steel chair, became the biggest heel in the company. The resulting grudge match at Shea Stadium drew 36,295 fans paying over half a million dollars, worldwide records that would both stand until WrestleMania III.

The empty arena (Jerry Lawler and Terry Funk, Memphis, 1981)

Funk claimed Lawler had an unfair advantage with his hometown fans, so he challenged him to a fight at the Mid-South Coliseum with nobody else there. In front of 11,000 empty seats, the two men brawled while a cameraman and Lance Russell looked on. After a lifetime performance on the microphone, Funk took control of the brawl only to mistakenly catch himself in the eye with a broken piece of wood, crying in agony while a disgusted Lawler walked away. Despite the angle failing to draw a big crowd for the next match, this incident became a cult classic.

The #1 contender (Ric Flair, Ted DiBiase and Dick Murdoch, Mid-South, 1981)

With world champion Flair due to visit the area to defend his title on television, various contenders battled to earn the title shot. The honour eventually went to heel DiBiase but, moments before the match, babyface Murdoch demanded he step aside. When DiBiase refused, Murdoch smashed him head-first into the ringpost. With DiBiase bloodied it seemed his title shot was lost. But he heroically returned and gave Flair a run for his money despite the heavy blood-loss, particularly when Flair tore a bandage from his forehead. DiBiase finally lost by countout and, as he lay at ringside, spent from the effort, found himself attacked by Murdoch with a neckbreaker on the concrete. Mid-South had a new lead babyface... and a new lead heel.

The jump (Stan Hansen, All Japan, 1981)

There's an old saying in wrestling about being in the right place at the right time. But at the final of the annual All Japan tag tournament pitting Bruiser Brody and Jimmy Snuka against Terry and Dory Funk, one man was very much in the wrong place. It was New Japan star Stan Hansen, whose switch of allegiance was a close guarded secret. He simply appeared at ringside, helped Brody and Snuka win, and then began brawling with lead babyface Giant Baba. It was a hell of a first impression.

The Ishingun (Riki Choshu, New Japan, 1982)

Since Japanese wrestling took off, the story had always been simple: heroic natives battled imposing foreign invaders. But one night, Riki Choshu turned on his partners Antonio Inoki and Tatsumi Fujinami.

Choshu formed an alliance with other wrestlers such as Masa Saito and Kuniyaki Kobayashi, turning legitimate backstage heat into the 'Ishingun' faction. It was a blurring of the line between heel and face. It was an angle based on reality. It was, when the group jumped to All Japan, an alleged 'inter-promotional' invasion. It was 'Stone Cold' and the nWo fifteen years early.

The coffee (Jerry Lawler and Andy Kaufman, 1982)

Perhaps the most forgotten part of this angle was that the big match had already taken place. When comedian Kaufman began challenging women to wrestling matches on his television spots, and then moving on to Memphis to repeat it live, he found Lawler offering his help to one challenger. Lawler then challenged 'inter-gender' champion Kaufman to a match, which saw the comedian win by disqualification when he was hit with two piledrivers. However, Kaufman was taken to hospital. The big angle took place when the pair appeared on the nationally televised David Letterman show. Kaufman demanded an apology. Lawler refused. Kaufman responded by throwing a cup of coffee in his face and beginning a brawl across the room. Letterman didn't have a clue what was going on. Indeed, it wasn't until the film 'Man on the Moon' seventeen years later that Lawler admitted what everyone thought, but nobody knew for sure. It was all an angle.

The door (Terry Gordy and Kerry Von Erich, Dallas, 1982)

On Christmas night 1982, Dallas hero Kerry Von Erich challenged Ric Flair in a cage for the NWA World heavyweight title. With previous matches between the two seeing Von Erich cheated by referee error, the promotion appointed recently arrived babyface Michael Hayes as the referee and placed his Freebirds partner Terry Gordy by the door of the cage to prevent interference. Slowly, little by little, Hayes began favouring Flair. But Von Erich still appeared strong and was seemingly about to win the belt when it happened. Flair 'accidentally' shoved Hayes, who 'accidentally' sent Von Erich crashing through the door. Gordy slammed the door on Von Erich's head. Flair took the easy victory. Von Erich and his brothers vowed revenge on the Freebirds. A struggling territory became the hottest promotion in the country overnight.

Santa Claus (Kevin Sullivan, Jake Roberts and Dusty Rhodes, Florida, 1982)

There was something about cages on Christmas night 1982. Sullivan and Roberts settled their feud inside the steel in St Petersburg that night with the loser to leave Florida for 90 days. A group of Santa Clauses were sat at ringside handing out gifts to the lucky fans. But wouldn't you know it, one of them suddenly passed a weapon through the cage to Sullivan. Three seconds later and Rhodes was gone (and the Midnight Rider began preparing for his debut). And a cameraman stuck his nose in the dressing room just long enough to see Sullivan talking to Jake Roberts... who was wearing a Santa outfit.

The piledriver (Randy Savage and Ricky Morton, Memphis, 1984)

If you throw somebody through a plywood table every week on television in 2002, it soon stops meaning very much. In 1984, when Randy Savage took what was billed as the most deadly and illegal hold in Tennessee wrestling, and performed it on Morton on a heavy ringside table, it was the closest thing to attempted murder as a wrestler could get away with.

The flag (Eddie Gilbert and Bill Watts, Mid-South, 1985)

Bill Watts' views on international politics were fairly simplistic in the 1980s. America was good. Russia was bad. So Eddie Gilbert managing Nikita Koloff and Kostia Korchenko and waving the Soviet flag didn't go down too well. One week Gilbert called Watts to the ring to apologise. He said he would no longer manage the Russians, and would instead turn his attention to the Blade Runners (who would later become the Ultimate Warrior and Sting). But as soon as Gilbert handed over the flag for Watts to destroy, the Russians stormed the ring and began attacking him. Gilbert showed his true colours, helping them beat him down with a not-so-subtly symbolic red shovel and chain. Meanwhile the Blade Runners blocked the aisle to hold off the various babyfaces trying to make the save. The last straw came as the Russians placed the Soviet flag over the beaten cowboy.

The Horsemen (Ric Flair, the Andersons and Dusty Rhodes, Mid-Atlantic, 1985)

Valour is not always rewarded in professional wrestling. Ric Flair had just defeated dastardly Russian Nikita Koloff in a cage match when Ivan Koloff burst into the cage and began a two-on-one attack while fellow Soviet Krusher Khrushchev guarded the door. Dusty Rhodes bravely came to ringside, and fought off all three Russians to make the save. His reward? Ole and Arn Anderson stormed the ring, locked the door behind them, and Flair showed his gratitude by helping to break Rhodes' leg.

The crucifix (Andre the Giant and Hulk Hogan, WWF, 1987)

It was such a simple thing. Hulk Hogan got a giant trophy to commemorate four years as WWF champion. Andre got a smaller trophy to recognise his successes. Commentators Bobby Heenan and Jesse Ventura started questioning why Andre had never had a title shot. Finally Ventura organised a summit on the Piper's Pit slot. Andre walked out with Heenan by his side and demanded a title match at WrestleMania III. 'I can't believe it', Hogan said. 'Maybe you'll believe this,' Heenan replied. Andre tore away the crucifix that hung around Hogan's neck. Hogan was left with a trickle of blood around his chest. The match made more than ten million dollars.

The haircut (Jerry Lawler, Austin Idol and Tommy Rich, Memphis, 1987)

After Idol and Rich posted Lawler crotch-first on a ringpost, the issue would have to be settled in a high-stakes affair. It would be a cage match (the cage surrounding the entire ringside area to prevent outside interference), with the loser having his head shaved, something that had never happened to Lawler despite taking part in several such matches. Any uncommitted fan was surely persuaded to attend by Idol's manager Paul E Dangerously (Paul Heyman) promising to refund the ticket money of every fan if his man lost. And that looked exactly what was going to happen… until Tommy Rich (who had been hiding under the ring since mid-afternoon) crawled out and attacked Lawler, leaving him defeated and bald. You haven't seen crowd heat until you've seen Idol, Dangerously and Rich leave the cage and literally run for their lives to the dressing room to escape the baying fans.

The slap (Hulk Hogan and Randy Savage, WWF, 1989)

Akeem and the Big Bossman had beaten up Randy Savage until Hulk Hogan made the save. Akeem and the Big Bossman had beaten up Hulk Hogan until Randy Savage made the save. A tag match was the only logical step. In front of a live NBC audience, Savage mistakenly crashed into manager Elizabeth at ringside. Hogan carried her backstage for help, leaving Savage to a two-on-one beating. When Hogan returned to make the save and leant into the ring for the tag, Savage replied with a slap to the face and walked out. After winning the match, Hogan returned to the medical area to check on Elizabeth, only for an enraged Savage to beat him to the ground. A woman in an English home laughed at the poor acting. Her 12 year old son, watching for the first time, took no notice. He was hooked for life.

The handshake (Terry Funk and Ric Flair, NWA (Crockett), 1989)

When Ric Flair fought Rick Steamboat at Clash of the Champions VI, former world champion Terry Funk came out of retirement for guest commentary. A month later, Funk sat at ringside as a judge as Flair regained the NWA title. After the match, Funk congratulated Flair and asked for a title shot. Flair pointed out that Funk was not a ranked contender. The two appeared to settle the quarrel with a handshake. But Funk then attacked Flair from behind and piledrivered him on the ringside table. The summer-long feud wound up with an I Quit match where, after Funk submitted, the pair made up with another handshake.

The hit and run (Jerry Lawler and Eddie Gilbert, Memphis, 1990)

Most wrestling promotions doing a hit and run angle would use stunt doubles. But not low-budget Memphis. Live on television, Eddie Gilbert ran his car straight into Jerry Lawler and drove off. When he later phoned the studio to check everything had come off right, he discovered several fans had called the police, who were now looking to question him. Meanwhile Lawler, who suffered legitimate heavy bruising to the hip, was underplaying his injuries to avoid his colleague missing future shows in favour of serving hard time.

The mask (Art Barr and Eddy Guerrero, AAA, 1993)

Art Barr's transformation from heroic technico to dastardly rudo, like most turns in Mexico, took plenty of time. He began the change by acting cockily on his way to losing a mask vs mask match with rival Blue Panther in EMLL. The pair then jumped to AAA and, in a hair vs mask rematch where 7000 fans were turned away at the door, Barr was disqualified for using the 'martinete' (tombstone piledriver). Suddenly the hottest heel in the country, Barr later found himself in a match with heroes El Hijo Del Santo and Eddy Guerrero (sons of long-time partners El Santo and Gory Guerrero). During the match, Barr attacked Santo and stole his mask. Guerrero didn't see this and turned round to see 'Santo' attack him. As Guerrero recovered from the beating, Barr put the mask back on the true Santo and encouraged Guerrero to avenge what he thought was a betrayal by his partner. The incident put Guerrero over the edge and, claiming he was stepping out of Santo's shadow, he formed the 'Los Gringos Locos' team with Barr that would rival the Hollywood Blondes for the title of greatest team of the 90s.

The outsider (Scott Hall, WCW, 1996)

One of the secrets of promoting wrestling is that what actually happens is nowhere near as important as how the promotion portrays it. And so, when Scott Hall walked out of the crowd and into the ring one Monday night, it was the way WCW announcers acted as if they had no idea what he was doing there that made the angle. By nothing more complicated than treating the angle (that Hall, and later Kevin Nash, were outsiders that should not be there) as if it were entirely legitimate, WCW began arguably the most lucrative two-year run the business had ever seen at that point.

The boss (Vince McMahon and Steve Austin, WWF, 1998)

McMahon and Austin had had problems ever since Austin dropped a Stone Cold Stunner the previous September. After Austin took the title, McMahon (playing off his real life chicanery in Montreal) ordered him to be a respectful champion. In a line stolen from Strangler Lewis, McMahon offered Austin the choice to do things the easy way or the hard way. Austin chose the hard way. One Monday night, McMahon took personal control and challenged Austin for the title. The match itself never took place that night, but the bait and switch was, for the first time in almost two years, witnessed by more viewers than WCW Nitro. The WWF was back in the race.

Wrestling Fan's Book (*Pro Wrestling Press*, November 2002)

My latest acquisition from the wonderful world of eBay is a 1952 publication from *The Ring* magazine titled *Wrestling Fan's Book* – it was the *PWI Almanac* of its day and not a bad buy for a buck.

The inside front cover mentions the curiously named Hillbilly Spunky (accompanied by Daisy Mae) and his tag partner the Bushy-Haired Elephant Boy with his 'spicy saronged' slave girl (who went on to be the Fabulous Moolah).

According to the book, television had just sparked off a major boom in the business, with 2000 active wrestlers and 100 towns running weekly shows while 500 more had occasional events. The book claims wrestling was outdrawing boxing, with around 24 million tickets sold in the United States in 1950.

The book profiles the 'big nine' stars of the day: Lou Thesz ('These days he is looking ahead to the time when he will retire'; hardly!), three-year pro Verne Gagne, Antonio Rocca (who allegedly killed a judo expert with a backbreaker... ahem), Frank Sexton, Gene Stanlee (2000 fan letters a week), former heavyweight boxing champ Primo Carnera, Mohawk Indian Don Eagle, Bert Assirati and Mildred Burke.

The next section profiles the rest of the top-line wrestlers of the era, including the wonderfully-named Steve Gob, Baron Michele Leone (who, a couple of years later, would drop his California version of the world title to NWA champ Lou Thesz in wrestling's first $100,000 gate), Mike Mazurki (who also starred in numerous films and formed the Cauliflower Alley Club for retired wrestlers), and Mr Moto (whose deadly abdominal stretch had just been outlawed).

This is followed by a 'Ones to watch' feature, with such up-and-comers as Fred Blassie, Mike DiBiase, Stu Hart (apparently of Scots-Irish descent), Don Leo Jonathan, Wladek Kowalski (who had apparently already been dubbed 'Killer', contradicting the later story that he got the nickname after mistakenly costing opponent Yukon Eric an ear), Harold Sakata (later Oddjob in 'Goldfinger'), and future WWF manager and agent 'Arnold Skoaland'.

Nat Fleischer, editor of The Ring, then picks his six greatest wrestlers of all time: Frank Gotch, George Hackenschmidt, Stanislaus Zbyszko, the Great Gama, Ed 'Stranger' Lewis and Jim Londos. A piece on great matches follows: the 'grudge' match between Lewis and Londos at Chicago's Wrigley Field drew 35,000 fans paying $96,302. At the time of the book's publication, a Lewis vs Joe Stecher match held the record for the highest-priced ticket at a whopping $25. And a main event with female grapplers Mildred Burke and Elvira Snodgrass had drawn 18,000 in Louisville.

Talking of the ladies, around 100 had turned professional at the time of writing. One was a 28 year old with 11 years in the business that had 'given Mildred Burke some of her toughest battles'. The lady's name? Mae Young. Also mentioned was Helen Hild, mother of Ted DiBiase.

An article on tag teams explains the then-standard 'Australian' rules, by which each fall of a match was fought elimination-style, with both partners needing to be beaten to end the fall.

Next up is an article on the likely outcome of a boxer vs wrestler match, where boxing legend Jack Dempsey explains that 'a boxer stands hardly any chance at all in the same ring as a wrestler, any time they tangle.'

A piece on midget wrestlers lists Little Beaver, which suggests he may be a candidate for the oldest competitor at a WrestleMania, having performed at the Silverdome thirty-five years after this book was published.

A listing of notable foreign wrestlers includes Bert Assirati, Alan Colbeck, George Kidd, Bert Mansfield and 330 pound Ray St Bernard.

The major moves of the day included the piledriver (closer in execution to a gutwrench powerbomb than the piledriver of today), the Jap sleeper (the same hold used as Ted DiBiase's 'Million Dollar Dream') and the backbreaker, which 'Dirty' Dick Raines claimed to have dreamt up while breaking firewood across his knee.

Some of the era's alleged incidents of heated crowds are detailed, with one wrestler receiving 273 stitches after meeting a mob of knife-wielding fans, a referee blinded in Detroit when a sharp object came flying from the crowd, a New Jersey referee making such an unpopular decision that he ended the night topless with his shirt literally shoved down his throat, and a crowd in San Diego so upset with the villainous Zaharias brothers that they burnt the arena to the ground!

Whatever happened to Gorgeous George?
(*Pro Wrestling Press*, January 2003)

There are many things to do in Manhattan. Among the less hip and stylish is to spend an afternoon in the New York Public Library reading out of print wrestling books. But that's what I did a couple of summers ago, and one of the publications I particularly enjoyed was the 1974 book *Whatever Happened To Gorgeous George*. While not actively breaking kayfabe, it certainly went into more insider detail than any other book of its generation. A couple of weeks ago I finally tracked down a copy of the book.

Among its fans were Lou Albano and Bert Sugar, who shamelessly lifted huge chunks without acknowledgement for their *Complete Idiots Guide to Pro Wrestling* shambles. Fortunately we at *Pro Wrestling Press* follow a strict code of ethics and have the decency to admit that all of the following quotes are plagiarised from *Whatever Happened To...* writer Joe Jares!

On the author's father wrestling a fellow heel: 'Pop came to the ring and showed off his ill-gotten belt. Still, the crowd obviously hated Spider more. So Dad shouted up to the black section, way up in the back, that he was tired of their being deprived and he was going to give them a close look at his belt. He did just that, delaying the start of the match fourteen minutes as he slowly wandered among them. By the time he got back in the ring the whites hated him as much as if he had sung 'The Battle Hymn of the Republic' over the loudspeaker.'

On Gorgeous George: ''I was alone at the arena, alone, and he comes up in this purple Cadillac, with his stooge', remembered ex-wrestler Dave Levin, who once promoted matches in Santa Maria, California. ''Hi Dave, how you doing?' he says and he steps back and the god-damned valet steps in and sprays my office there. Then and only then George steps in. It's only us there, but he has enough brains to know I'm going to tell this story a thousand times around, you see?''

Another Gorgeous George story: 'In the early forties he boarded a luxury liner to Honolulu with only his ticket, no money. He threw his wallet on the floor in one of the men's rooms and reported that it had been stolen during the bon-voyage parties. It was found later that day:

empty, of course. The captain and the other passengers took pity on him and he got free drinks all the way to Hawaii.'

On the various wrestling 'Lords' in the Los Angeles: 'When all these fellows and their seconds were working the territory, there should have been a local edition of 'Burke's Peerage' to keep them all straight. Instead there was a stiff note from the British consulate general in L.A.: 'No member of the British peerage is participating in any wrestling or similar exhibitions in the Los Angeles area...' The fans cared not a fig for what the consulate general said; they formed a Lords of the Mat Fan Club, with a swell newsletter called the 'Nobility News'.'

Eccentric promoter Jack Pfeffer hyping his latest twist on the ugly 'Angel' gimmick, a Lady Angel: 'She is bald on account of she escaped from the fiends who invaded her native country by taking the guns from the secret police who came to arrest her and members of her family and throwing them into the river from vich there was no escape. She lost her beautiful hair in the battle and decided to stay bald as vat was a good disguise. Also it helps her wrestle. Any clown who tries a headlock on the Lady Angel finds it is like trying to hold a bowling ball dot has been covered with butter.'

And Pfeffer explaining why she was unavailable for interview: 'The Lady Angel comes from an old Central European family. And members of the family would disown her if they learned she vas wrestling. They think she is sending them money from vat she makes hanging by her hair in a circus act.'

On the first leading female wrestler, Mildred Burke: 'In Toledo, Burke kicked the referee, and a representative of the athletic commission immediately announced that she had been fined $5. A fan sent up a $10 bill to pay the fine, so, being $5 ahead, she took another kick at the ref.'

A promo by 'Wild' Red Berry: 'Let these hams primp there feathers and strut their plumes. I will proceed to maltreat and obliterate them. I will turn loose such terrific voltage and velocity end elliptical trajectory that when it lands on the cleft of their chin it will tear loose their medulla oblongata from the pericranium, cure them of chronic dandruff and knock out four of their impacted wisdom teeth.'

Pfeffer's favourite phrase that he added to every signature: 'Life is just a bowl of pickled herring. You must taste it to like it.'

Pfeffer's logic for using front men rather than getting his own promoting licence: 'If I don't have a licence, dey can't take it avay from me.'

On money-grabbing promoters: 'Joe Malcewicz of San Francisco always tried to have a main event in Salinas that would appeal to the many Filipinos in that town because they have narrow rear ends and he could squeeze more of them into the little arena.'

And on crowd heat: 'When The Sheik went through his bowing-towards-Mecca routine before a match in Boston, he was bombarded with tomatoes, a pear, flashbulbs, hat pins, batteries, beer cans, soap, onions and eggs. The situation got so bad in Boston that promoter Abe Ford installed a seven-foot-high Plexiglass barrier around the ring with one passageway in and out. He borrowed the Plexiglass idea from ice hockey, and it at least takes away the good throwing angles from all but the balcony fans.'

Unpublished article (for *Pro Wrestling* Press, July 2003)

(*This piece never made it to print as it was deemed unsuitable given that Premier Promotions were advertisers with the publication.*)

Jackie Pallo once wrote that the promoter's greatest fear was to arrive at a venue and find a pile of posters for the show sat behind the desk. Such a fate befell John Freemantle of Premier Promotions on the afternoon of Sunday 23 March. He arrived at Crewe's Victoria Centre to find his publicity material had not been distributed and, instead of the crowd of around 200 that came to his last visit to the town, a mere 41 people had come through the doors.

It was to be an expensive day out for the veteran promoter, who normally sticks to his home territory along the south coast, including weekly visits to Worthing. Under the circumstances, the only thing mitigating the show from a financial disaster was that Freemantle, who has promoted since 1987, does not follow the 'new-school' philosophy of spending freely on imported 'name' talent and pyrotechnic displays; instead he practices the traditional technique of drawing what you can and hoping to spend less.

The old-school approach is also present in the format of the shows: two out of three fall matches over five minute rounds, with tag matches and rumbles the only specialty matches. And the style itself is perhaps the strongest remaining link to the traditional British genre, with matwork and strong basics mixed in with constant crowd interaction. Such interaction proved a vital part of this event; a detached 'pure' display of athletics before such a small crowd would have verged on the surreal.

The first match of the evening saw Baxter Burridge and the Masked Emperor take on 'Flying' Phil Powers and Jonathan Allen. Burridge was, to put it mildly, an admirer of Adrian Street. I must admit this was the first time a villain has stroked my cheek while pouting... Powers, a former Hammerlock trainee, is best known for his days on L!ve TV's UCW broadcasts, and despite his young age is now something of a veteran figure. He played this role throughout the match, with Allen in the slot of the up-and-comer; the worst that can be said of the youngster is that his enthusiasm and effort is not yet matched by experience.

With tag matches considered a special attraction, it is unusual for one to open a traditional British show. On this occasion, however, it proved a blessing; the prospect of 2-on-1 beatings is one of the more productive ways to build crowd heat, and this helped get the small crowd into the swing of things.

Those involved didn't mess with the traditional tag match formula, with double-teaming, blind tags and hot comebacks aplenty; unlike the stereotype of endless headlocks, there was barely a moment of inaction. The only limiting factor was that the small ring made it difficult to create a sense of urgency in struggling to reach a partner for the tag.

The Emperor took the first fall on Allen with a Samoan drop, while Powers pinned the masked man for the equaliser. The highlight of the final fall was Allen pulling off the classic Johnny Saint 'double lock-up broken with the foot and the arm twisted over the head into a duck between the legs followed up with a leapfrog and a 180 degree turn into an armdrag'. You'll know it if you see it!

The end came with Powers going for a cross-bodyblock but being caught by both opponents; never to fear though, as Allen got down on all fours for the old schoolboy trip leaving Powers to pin both men. As Freemantle announced, it was a win by three falls to one!

Next up was perhaps the simplest to explain rivalry that could be found at this venue. Mike Weaver is from Crewe, which is good. Keith Myatt is from Stoke, which is bad. Both are veterans, with Myatt known for his work at his hometown's GBH promotion, while Weaver was part of the 'parade of legends' at a recent All Star event at Hanley's Victoria Hall.

The match was inevitably slower-paced than the opener and, under normal circumstances, might have been better served in the opening slot. The pair (aided by a strong performance from the referee) played to their strengths, interspersing villainous attacks and heroic comebacks with the kind of true wrestling comedy that many promotions have lost sight of as they concentrate on television style punchline delivery. One priceless exchange came after Myatt took the first fall with a 'Stone Cold Stunner' style chinbreaker in round two and began walking to the dressing room.

"Where are you going?" enquired the referee. "It's best of three falls."

Replied Myatt: "Come on ref, you won't see one better than that"

Fortunately the crowd went into the interval happy, with Weaver coming back in the fourth round with a sunset flip and then taking the winning fall in round five with a powerslam.

After the crowd lost by submission to the halls' notorious heel vending machine, the show restarted with the billed main event, Premier's heavyweight champion Flash Barker against Robbie Brookside. As Gorilla Monsoon so often said, "that's a main event anywhere in the country". After recovering from a recent medical scare, and appearing before a crowd that barely stretched to a second row, Barker probably deserved more sophisticated heckling than one fan's suggestion of "Go back to London, you Londoner. We don't want your London types round here."

To his credit, Barker and his opponent worked an excellent match in the true traditional British style; not belly bumps and granny-baiting, but tight, credible matwork with logical but compelling submission attempts. Inexperienced grapplers often talk of 'working stiff' with a misplaced air of pride, but this match showed that skilled wrestlers can work 'solid' matches without being reckless. As Brookside's old friend William Regal told the contestants on MTV's Tough Enough 2, "I hit people very hard in safe places."

The bout went into a fourth round and was thus approaching the twenty minute mark when it came to an unsatisfying conclusion with Barker disqualified for refusing to halt an attack on Brookside in the corner. Had this been a regular venue, it would have served to set up future rematches; as it was, it felt as if a top-notch contest had been needlessly cut short. That said, the outcome was not without purpose; Brookside made the point that he had been prepared to wrestle scientifically, but if Barker wanted to mix it up, then all rules were out the window. And wouldn't you know it, the final match of the evening was a battle royale.

The match itself went merely eight minutes, and you can hardly blame those involved for wanting to get the afternoon over with. Among the significant points were all eight wrestlers on the bill appearing, including the Masked Emperor, proving nobody had pulled double-duty under the hood; and the slightly surreal experience of PJ and Duncan's 'Lets get ready to rumble' playing throughout the entire match, New Jack/ *Natural Born Killa* style. Given the finish of the main event, you will not be surprised to learn that Brookside eliminated Barker for the win.

It was a show of mixed emotions. There was a heavy air of depression at the turnout and the inevitable financial woes that the event would bring John Freemantle. But there was also a feeling of reassurance that an audience, with a healthy mix of age and gender, could still be taken on an emotional ride by the traditional art of British professional wrestling. And most of all, there should have been a feeling of pride for all involved that eight wrestlers would put on their best effort to entertain a crowd, however small in number.

Chokehold: A critical analysis (*Pro Wrestling Press*, November 2003)

When Wrestling Observer editor Dave Meltzer praises a book as "the best researched book on pro wrestling ever written", it's a safe bet it may be worth a read. But when an administrator on the historical-based Wrestling Classics site describes the book's author as "a curtain jerker who made zero impression on anybody except for some people having vague memories of his being abysmally bad... his claims of how much money he was making and what he was 'promised' because of what a big football star he was have always seemed like the ravings of a lunatic to me", it's clear there is more to the book than meets the eye.

Chokehold is the work of former All-American college footballer and Georgia-based pro wrestler Jim Wilson. The 538 page book is a combination of autobiography, history of the business since the 1940s, and a campaigning piece to 'clean up' the wrestling business. At the heart of the book is a simple message: the way professional wrestling is treated as a joke by mainstream society has allowed it to escape the scrutiny faced by 'legitimate' industries.

The book starts with an account of a 1985 incident when ABC's investigative news show *20-20* covered the pro wrestling business, a matter of weeks before the first WrestleMania. Guests Jim Wilson and Eddie Mansfield had spoken to reporters in the hope they would cover what they saw as an abusive industry; one where promoters held all the power and wrestlers followed orders or faced black-balling. Instead the show concentrated on the (shock horror) revelation that wrestling matches were fixed. Indeed, the broadcast was later remembered solely for the incident where WWF star David Schultz assaulted journalist John Stossel when he "dared to ask the tough question whether it was all fake". It's ironic that nearly 20 years on, Vince McMahon now uses 'openness' on this largely irrelevant issue to distract from his lies about issues that truly matter. Or as he calls it, *WWE Confidential.*

The book's then covers four main topics. The first is Wilson's own experiences, leaving football to work as a wrestler and then move to Georgia. Eventually, according to his account, he turned down sexual advances from promoter Jim Barnett in Australia and found himself sent back to the United States and unable to get work in any NWA territory. Barnett's counter-claim is that Wilson caused an embarrassing public incident with a married stewardess. Other wrestlers of the time claim Wilson's 'black-balling' was more to do with his refusal to lose matches. Wilson replies that he only refused to do the job when asked to do so in a deliberate attempt to damage his marketability. Whatever the truth (and in most cases it turns out to be a little of everything), Wilson's own story shows that a wrestler who got on the wrong side of the NWA cartel was looking at a far less successful career.

The second strand of the book is the infamous 'Battle for Atlanta' when NWA promoter Ray Gunkel's widow Ann was edged out of control of the Georgia territory and began running opposition shows. The NWA's response began with a conference call with NWA promoters Paul Jones and Lester Welch (Georgia), Eddie Graham (Florida), Sam Muchnick (St. Louis), Fritz Von Erich (Dallas), Mike LeBell (Los Angeles), LeRoy McGuirk (Oklahoma, Louisiana and Mississippi) and Vince McMahon Sr (WWWF). It took in methods from the perfectly legal (running shows in opposition; bringing Gordon Solie in for commentary) to the ethically dubious (banning wrestlers in every NWA territory from working for Gunkel; persuading big stars to take bookings for Gunkel solely so they could cause an embarrassing no-show) to the flat-out illegal (vandalising the car of a local promoter who supported Gunkel; bribing arena staff to refuse to rent buildings to non-NWA promoters). And it ended with Gunkel defeated and the NWA monopoly restored.

From here the book expands to look at the long history of the NWA, from its formation, through the 1956 legal decree where the NWA members promised the U.S. Justice Department that they would cease all attempts to exercise monopoly power, through the countless times the organisation simply ignored this promise (and the countless government investigations of this abuse that mysteriously ran out of steam), right through to the NWA's collapse when Vince McMahon beat them at their own game. This section of the book benefits from extensive research, including transcripts of several major legal cases between the NWA and 'outlaw' promoters that Wilson obtained under Freedom of Information regulations.

The final section of the book looks at more recent issues in the business, from the long list of drug-related deaths, to the steroid scandals of the mid-90s to the numerous sexual abuse allegations. It also looks at the ridiculous system by which wrestlers are considered 'independent contractors' by promoters, despite the fact that, for example, a WWE contract gives the company complete control over where a wrestler works, under what name, in what circumstances, on what dates, and even what they are paid. The simple fact is that if a WWE wrestler is not allowed to take independent bookings (which applies to virtually every contracted talent), they are an employee. But to admit this would leave the company liable for healthcare benefits, pension funds, sick pay during injury layoffs and, perhaps worst of all for the corporation, they would have to pay the United States equivalent of National Insurance taxes.

While the book as a whole is an absolute must-read, with some uncomfortable truths about the way the business has truly operated, it does have some weaknesses. Most notable is the gross disparity between Wilson's assessment of his own skills and potential, and that of those who saw him in action. Wilson believes he was a genuinely strong candidate for the NWA title, a view shared by virtually nobody else. It's particularly ironic that Wilson seems to have fallen victim to the very same pattern he so readily recognises in others: a wrestler stays within the system (or as Jack Brisco puts it in a conversation with Wilson, "goes with the program") blinded by promises of fame and glory and a headliner slot; promises that a promoter is in fact making to everybody in sight. While it is perhaps little more than comical to read of WWF jobber Barry 'O' honestly believing he was a future world champion, how many modern-day interviews with disillusioned WWF departees tell of an initial meeting with Vince McMahon where they were 'promised' an eventual main event slot? This lack of perspective on Wilson's part is a particular shame as it gives ammunition to those who attack the messenger rather than take issue with the message.

The people responding in this way can also point to Wilson's recounting of a popular story that Tommy Rich received an NWA title run after acceding to Jim Barnett's sexual demands. Virtually nobody of note believes this to be true, but the title reign's background remains unclear and Wilson may have unintentionally stumbled across a previously unspoken explanation. As the book explains, Barnett's NWA colleagues were suspicious about his control of the Georgia group's national cable TV slot on TBS and it was hardly the first time he had been suspected on plotting a national expansion. So it is certainly plausible that Barnett (who controlled the NWA title) booked the title changes from Harley Race to Rich, back to Race and on to Dusty Rhodes with the intention of boosting his local business at the expense of the other territories; for a title that changed hands rarely to suddenly see three title switches in two months, and all in the same state, does certainly raise questions

The more recent material is weaker than the NWA stories, partly because Wilson had largely stopped following the business and partly because the book was originally written in the 1980s but failed to find an audience. The major problem with this section is that it tends to simply list every allegation going without taking a truly objective look at their validity. While, for example, the list of early deaths is indisputable (and makes chilling reading), the outcome of the WWF steroid trial is grossly misrepresented. Wilson claims the jury was conned by Vince McMahon into dismissing the charges simply because wrestling was fake and thus irrelevant; in reality the trial demonstrated a strong culture within the company of encouraging steroid abuse, but the prosecution case was so inept that the specific charges laid before the court ranged from unproven to logically impossible.

The book similarly falls into an oversimplified 'good guys vs the evil business' trap when it deals with Owen Hart's death, highlighting Minnesota governor Jesse Ventura's call for a wrestlers union in the days after the tragedy, but failing to mention his sudden silence when, just three months later, he took a refereeing gig for the company. One of the striking points that becomes clear reading the book is that, ultimately, virtually every wrestler who goes against 'the system' winds up back on the inside. Indeed, one of the cases mentioned in the book has had such an outcome since its writing. Sable, who sued the WWF for $140 million in a sexual harassment case, is now back in the company playing a character who apparently sleeps with the chairman. Can you seriously picture this happening in any other business traded on Wall Street?

But despite its faults, the book makes a powerful case that the wrestling business falls far short of the basic standards that are commonplace in any 'legitimate' industry. Wilson makes three specific suggestions for changes he feels are needed to 'clean up' the business.

1) Basic health and safety standards. Because there is no national equivalent of our NHS, people in the United States generally have a health insurance policy. In virtually every industry, this policy is paid for by the employer as a standard benefit of working for the company. Yet in wrestling, where performers are 'independent contractors', there is a long-standing tradition of injuries and health being 'your problem, not ours'. Not only do wrestlers have to pay their own hefty medical bills (NWA-TNA has just become the first major promotion to offer health insurance), but they face lost earnings if they miss matches, even though they suffered the injury at work. Of course, none of this matters in the real world, because we all know nobody gets hurt in these phony matches...

2) A union for wrestlers. Whatever the make-up of the wrestling industry, wrestlers have always been disposable if they are seen as troublemakers. In the territorial days, there were always new stars to bring in from other areas. Today, there are far more qualified wrestlers than there are slots available on the WWE roster. It has always been a case of 'like it or lump it'. According to the book, the share of WWF/WWE revenue that has gone to wrestlers in salaries has constantly hovered around 12 to 15 per cent. To put this into perspective, Nationwide League football clubs in England were recently ordered to limit players' salaries to 60 per cent of the club's revenue. But in reality, a union will likely never happen. The hierarchy of wrestlers payoffs will always mean that the main event stars who would give a union true power in the event of a strike are the very people who make the most money and have the least personal interest in getting a fair deal for everybody.

3) A return to state athletic commission regulation of the business. Over the years, athletic commissions have played many roles in the wrestling business, from 'those people you bribe to recognise your choice of champion after a double-cross in the ring', to 'those people you bribe to make sure nobody else can hire your favourite building',

to 'the people who paid for a drug-dealing doctor to attend the shows', to 'those people we shouldn't have to pay taxes to because we're not a real sport'. The role of 'those people who make sure the business operates in a decent and legitimate manner where everyone gets a fair shake' is one that athletic commissions may never play. If nothing else, a credible commission system could end the problem of WWE stars being released when their personal problems get out of hand only to be snapped up by independent groups and continuing to wrestle rather than deal with their issues.

Writing on the Wrestling Classics site, Jody Hamilton (who wrestled as the Assassin, helped book in WCW and is the father of referee Nick Patrick), gave a particularly frank opinion on both sides to the book's arguments:

"Some of the conditions described by Wilson really did exist, and had existed long before Jim Wilson ever attempted to become a pro wrestler.

"Everyone starting in the business knew up front there was no insurance, no pension plan, only a very select few had a money guarantee, and some of the equipment we had to work on sometimes was very poorly maintained. There were promoters that fell far short of an accurate accounting of the gate receipts. 'If you didn't like it don't get in it' was more or less the accepted attitude.

"Now I would be the last person in the world to condemn anyone for attempting to improve themselves or their working conditions. As a singles wrestler and as a tag team wrestler I had more than my share of run-ins with promoters about payoffs, finishes, poorly maintained equipment, and generally poor working conditions.

"Yet I was never 'blackballed' or 'blacklisted.' Why didn't this happen? Because I had a reputation for drawing big money wherever I went. Promoters all over the country hated Buddy Rogers, but when they would find out he was available they all jumped at the chance to book him, because he always drew money.

"The real reason promoters quit booking Wilson is because he was an egotistical, glory happy, didn't want to do business, never wanted to lose pain in the butt whose performance in the ring left a lot to be desired. However, if Wilson had ever proven himself as a bona fide attraction capable of drawing money, promoters would have used him regardless of what he did."

Ultimately, the truth about *Chokehold* is that much of what it says about attitudes to professional wrestling will be demonstrated with cruel irony. The book will make no difference to the way the business operates.

Promoters will dismiss it by attacking the author, not his message, and they'll continue to protect and abuse their powers.

Wrestlers will continue to chase illusory dreams and think they will be the exception to the grim rule that the book describes.

Fans will largely ignore the book, having been educated to a culture where all that matters is the next pay-per-view, with history not even an afterthought.

And the book won't even register a blip on the radar screen of the 'real world'.

Because wrestling is fake, don't you know?

Behind the small print of a WWE contract
(*Pro Wrestling Press*, March 2004)

Have you ever wondered what a WWE wrestler's contract involves? Well here's a plain English version of the legalese-filled standard wrestler booking contract. The particular example this comes from is that of Vince McMahon (as an executive, his has to be publicly available). However, this is used for everyone (with any alterations you can negotiate).

It starts off with some standard background blurb, including the news that "the professional wrestling exhibitions arranged by (WWE) constitute demonstrations of wrestling skills and abilities designed to provide athletic-styled entertainment to the public, and such wrestling exhibitions constitute entertainment and are not competitive sports."

Section 1 (Booking) gives WWE exclusive rights to use the wrestler for matches, televise his matches, sell them on video and exploit intellectual property rights (that is, make cash off the gimmick).

Section 2 (amusingly titled 'Works') gives WWE exclusive rights to the video, photographs and so on of the wrestler's matches. The moment the contract ends, the wrestler has to give back "All gags, costumes or parts of costumes, accessories, crowns, inventions, championship, title or other belts (if applicable), and any other items of tangible property" that the WWE has given them.

It also says that the WWE has the rights to "all incidents, dialogue, characters, actions, routines, ideas, gags, costumes or parts of costumes, accessories, crowns, inventions, championship, title or other belts (if applicable), and any other tangible or intangible materials written, composed, submitted, added, improvised, or created by or for" the wrestler. WWE also has the right to obtain trademarks or copyright in their own name for anything the wrestler comes up with.

Section 3 (Intellectual Property) deals with anything the wrestler already owns the rights to such as 'legal name, nickname, ring name, likeness, personality, character, caricatures, voice, signature, costumes, props, gimmicks, gestures, routines and themes'. All of these are exclusively licensed by the wrestler to WWE during their contract. The wrestler gives WWE permission to trademark and copyright any of this intellectual property.

Anything they don't already own will belong to WWE forever. WWE also has the right to carry on using the intellectual property after the contract ends (cough new Razor Ramon cough).

Section 4 (Merchandising)
WWE has the exclusive rights to market any merchandise related to the wrestler.

Section 5 (Exclusivity)
Anything the WWE has exclusive rights to really is exclusive, even if this is at the expense of the wrestler's rights.

Section 6 (Term and territory)
The contract applies anywhere in the world. There is also a specified time for the contract term (in Vince's case it is the same period as his separate permanent employment contract as an executive).

Section 7 (Payments and royalties)
For a non-televised show, WWE will pay the wrestler "an amount equal to such percentage of the paid receipts for such House Show from the live House Show gate receipts only as is consistent with the nature of the match in which the wrestler appears, i.e., preliminary, mid-card, main event, etc. and any standards WWE establishes specifically for such House Show. However, such amount shall not be less than One Hundred Fifty Dollars ($150.00) per House Show."

For a televised show, including PPV, the WWE will pay the wrestler "an amount not less than Fifty Dollars ($50.00) for each day of TV Taping, if any, on which TALENT renders services hereunder in connection with the production of the TV Taping."

Aside from this, WWE "shall not be liable in any way to pay royalties, residuals, fees, or any other compensation whatsoever".

(This said, since 1996 it has become standard practice for the wrestler and WWE to sign a separate downside agreement by which, at the end of the year, the wrestler has earned less than an agreed fee, their 'downside', they will get a one-off payment to make up the difference. Several paragraphs are blanked out in the public version of Vince's contract; these presumably deal with his specific downside details.)

If WWE hires out the wrestler to a third-party (e.g. for an advert or film), WWE and the wrestler shall agree a fee.

If the wrestler does commentary or production work, they get nothing for it, and the WWE owns the rights to their work.

There is no payment for appearances in WWE publications, including magazines and the website.

Section 8 (Company obligations)
WWE will get any licenses the company needs. If they help the wrestler get a wrestling license, they can charge them a fee.

WWE will pay the costs of running a show, such as venue hire, taxes, promotion and so on. They will also pay the costs of producing and distributing TV shows.

Section 9 (Wrestler's obligations)
The wrestler must get his own wrestling license.

The wrestler must take responsibility for his physical training, including paying the cost, and this must not interfere with his work schedule.

The wrestler must pay his own transport costs.

The wrestler must pay for his own ring attire and props.

The wrestler "shall use best efforts in employing his skills and abilities as a professional wrestler and be responsible for developing and executing the various details, movements, and maneuvers required of wrestlers in a professional wrestling exhibition."

The wrestler "shall take such precautions as are appropriate to avoid any unreasonable risk of injury to other wrestlers in any and all Events. These precautions shall include, without limitation, pre-match review of all wrestling moves and maneuvers with wrestling partners and opponents; and pre-match demonstration and/or practice with wrestling partners and opponents to insure familiarity with anticipated wrestling moves and maneuvers during a wrestling match. In the event of injury to the wrestler, and/or his partners and opponents during a wrestling match, he shall immediately signal partner, opponent and/or referees that it is time for the match to end; and he shall finish the match forthwith so as to avoid aggravation of such injury."

The wrestler must perform to the best of his ability and "agrees all matches shall be finished in accordance with the WWE's direction." If you refuse to do a finish, you don't get paid and you can be fired instantly.

The wrestler must take part in any publicity work the WWE says, and there's no payment for this.

The wrestler agrees WWE can make any legal decisions about gimmicks and names (except for their real name). The WWE can sign any legal documents on the wrestler's behalf in terms of intellectual property.

The wrestler accepts legal responsibility for anything they do, pretty much anywhere, and must cover WWE's costs for any legal action that results.

The wrestler must pay all his own taxes.

The wrestler must arrange and pay for his own insurance.

The wrestler accepts full responsibility for any injuries he suffers.

If the wrestler is seriously or permanently injured, or killed, because of a match, they have no right to legal action, even in cases of negligence (except where the law says otherwise).

If a wrestler is injured and misses matches, they have no right to compensation for lost earnings.

If the wrestler does anything wrong in terms of bringing himself "into public disrepute, contempt, scandal or ridicule", damages his reputation, insults or offends the community or any employee, agent or affiliate of WWE or otherwise damages the wrestlers marketability, WWE has the right to fine, suspend or fire the wrestler at WWE's discretion.

Section 10 (Waiver)

The wrestler promises there is nothing they have not mentioned that could affect the contract, including any immigration or government issues.

The wrestler promises they are of sound mental and physical condition and definitely on no illegal drugs. And they agree to follow the WWE drug policy and have an annual medical check-up by a WWE appointed doctor. The WWE can also order a check-up at any time.

The contract overrides and previous agreements, written or oral. (So if Vince brought you to his office and promised you the WWE title, you can't later sue him when you end up on *Velocity*).

Section 11 (Early Termination)
The contract can be ended at any time if the wrestler and WWE both agree.

If the wrestler dies, the contract ends and there is no further payment to the wrestler's heirs.

Section 12 (Breach)
To cut a long story short, if the wrestler breaches the contract, WWE can sue the living crap out of them for every penny they can get, even if it's not over a direct loss.

Section 13 (Miscellaneous)
The wrestler is definitely not an employee. They are an 'independent contractor'. (This means they get no legal employee rights such as a pension, health insurance, redundancy and so on, and that WWE doesn't have to spend money on things like employee taxes or social security).

There's the usual legal drill about if any part of the contract is found to be legally unsound, the rest of it still applies.

Section 14 (Confidentiality)
The wrestler can't reveal squat. In particular, they mustn't give away or share "reports, business plans, sales information, cost or pricing information, lists of suppliers or customers, talent lists, story lines, scripts, story boards or ideas, routines, gags, costumes or parts of costumes, accessories, crowns, inventions, championship, title or other belts (if applicable)".

Having your cake and eating it (*Pro Wrestling Press*, April 2004)

It's taken us a couple of years to be allowed to publish this article, but *Pro Wrestling Press* is finally able to give you the exclusive details of the real story behind British Wrestling Limited.

This curious story began when every wrestling promoters in the country received a letter on BBC headed notepaper explaining that, with the departure of director-general Greg Dyke, the corporation was now interested in broadcasting professional wrestling. The letter invited them to a secret location for further talks.

When the men arrived, they were intensely irritated to find their 'rivals' as company, and the mood stayed ugly when no BBC representative appeared. It wasn't until one promoter tried to leave that the crew realised they were locked in a windowless room. Even stranger, the room contained an oven and a fridge with a packet cake mix and all the necessary ingredients.

Eventually the men became hungry and old grudges fell aside as they worked together to bake a tasty cake which they then sliced evenly and served up. This was enough to keep hunger at bay until a cleaner let them out the next morning. Relieved to have survived the ordeal, the men made their way to a local cafe where they continued the discussions they had struck up with one another.

The rest is, of course, history. Following the ordeal, the promoters put their differences aside and formed a new company, 'British Wrestling Limited'. Brian Dixon (All Star), Elisar Cabrera (FWA), Andre Baker (NWA-UK), Ricky Knight (WAW), John Freemantle (Premier Promotions) worked as equal partners in the company and began pooling their resources. To boost their numbers, they drafted in MPW trainer 'Majik' to co-ordinate with smaller groups in the Midlands area. Lee Butler of Garage Pro Wrestling joined the cause and brought in several smaller promotions in the North West. Gary Graham's WrestleZone Wrestling came aboard, as did the Nottingham and Enfield-based Revolution British Wrestling. Knight got in touch with groups across East Anglia. And All Star despatched Chic Cullen to help settle the differences between several promotions across Scotland.

The first major policy decision taken by the new company was to establish two distinct schedules for live events, which were seen as the heart of the group's activity. The first schedule involved a co-ordinated effort to build up local circuits of regular venues such as Croydon, Stoke, Enfield, Morecambe, Bristol, Liverpool, Coventry and Nottingham. The plan was always to start with monthly dates but, as you now know, several of these venues are running once a fortnight, with the most successful scheduled to go weekly next year. The regular dates were built up not just by consistent monthly storylines, but by measures such as booking long-term schedules to benefit from greater advance publicity, and rewarding loyal fans with discounted tickets and the chance to reserve a particular seat. When reviving 'old time' venues, the company worked with the organisers of the annual British wrestling to track down local stars from the *World of Sport* days. These local legends were brought in as regular guests of honour and billed as local matchmakers and used whenever a storyline required an authority figure. They also acted as goodwill ambassadors for the company, gaining valuable local press and broadcast publicity.

While the local venues were largely storyline-driven and filled with local wrestlers and rookies (who were able to work part-time because of the weekend dates), with perhaps one or two full-timers, the other half of British Wrestling Ltd's live business was touring dates. The company began booking 'spot shows' or 'one night stands' around the country. Thanks to their co-ordinated efforts, the promoters were able to put together dates with a more tolerable travel schedule: no longer would a wrestler need to travel from Plymouth to Liverpool to Kings Lynn to Edinburgh on consecutive nights to make ends meet. The combined efforts of the new alliance meant that, as well as having enough work for the country's growing band of full-time wrestlers, it became much more efficient to bring in overseas workers; international flight costs could now be recouped over perhaps seven or ten shows around the country, rather than promoters having to jack up ticket prices and bill the one-off appearance as the 'biggest show ever'.

Television was, of course, an important part of the company's plan. The promoters used the production facilities and timeslot of the former FWA to put together a weekly one-hour show on The Wrestling Channel that was carefully designed to expose as many top-line wrestlers as possible to the viewing public, while having episodic storylines which were reflected in timely line-ups on the spot shows. Rather than try to ape America's WWE by building up to a single match (which would be ineffective for a relatively small audience dispersed around the country), a feud could now draw fans around the country.

The company was also able to pool its resources to get more effective publicity in other fields. They purchased advertising space in *PowerSlam* to promote both touring and regular dates, including details of the imported tourists who would already be familiar to the magazine's readers. The magazine, now dealing with a central office rather than dozens of small-time promoters, responded by giving greater coverage of British shows, including sending photographers to the eventful TV tapings. The Sun Online website came to a barter agreement where they exchanged increased coverage for the promoters displaying advertising banners at live events. And perhaps most importantly, the promoters clubbed together to hire a full-time webmaster to produce a single website that included a comprehensive calendar of upcoming events.

Promoters working together helped settle many of the long-term problems that had plagued the business. With a co-ordinated schedule, there was no longer any question of wrestlers being double-booked. Those wrestlers who did choose to repeatedly fail to appear for scheduled matches soon found themselves out of work across the country. With more long-term planning, the problem of false advertising, whether deliberate or inadvertent, was largely wiped out. And when wrestlers were unable to appear for legitimate reasons, suitable replacements could be booked more easily thanks to the support of promoters across the country.

Of course, with a single major employer, the wrestlers themselves finally put personal differences and paranoia aside for the sake of protection. This is the reason that the world's first ever wrestlers union was set up, with Doug Williams, Phil Barker and Rob Brookside representing the profession at monthly meetings with British Wrestling Limited's board of directors. Among the agreements they negotiated with the company was a reasonable wage structure. Full-timers are now guaranteed to get at least a living wage, with bonuses when business is strong. And at the other end of the pay scale, a part-timer or trainee will no longer work for nothing; at the very least they will get reasonable travel expenses (outside their home base) and a payoff equivalent to the national minimum wage for the hours they are required to be at the venue. Any promoter looking to pull a fast one knows that top-line talent will band together and refuse to work until any outstanding debts are paid off.

But such potentially hostile relations are rarely needed. Indeed, wrestlers and promoters have responded to the greater efficiency and strength of the business by establishing a scheme where the company (with one eye on the tax breaks) matches the union dues paid by wrestlers to fund a group medical insurance scheme which makes sure those injured in the line of duty can afford to get professional treatment. The days of wrestlers taking unnecessary risks and developing permanent injuries through a fear of starvation are over. And one of the unsung achievements of the promoter-wrestler partnership was the recent introduction of a 50 pence increase to ticket prices across the country which goes directly to a fund for retired wrestlers suffering financial or physical difficulties.

OK, that bit was probably pushing it too far. Clearly no *PWP* reader is going to buy the idea that the wrestling business is going to develop a sense of compassion. And yes, this entire story has been a work of fiction. Except for the part about the promoters being locked in a room, which was almost true.

Everything up until the discovery of the fridge was just as written. But what really happened next was that, as the cake mix was opened, the men fought to grab the contents for themselves and, amid the scrambling, the crumbs fell to the floor. The promoters continued their fighting, apparently more concerned with making sure nobody else got their hands on the cake mix. When the fighting ended, each man had a bloody nose, a black eye, and a pile of trodden crumbs mixed with dirt and dust.

And the next morning the cleaner found a group of starving men.